D1603991

They Said It
Couldn't Be Done:
The Incredible Story of
BILL LEAR

VICTOR BOESEN

They Said It Couldn't Be Done:

The Incredible Story of
BILL LEAR

DOUBLEDAY & COMPANY, INC., GARDEN CITY, NEW YORK
1971

Unless otherwise credited, all photos
in this book are by Art Alanis or from
the Lear collection.

FOR NANCY

CHAPTERS

They Said It
Couldn't Be Done:
The Incredible Story of
BILL LEAR

1: WE GOT A LIVE ONE!

The Lear Jet sat out on the field, a block or so from the doors of the Flying Tigers hangar. Sleek and snow white, with the back-swept lines and high scorpionlike tail, the ship had an up-on-its-toes look, as if keeping only the most tentative contact with the ground and might go skittering off any moment like a big dragon-fly.

As it turned out, it almost did, without me.

Take-off was at nine o'clock, a half hour from now. I wandered briefly around the hangar. When I got back to the door, a Cadillac had pulled alongside the Lear Jet. People were hurrying out of the car and into the airplane. It looked like a getaway from a Chicago bank job.

The door closed and the engines howled. I waved and yelled like an overlooked passenger on a sinking ship as the rescue craft pulls away. I went banging along with my free-lancer's cardboard suitcase, making the best time I could. The engines slowed. The door opened and I scrambled aboard.

Down went the door once more, up went the engines, and the ship began to roll. The legendary Bill Lear himself, in white shirt sleeves and visored cap, bluish-gray hair showing around the edges, was driving. He turned left onto the runway, picking up speed at the same time, and before you could say William Powell Lear, we were going upstairs so fast there seemed a likelihood of being pulled through the seat.

In the dazzling light of forty-one thousand feet, far above the tobacco stain which marks Los Angeles for aviators, I went the other way on the seat from inverse gravity as Lear leveled the ship off and pointed her nose north to Reno.

"Nothing climbs like a Lear Jet," smilingly observed the trimly built white-haired fellow in a gray glen plaid suit and sandals in the seat by the door, "not even military planes." She was fast, too, continued my informant, who spoke with an accent and said something about being a musician, playing the piano. "We clip off about a hundred miles every ten minutes."

It usually took about forty-five minutes to get to Reno. Today, though, "it might take a little longer due to some very unusual winds," my man said. "The jet stream, which normally moves from west to east, has reversed itself."

For a piano player he seemed to know quite a bit. Well, I knew a thing or two myself. "You know, the Stockton Delta is a very interesting place," I threw out as we passed a hundred miles east of the Stockton Delta.

"Yah!" he said, leaping at the comment and grinning eagerly.

I plowed on about the seventy-five thousand acres of peat, the raised waterways, the fires and floods, other dramatic facts about the area. He kept nodding and saying, "Yah! Yah!" He knew all about that, too.

He proved to be Professor Gunnar Johansen, the internationally known Danish concert pianist and long-time artist-in-residence at the University of Wisconsin, a post created especially for him. A few months before, he had been written up in *Time* for walking onto the stage of New York's Philharmonic Hall as a last-minute substitute and flabbergasting the critics with a masterly performance of Beethoven's Piano Concerto in D Major, playing music he had never seen until that afternoon. He lived in Santa Rosa, California.

The lady passenger was Moya, Lear's wife of twenty-seven years. With classical features, a ready smile and warm, shining eyes, she strikingly resembled her father, the late Ole Olsen of Olsen and Johnson comedy fame.

She was delighted at this new interest of her husband, building a steam automobile. "It's so exciting!" she said, "and absolutely fascinating to have a ringside seat!" At this stage of his life— his 67th year—he was going to "make economic history." She told how "Eddie" Cole, president of General Motors, had sent a telegram inviting Lear to Detroit next day for lunch and a press conference.

This represented a turnabout by the auto industry. Up to now they had given Lear the cold shoulder. "At first, they played it very cool," Moya said. "They refused to give him cars to work with." They wanted no publicity without their approval. Now they're more respectful. "Oh, boy, are they!"

Over Yosemite, Lear suddenly stood the plane on its left wing, then the right, giving his passengers a clear view of Bridal Veil Falls, spilling Lilliputian-like over the precipice eight miles below.

We passed over Reno and landed at the site of the former Stead Air Force Base in mountain-hemmed Lemmon Valley, ten miles north of the city. Wobbling a little from fresh-air trauma, I heeded Lear's command "Follow me!" as he headed for a tour of his plant in a couple of renovated Air Force buildings. He carried his arms slightly crooked and out from his sides, like a wrestler stalking his opponent.

He did a fast turn around the art department, where two artists were rendering new steam era designs in cars and buses, then he burst into a room across the hall and pridefully displayed a new automatic pilot. Smaller than a shoe box, it was lighter, more reliable, and would do more things better than any other automatic pilot in existence. No, the airlines would never use it. "It's too good, too small, and too light," he said sardonically.

In the machine shop, filled with $375,000 worth of lathes and other equipment from Japan, Germany, Italy, and Czechoslovakia, we were joined by a tall, dapper man in a blue jacket and fine-checked gray trousers which arrived a little early above his well-polished buckle shoes of alligator hide. He had grown up through his hair, leaving a fringe at the ear line. He looked at me with gray, questioning eyes.

"This is my parole officer," Lear said, presenting Clarence W. Nanney, administrative vice-president of the company, known as "Buzz" because his kid brother long ago couldn't say brother. As the three of us moved on, Lear hefted a dummy of the steam motor they were developing. It was delta-shaped, weighed about the same as the equivalent internal combustion engine used in automobiles, but was only about half the size.

The place abruptly filled with uproar as the functional version of the motor was put to a load test on the dynamometer. The crew stood respectfully back from the test cell, watching through the open doors and the glass panel of the control booth.

The tour presently included a quartet of Japanese from the Datsun plant in Yokohama, Japan. With another "Follow me!" Lear split off with the visitors from the Orient, leaving me in Buzz's charge.

Buzz set forth some basic facts about engines. There are two kinds: the internal combustion engine and the external combustion engine. In the first kind, the fuel is burned on the inside, by explosion in the cylinders. It isn't burned very well, only about two thirds of it getting used, the rest going out the exhaust pipe.

In the other engine the fuel is burned on the outside, in the open atmosphere and, therefore, with almost total combustion. This is the steam engine.

He told what the big problem has been with steam through the years in its application to automobiles. "The tea kettle is a very inefficient way to boil a pot of water because of the steam that escapes through the spout," he explained. "It's the same way with the old steam car—too much steam got away."

If the steam could be captured—if the spout could be turned back into the tea kettle—it obviously wouldn't be necessary to keep replenishing the water. The steam system could be sealed like the Freon system in your refrigerator. This was the trick. There were enormous problems, but with the help of space-age technology, there was no doubt it could be done, he said.

"This is what we're doing here in Reno."

Cool breezes sweeping down from ten-thousand-foot Peavine Mountain, still cradling snow in her folds, tempered the warm May sun as we walked over to the University of Nevada cafeteria for lunch. Thousands of computer calculations had been made just for the steam generator alone—that is, the boiler, Buzz said. What size tubing to use, how much, what the material should be, pressures, temperatures—all these and more had been studied. In the end, with tens of thousands of variables calculated, the maneuver area left in which to confine the design had come down to the size of a postage stamp relative to an area that had been as big as the wall of Buzz's office.

"This has never been done before," Buzz said. "Backyard inventors have gone at it trial and error for years. They've probably contributed very little to the technology. In a large sense, it is a completely new field of endeavor."

The delta motor they were testing had already been redesigned five times. It would be noiseless, since there were no explosions and there was no transmission. The motor was connected directly to the wheels. "When you turn the key and step on it," Buzz said, "you better be sure things are clear up ahead, because here you come."

The new motor would be applied not only to automobiles but to trucks, tractors, buses, airplanes, and whatnot. "We are devoted to the advancement of this new power source and adapting it to all present internal combustion engine uses," Buzz said.

Bright fellow—this Nanney. He must have several engineering degrees? He had none. He was a former policeman. He put in twenty years on the Los Angeles force, fifteen of them as a detective. What he knew about engineering he learned from doing several years of moonlighting for Lear in "security work" and from reading.

Lear called over from the door of the cafeteria as he was leaving, "Don't tell him everything," smiling for the first time.

In midafternoon Lear roared off to Detroit and his luncheon appointment next day with General Motors' Edward Cole. With him were Moya and Gunnar Johansen. Because of the wind direction, the take-off run was upslope, and with a full load of fuel to lift, he took his time before leaving the ground, in contrast to the rocketlike departure of the morning in Los Angeles.

Airborne at last, he skimmed the brush until the ship was a speck against a distant ridge. "Look at the son of a bitch," grunted Buzz, who wanted to show me what a Lear take-off looked like from the outside, "holding it right on the deck till you can't see him any more!"

As the sound of Lear's engines beat down on Reno and Sparks, the 130,000 residents could wish him Godspeed on his flight east, for it might well be that much of their future rode in the cockpit with him. When Lear came to town the year before, things were not good. The closing of the Stead Air Force Base had driven ten thousand people out of the community, thrown four thousand houses onto the market, and dropped retail sales $34 million the first year. "It flattened us out," one townsman said.

Washoe County was trying to make a go of it chiefly on the

$94 million a year which tourists left behind in exchange for being allowed to gamble and do other things they got arrested for at home. It wasn't enough.

Then Lear bought 3500 acres of the old base and set up shop there. Already it was easier to borrow money—significant in view of the usual precept for credit eligibility that the borrower establish the fact he doesn't need the money. "A little while before," said Judd Allen, manager of the Chamber of Commerce, "if you mentioned to an Eastern moneybags that you were from Reno, he laughed at you."

But besides a new and less spindly leg under the economy than gambling, Lear brought the promise of respectability. "This is a dramatic way to change Reno's image," Allen said. "The townsmen want to alter the old notion that Reno is a place where you don't bring the family, to a place where you *do* bring the family," Allen explained. "They long to expunge the old picture of wickedness lingering from the days when Reno was the 'divorce capital' of the country."

There would still be gambling, of course, but the presence of Lear would have an Airwick effect. The whole of Nevada had benefited when Howard Hughes, "a responsible corporation man all his life associated himself with gambling down at Las Vegas," Allen said. "It's different having Howard Hughes own it instead of the syndicate." In other words, it's not so much what goes on at the whorehouse as who owns it.

"Unfortunately," Allen went on, "Hughes was also submerging the north. We needed a Hughes of our own to balance him off." Bill Lear is Reno's Howard Hughes.

And in the long run, Reno expects to do better with Lear than Las Vegas with Hughes, Allen indicated. "Lear is outgoing," he noted. "He is not a recluse. He doesn't necessarily seek but he attracts publicity. We feel we have the horse's mouth and Las Vegas has some other part of the horse."

Lear was promptly admitted to a tight little circle which gathers with ritualistic regularity each evening at five at a small round table in the lobby of the Holiday Hotel. No more than four feet in diameter and placed just outside the door to the ladies' room, the table bears a permanent "Reserved" sign. The group drinks until six, then goes home to dinner. What happens next day in Reno may be shaped by this hour of wassail, for these knights of the Holiday round table, some say, are the *de facto* wheels of the city, if not of all northern Nevada.

One thing they can't do much about is to affect the land ownership of the valley. A good deal of the land is owned by Italians, descended from gold seekers at Virginia City, and they are hanging onto it. This is frustrating. The story is told of a sulky local banker visiting Rome, who sent back a post card reading, "Christ, I haven't seen so many wops since I left Reno!"

A regular at the round table is tall, silver-haired Norman Biltz, "Duke of Nevada," who built the Holiday. Once of Wall Street, Biltz occupies a small office on the second floor of the hotel and still gets inquiring calls about the stock market from Wall Street where, as he says, "It's a misdemeanor to tell the truth."

Another face nearly always on hand is that of John Heizer, mining engineer and amateur anthropologist, who is proud to mention that his brother heads the Department of Archaeology at the University of California at Berkeley. A third faithful at the table is Bob Helms, whose name appears on heavy road-building machinery and highway barricades far and wide from Reno. A short, balding man, Helms is the one with his hat on.

Whatever the composition of the circle, whose diameter sometimes is so great that the table in the center is out of reach to hold the drinks, the attendance runs heavily to millionaires. "I've seen as much as a half billion dollars sitting there at one time," Buzz Nanney said.

Nobody butts in except an occasional out-of-towner led astray by the open-shirted informality of the group—like a lady one winter evening who rushed up and asked Bob Helms, wearing an old windbreaker and the usual hat, his fist filled with $100 chips, "Pardon me, but did you folks just come in on the bus?" She was a Californian who wanted to check on snow conditions in Donner Pass before heading back.

Material for this Croesus club is amply provided by the high assay of millionaires who live in Reno, enjoying Nevada's hospitality as "a cyclone cellar for the tax weary." The state exacts no income or inheritance tax, balancing these and other tax indulgences with a sales and food tax. Buzz Nanney said there are ninety millionaires in town. Broker C. V. Emmons, thirty-two years on the scene and sometime guest at the Holiday round table, said there are more than ninety. He said it as if only ninety made it a poverty area.

The newcomer's fate largely rests on what the round table thinks of him. He has to sweat it for a while. "You don't join this club in twenty-four hours," one member said. If the answer finally is thumbs down, that's the end of it. "You may as well leave town."

The test is not whether he has money. That the members have plenty of, and they've seen hustlers come and go. The test is what kind of fellow he is. "This is handshake country," said Paul Garwood, vice-president of Nevada's Bell Telephone Company. "It's a hangover from the old days when you dealt with the good guys and shot the bad guys."

"I've seen three- and four-million-dollar deals sealed with a handshake many times," Bob Helms said.

When the candidate passes muster, internecine differences are forgotten and the word goes out: "Don't let him get out of town! We got a live one!"

Bill Lear was a live one.

"This thing's bigger than Virginia City," said Helms, comparing the potential in Lear's steam project to the $1 billion Comstock Lode at his home town, thirty miles away. "When it comes, people will have to live in tents."

At Harrah's, "Lamb Chops à la Lear" became a popular gourmet item. This resulted when Lear, finding his own dinner chops not to his liking, went into the kitchen and showed the chef how to prepare them. "You have to use Lawry's seasoning salt—not something else," he said. "Smother them with it."

He was made an honorary sheriff, perhaps the next best certification after acceptance at the round table, but in this case carrying with it an uncommon hazard. Lear stuck the usual pistol in his belt. This normally works fine, but Lear, a fast dresser, is prone to stuff his shirttails inside his shorts. Sitting with his new friends at the round table one evening, he lost the pistol down the interior as he stood up, presenting the infrequent spectacle of a man's pants sagging in the seat from the presence of a loaded .38.

"You dumb bastard!" Buzz Nanney scolded in alarm. He described a highly personal injury which he said Lear was risking to himself.

Next day Buzz bought Lear a holster. His credentials were complete.

In the handshake country of the old West nobody asked questions about origins—about the child who became father of the man. That is what Boswells are for.

2: MY DESTINY I WILL MAKE FOR MYSELF

On a spring day in 1917, an outlandish figure with a round face and snub nose presented itself to the receptionist at Rotary International headquarters, 910 South Michigan Avenue, Chicago. Instead of being in the usual knee pants and black stockings, the boy was swathed in a pair of men's trousers, pulled high under his armpits by suspenders, overlapped a half turn at the waist, and rolled up at the bottoms. He looked as if he might have wandered in from scarecrow duty at the nearest cornfield.

"My name is William Lear," he said, fixing her with remarkably blue eyes. "I have an appointment with Mr. Perry."

Questioned by the secretary, the caller confessed, "I don't actually have an appointment, but I know he needs an office boy and I thought if I could get in to see him I could get the job."

The secretary ushered him into the office of Chesley A. Perry, secretary of Rotary International. "Young man, who sent you here?" Perry asked with friendly interest.

"My Sunday-school superintendent, Ed James," the lad replied.

Thus William Powell Lear began his career in business. While he would become known for having his own ideas of how things should be done, the sartorial unorthodoxy at the start was his mother's. "If you're going to ask for a job you've got to look like you needed it," she said.

Fibbing about the appointment reflected the influence of Horatio Alger, whose books had made him believe "there was nothing I couldn't do if I had the will to try."

From the same inspirational source, he also knew the value of identifying himself with Sunday school. A man who seeks the Lord is considered unlikely to hang around big city hell holes like pool parlors, dance halls, and other such resorts of Satan.

He needed the job. His mother kept harping at him that he was a free-loader who didn't appreciate what a generous, loving parent she was. She allowed him a quarter weekly, and he blew this entire amount on Sunday. A nickel bought him carfare from his home on Chicago's Southwest side to the Moody Bible Institute Church on the North side. A second nickel bought a chocolate nut sundae at the Buffalo ice cream parlor across the street from the Lane Technical High School on Division Street enroute to the Moody Tabernacle, a mile away, following church and Sunday school. A dime for dinner at the Greek Restaurant left the final nickel for his return home after the day's debauchery.

A job would bring economic improvement and this, in turn, would enable him to get out of the house more. Truth may be what makes you free, as he had read, but he had seen that a little money mixed with it didn't hurt any. While he and his mother violently disagreed with each other, Aunt Minnie fought with both—and with the world at large. At the Stockyards Restaurant, where she worked as a waitress, she was prone to throw the steak on the floor and then, retrieving it, ostentatiously wipe it off with her apron before serving it to the customer who forgot to tip last time.

Caught in the incessant cross fire of the household was Otto Kirmse, its nominal head. A man of peace and Job-like patience, and the worshipful slave of Gertrude Elizabeth Powell Lear, young Bill's mother, whom he called "the kid," Otto had taken mother and son into his bachelor home when the two were living with Aunt Gussie Bornhouser in Dubuque, Iowa, all moving to Chicago later. The mother had abandoned Reuben Marion Lear, a hardworking man for whom success came in inverse ratio to the effort he put forth. This was two or three years after young William was born at Hannibal, Missouri, June 26, 1902, perhaps destined to become as famous in his way as that other son of Hannibal, Mark Twain.

For the boy, among the enrichments of life that came from living with Otto, whose home was next to a brewery in north Dubuque, was the chance to ride beer cases down the roller ways at the loading platforms and to get the smell of yeast implanted in his nostrils for life. Otto, one of the best lathers in the country, brought a measure of tranquillity to the home. Ever on the lookout for common ground for the mother and boy to stand on, he kept a desperate neutrality himself. To Otto, peace was cheap at any price. Long afterward, Lear would still speak of him with respect and affection.

It was partly in quest of the same peace as Otto sought that young Lear took to going to church. He attended the Moody Bible Institute all day Sunday, prayer meeting Wednesday night, Young People's Friendship Club Friday night, and all special occasions in between.

While he may not have gotten too much salvation out of it, he did gain some other things of value. From listening to evangelist Paul Rader, of the Moody Tabernacle, he learned grammar and how to speak. He found out how to meet people, how to shake hands, and what to say when he did so. The first time he had shaken hands, he was chided, "Look, don't give me a cold fish! Look me straight in the eyes and give me a firm hand." In church, in short, he made contact with the world and saw how people normally behaved toward one another.

He learned about hypocrisy, too. When Lear innocently remarked to mutual friends that his girl missed the Sunday-school picnic because "she was sick," his Sunday-school teacher chose to misinterpret his words, causing Lear to lose the girl. The experience soured him on those who preached forbearance and understanding on Sunday only to turn their backs on it Monday. The church has seen little of him since.

There was something else on his mind that day when he asked for the job at Rotary International. This was Irene Roberts, who had graduated two classes ahead of him at the Kershaw Grammar School and was now a junior in high school. Irene, a petite little brunette, was the loveliest, smartest girl he had ever seen. He had held her hand and found the experience full of exquisite promise, which he meant to explore.

This brought him into even more violent conflict with his mother. She warned that girls were evil and must be shunned like Satan himself. She painted a black image of marriage—of dirty diapers and squalling kids in the night—which haunted him for years. It wasn't until the birth of Tina, his seventh child, more than half a century later, that he began to get the full enjoyment of fatherhood. His mother threatened that if ever she found him with one of these skirted hellions who were beginning to excite his budding manhood, the punishment would be awesome.

How fiercely she meant it he learned after he took Irene Roberts for a ride on his new bicycle. The bike was a Christmas present, his first with tires on it, but it remained in the store until it was fully paid for, on his birthday, June 26.

Meanwhile, he daily rode the bicycle on its stand in the store. With envious friends watching, he sat on the seat and furiously pedaled, holding out his hand to signal right turns, left turns, applying the brakes in fast stops, and otherwise filling his life with make-believe until things became real.

On the enchanted day when at last the bike was his, he wheeled straight over to Irene Roberts' house and, with Irene perched on the handlebars, proudly pedaled past his own house. When he arrived home, he walked into an airplane propeller in the form of a broom handle in the hands of his mother.

"Now, kid, take it easy," said Otto with distress, stepping between so that the blows fell on him instead of the boy. But there was nothing Otto could do about what she did next. This was to take the bicycle away, with strident warnings that if he ever rode another girl on it, far worse and more permanent punishment awaited.

For the first time the apron strings that bound him to his mother with a security that terrified him felt loosened. He dared to doubt her authority and to think she was unfair. "Are you a man or a mouse?" he asked himself.

As a solution to poverty, the pay he brought home from Rotary proved to be disillusioning. Except for fifty cents, his mother made him turn over his earnings of $15 a week toward his keep. He cannily saw a way out by resolving to keep quiet when he received the next raise, but when it came, pride got the better of him, and the secret lasted only until he reached home. Into the kitty went the new money along with the old.

In the fall, mindful of Horatio Alger's stand on education, Lear enrolled at Englewood High School, but soon encountered a problem Alger hadn't prepared him for. In electrical class one day, the teacher said, "The ammeter has to be connected to the positive side of the circuit because the current flows from negative to positive."

"Pardon me, sir," objected Lear, who had read all the books on electricity at the local Hiram Kelly Library by the time he was ten, "but that isn't so. You can connect it at either side. It makes no difference."

The teacher's eyebrows lifted. "Well, now, Mr. Lear," he said, "suppose you just show us how it can be connected at either side."

Lear stepped forward and made the connection first on one side, then the other. It worked either way, just as he had said.

"Since you're so smart," the teacher said coldly, "you won't need to come back to this class."

Then it was necessary to set the physics teacher straight on something, with the same result: He was made to feel free to keep away from that class as well. Finally, he found a number of things wrong in shop. Within six weeks, Lear was out of school altogether.

He then landed a job with the Multigraph Company and made some important additions to his knowledge. As office boy, he sat in the corner and listened to his boss, Warren B. Houghton, dictate to his secretary, talk on the telephone, negotiate deals. But what he would remember best was what happened to a fellow being interviewed for the post of new assistant manager. The job paid $9000 a year, tremendous money in those times. To alert office boy Lear, knowing what Houghton wanted, the applicant seemed just the man for the post. Then the damn fool threw the opportunity away. "I can't accept the job before I talk it over with my wife," he said hesitantly. "I always discuss everything with her before I make a move."

"In that case, forget the offer," Houghton said. "I can't hire both of you and since you can't make decisions by yourself I'll have to find someone who can."

Sitting over in his corner, young Lear was stunned. Because this man was spineless, he had muffed a chance he would probably never get again. Houghton's logic was plain; for Lear it was a lesson to remember.

As the owner of a small printing press and several fonts of type when he was twelve, Lear had set up for business printing calling cards. Something less than a stampede developed for the junior Gutenberg's services, but his fascination with printing lingered, and as a Multigraph operator he learned to run the rotary typesetting and printing machine. Being mechanically inclined, he was soon able to see what was wrong when it went wrong and fix it, metamorphosing from office boy to repair man.

But with all the hard work and no money he could call his own, except the fifty cents his mother let him keep each week, he came to feel like the character in "Ol' Man River" who lamented the short returns on one's sweat and toil. Lear visited his father in Oklahoma, spending the summer with him on what was left of the land his grandfather, John Lear, had homesteaded in what became the heart of Tulsa.

His father, now demonstrating his talent for converting hard work into backward movement in the trucking business, all the same gave the boy a silver dollar each day. The lad couldn't help wonder what the largesse might have been if his father, a generous, warmhearted man, had inherited the gifts of his grandfather, a real horse trader. His grandmother, a kind and wise, but frail little creature with a shimmering sense of humor, told how, when things got tough in the old days, Grandfather John would drive into town with a team and wagon and come back with two teams and two wagons, plus a couple of hundred dollars on the side.

Saving the daily dollar, Lear was soon able to buy his first automobile, a Model-T, for $11. He stripped the machine down to its chassis, putting a box on top of the gas tank to sit on and, with the muffler removed, drove around town making more noise than an Indianapolis 500 racer. None of the scores of cars he would own through the years gave him so much satisfaction.

Upon his return to Chicago, his mother accused him of being just like his father.

To young Bill, his father had seemed like a nice guy—not at all as his mother had painted him all these years. Lear gave her no sass. He went to his room, stuffed an extra pair of BVDs, stockings, and a shirt in his waist and silently walked out the door.

He paused and sniffed the wind. "Go West, young man!" He heard the words, supposedly spoken by Horace Greeley, as he had read them at the library. With ten painfully hoarded dollars in his pocket, he headed for Des Plaines and west. He rode the streetcar as far as it went, then hit the Lincoln Highway, a 3384-mile trail of brick and dust leading from Philadelphia to Sacramento, California. That would be his destination: Sacramento, where the Pony Express went.

Under the broiling summer sun of Nebraska, he shocked wheat. The sweat ran into his shoes, making squishy sounds as he walked, and the tiny sawtooth beards stuck in his clothes, prickling his skin like a hair suit. But at two dollars a day the pay was good.

In Denver the money ran out and there were no jobs. Seemingly no one ever quit, died, or was fired in Denver. But, come what may, he would not break silence. He remembered the beatings he used to get when he came home a half hour late and it gave him bitter satisfaction to imagine the scene when he didn't show up at all one night—or the next night or the next night. . . . There was a lot more time to go. He was bound to keep the apron strings broken. "My destiny I will make for myself," he thought.

All else failing, he lied about his age and joined the Navy. But instead of showing him the world, as it promised, the Navy sent him back to Chicago, to the Great Lakes Naval Training Station.

In Preliminary School for instruction as a wireless operator, he ran into an old problem: The teachers knew less than he. Lear had been fascinated by wireless since it brought the *Carpathia* to the rescue in the *Titanic* disaster of 1912, and he had read widely on the subject, including the works of Nikola Tesla, the Croatian wizard. He had even built a radio set, based on a twenty-five-cent Galena crystal which he sent away for, and he had learned the Morse code, the fun ending when some patriot took his antenna down. Anyone listening to the wireless (it wasn't yet "radio") must be a spy tuned in to Berlin, although no transmitter yet reached across town.

In building his wireless receiver, Lear was inspired by a neighbor boy, Shawgo, whose father worked for one of the city utilities. His basement was an eye-popping wonderland of things electrical: Leyden jars, helixes, Tesla coils, transformers, telegraph sounders and relays, batteries, and whatnot, the whole charged with the delicious smell of ozone. Shawgo even had a sending station, which he was forced to take down for fear he would be getting in touch with the Boche.

Additionally, as sailor Lear sat in Naval Preliminary School listening for something he didn't already know about wireless, he enjoyed the benefit of his experience as one half of the erstwhile Laso-Rael Company. This had been a basement enterprise next door to his home, in which Lear and Lawrence Sorenson manufactured radio loose couplers, selling them to Warshawsky's, the big war surplus store. "Laso" was of course short for Lawrence Sorenson and "Rael" was Lear spelled backward.

Finally, Lear had hung around a five-watter atop the Congress Hotel taken over from the Navy after the war and built into one of Chicago's first broadcasting stations by Commander Eugene F. McDonald, Jr., who became president of the Zenith Radio Corporation.

Appreciating Seaman Lear's sophistication in the field of wireless, the Navy took the unusual step of making the best use of his qualifications. It made him an instructor in wireless.

This gained Lear a number of good things—more pay, better quarters, a greater freedom. He was able to come and go almost as he pleased, spending weekends in Chicago. Yet, although he seemed well on his way to making admiral, having passed everyone he joined up with four months before, he decided the Navy was too limiting for him.

Besides, there was Ethel Peterson. He hadn't spent those weekends in Chicago just walking around looking in Marshall Field's windows.

Back with his mother and Otto, who had come to see him after he surfaced at Great Lakes, his mother chastened and much too glad to see him to scold, Lear once more tried the Horatio Alger road to riches. He worked for a number of companies, staying with each only until he reached top pay in his department, then moving on before he got stuck with being president.

His maternal grandfather died, leaving his mother the eighty-acre farm at Barry, Illinois, and under Lear's deviling, the household moved there. While it was good to be away from Aunt Minnie, who was still coming over to the house and raising hell, the glamour of life in the country quickly faded, and after a month or so Lear walked to Quincy, on the river, twenty-five miles northwest. He walked to Quincy because there was no other place to walk to.

Going into Clifford Reid's auto supply store, drawn by some radio paraphernalia in the window, Lear told Reid he was a radio engineer. He qualified himself on two points: He knew more about radio than anybody in Quincy, and he was quite a distance from home, the difference between a radio engineer and a radio repairman being a matter of whether the prophet was far enough afield to claim the honor denied to him in his native heath.

Lear had little trouble persuading Reid to take him on as head of his radio department. Besides his background as an expert, he had nature going for him. Radio reception was at the peak of its eleven-year sunspot cycle, half of which time it gets better and the other half worse. Owners of the crude wireless receiving set of the day were hearing broadcasts from fantastic distances.

"I picked up KDKA last night," the farmer in, say, middle Indiana would crow to his neighbor, referring to Pittsburgh. Or maybe it was WGY, Schenectady; or WWJ, Detroit; or faraway Jefferson City, Missouri, where lifer Harry M. Snodgrass, "King of the Ivories," held forth nightly on his piano at the state prison as the first radio star, giving his fans such favorites as "Kitten on the Keys," "Canadian Capers," and "Three O'Clock in the Morning."

As a consequence of this chance conjunction of an advancing technology with a time of favorable conditions for reception, but for which the development of radio might have still been long deferred, receiving sets became the rage. The elite went first cabin with a loudspeaker, an independent horn by which the scramble of words, notes, and static could be hand-carried about the house, routing peace from all rooms, while the hoi polloi, with palpitating hearts, strained their ears with headphones.

Contractor Julius Bergen was so excited with the set he bought from Lear that he said, "Why don't we go into business together?"

Quincy Radio Laboratories, in a tidy store on Hampshire Street, became an absorbing interest for Lear. When he married Ethel Peterson one afternoon, he promptly left her at the hotel, saying, "I'll see you later," and hurried back to the shop.

Getting home well into the night, Lear found Ethel rather relaxed about the whole thing herself. It took the bridegroom knocking at the door, the neighbors on either side beating on the connecting doors, the telephone operator downstairs ringing the phone, and in the end a bellboy crawling through the transom to wake her up.

"Hello," she said, drowsily peering up at the crowd standing over her.

"Have you been asleep?" Lear asked. In the depth of his relief, it was the best he could think of.

Tragedy would come, but in a different form. William P. Lear, Jr., their first child, lived but two or three months before he smothered in his blankets. With its reminders of little Bill, the house became oppressive and the parents moved to Tulsa, sharing the home of Lear's father and grandmother.

While he worked in a hardware store for grocery money, Lear kept his hand in radio by founding Station WLAL for the Christian Church, destined to become an anchor broadcasting facility as KVOO. It would not be the last time he set up an enterprise which grew to importance for others.

Also at this time, with baby Mary Louise a new member of the family, he decided to complete his high school education. Starting a radio repair shop in his home, which he could tend nights, he enrolled at Tulsa Central High School, taking eight solids, heavy on math. He was at the point of wrapping up the entire four-year curriculum in one when he came a cropper of an old obstacle.

In geometry there was this Mr. Fisk, a whiz in the subject but disliked by his pupils, who one day confronted the class with a classical proposition. "I'm not going to ask you to work the problem," he said, "because you're not far enough along, so I'll work it for you. You'll see that there is only one way to do it."

As Fisk worked, Lear prepared to ride back into the valley of death. Up went his hand when Fisk was finished. "I'm sorry, sir, but there is another way to work it," he said.

Fisk eyed him with shocked surprise. "All right," he said at length, "come to the blackboard and show us!"

Lear stepped forward and began from a different premise. "Therefore," he said as he concluded all the steps and arrived at Q.E.D. (*quod erat demonstrandum*), "there *is* more than one way to work the problem!"

Fisk had been bested and it couldn't have happened to a more deserving fellow. Shouting and cheering, the class marched and stomped around the room. They threw their books into the air.

And Fisk threw out Lear.

Taken together with the need to lend guidance to the machine-shop instructor, who kept going wrong on the installation of a new machine, that pretty well shot formal school days for the young man from Hannibal.

Tulsa palled on him, as did Ethel, and on a day in 1924 he chugged into Chicago in an old Ford with a flat tire, five cents in his pocket—and a new wife, Madelaine, who had become his Lady Elaine the minute he met her in a Tulsa drugstore. In Hyde Park he checked into the Dornel apartment hotel, which was so glad to see a new tenant that it invited him to send in groceries, paying for them and putting them on his bill.

With the problem of food and shelter thus quickly disposed of, Lear hitched a ride downtown to the Coliseum, where there was a radio show going on. As he stood at the gate, wondering how he might get in, out came an old friend from Quincy, Howard Sams, who gave him a pass. Lear wandered around a while, getting his ears beaten down by the cacophony pouring from receivers played at top volume to outdo one another, volume in those days being the measure of excellence. He marveled at things he hadn't seen before.

Having savored the show, he decided to put on a big front and presented himself to Howard Sams's boss, R. D. Morey of the Universal Battery Company. "I can build you a B battery eliminator," he said confidently.

Morey's ears waggled. "B" batteries, which supplied most of the current to operate the receiver, were the bane of the radio business, holding back sales. They cost a lot of money and they didn't last long. Anyone who could find a way to do without the B battery could write his own ticket—as Lear did, for $125 a week, $50 of it paid under the table because it was that much more than the company's chief engineer was paid. In 1924 only sultans and bootleggers made that kind of money.

He soon proved he was worth it. He devised a way to substitute the house current as the source of power for the receiver, converting it to direct current. Lear's B battery eliminator became a prime item in the company's sales line.

Then he met Waldorf Astoria Smith, chief engineer for the Carter Radio Company, makers of radio components. A graduate engineer, Smith taught him more about the application of Ohm's law, named for Georg Simon Ohm, the nineteenth-century German physicist. One ohm is the unit of electrical resistance it takes to make one volt pass a current of one ampere.

Knowing Ohm's law, basic to the radio engineer, helped Lear when he set about building a radio set around a powerful new rectifier tube which had just come out, this being a tube which converts alternating current into direct current. When he was finished with the set, working at night in his two-room apartment, he invited Tom Fletcher, head of the QRS Company, makers of the new rectifier tube, to come and see it.

"I'll give you $200 a week to come to work for me," Fletcher said when he had seen Lear's new receiver.

Lear thereupon had a meeting with his boss at Universal Battery, R. D. Morey. "R.D.," he began, with the confident air of a man negotiating from strength, "I've got a brand-new wife, an ex-wife and child I'm supporting, and you know, I'd just like to live a little better than I am. I wonder if you can pay me more money?"

Morey looked him up and down. "Lear," he replied, "your problem is, you have a champagne appetite and a beer income."

"You certainly hit the nail right on the head," Lear retorted brashly. "I feel I can do something about the income. I don't think I can do much about the appetite."

"More power to you!" Morey said with a wave of the hand. "See you around."

So Lear went to work for Tom Fletcher at QRS. There was an SOS call from the Grigsby-Grunow-Hinds Company, which had just discovered that sixty thousand B battery eliminators they had built didn't work, causing so much static in the set that it drowned out any reception.

The company was desperate. Did Fletcher have any suggestions?

"I've got a bright young fellow working for me," Fletcher answered. "I'll send him over."

Lear promptly found the trouble and fixed it.

"I'll pay you $1000 a month and throw in 2500 shares of stock," Bill Grunow offered. "All I want you to do is think up things to do."

Lear was sitting around thinking—those passing near could feel the undertow—as it came time for the 1925 radio show, the first event to be held at the newly opened one-thousand-room Stevens Hotel on Michigan Boulevard. Since the hotel was on direct current, while all radio sets of the time operated on alternating current, big inverters were installed, with wires branching off to the various display rooms so that the participants, members of the fledgling Radio Manufacturers' Association, could demonstrate their wares.

Alas, with the inverters installed, nobody thought to flip on a radio and see how they worked until almost the eve of the show's opening. The racket buried all other sound, including the distraught words of the radio men. If anybody had a competitive advantage, there was no way of knowing it. It was an emergency of disastrous dimensions.

Waldorf Astoria Smith called in Lear, who directed a balky and disbelieving Smith in making remedies. "That's absolutely crazy!" Smith would protest as Lear proposed a step not in the book. "That can't possibly work!"

"Let's try it anyway," empiricist Lear replied, in words that would become a hallmark in the years to come. And, as in the future, it worked.

The people who had built the inverters gladly arranged to pay Lear a royalty for the use of the invention by which he made them function, beginning with a lump sum of $2500. For years the monthly check for $50 to $125 paid for the Lear groceries.

At the next radio show, likewise at the Stevens Hotel, the hit of the occasion was an innovation called a loudspeaker, developed by the Magnavox Company. Lear talked their man into letting him take one of the speakers home, now a little apartment at 80th Street and Cottage Grove Avenue, for experimentation.

Working in quarters made no roomier by the recent arrival of a second little Bill, Jr., Lear put the speaker into a wooden dry goods box, in the side of which he first cut a hole to fit the mouth of the horn. He added supporting components, including a built-in amplifier, and then hooked it all to a portable phonograph playing a Broadway hit. No musical recording had ever sounded like this.

He took the combination downtown, set it up in his office, and turned on the music. Bill Grunow came racing in from his own office next door. "What in hell is that?" he demanded excitedly.

"That's a dynamic speaker," Lear replied, looking pleased. "Boy, that's great!"

A handsome new cabinet radio set was designed around Lear's enclosed speaker and named Majestic. Made in a high-boy and a low-boy model, it brought jostling lines of distributors to the door with rolls of cash in their hands, and in due course the 2500 shares of stock which Bill Grunow gave Lear when he hired him, worth $25 a share then, went to $1600—only not for Bill Lear. He had unloaded it long ago.

Instead of living the life of the millionaire he could have been, Lear was hard at work with Ernie Tyrman of the Tyrman Electric Company building radio sets which infringed the patents of RCA, General Electric, Westinghouse, and Western Electric. These were the "Radio Trust," to whom Grigsby-Grunow paid millions in royalties annually before going broke in 1934, and they were inclined to be hard-nosed toward claim jumpers.

Besides being troubled with visions of police arriving in the night and dragging them off to jail, Lear and Tyrman developed a severe burning sensation in their gastric systems, which subsided with a half hour's ingestion of food, but then got worse than ever. The doctor said the only answer was to operate.

Tyrman went first and died. Disquieted by this result to his partner, Lear looked for some other form of cure. He read up on the causes of ulcers. He discovered that citrus juice makes the system alkaline, overcoming acidity, which he knew was his problem when the piece of litmus paper he put on his tongue turned red. He began eating oranges and grapefruit and drinking Vichy water, whose alkali content stays in suspension. There were no more stomach pains.

His champagne tastes were giving his income a hard race, and he decided the time had come to start his own business. He had paid off the mortgage on his mother's house on 65th Street, and with her and Otto back on the farm, he set up Lear Radio Laboratories in the basement.

He proposed to make something which wasn't supposed to work, using an unavailable material which wasn't suitable. This was a radio coil only half the standard size—1⅛ inches in diameter by the same in length. Professor Morecroft, whose book was considered authoritative, said the coils had to be 2¼ by 2⅜ inches to be any good.

Moreover, according to Morecroft, the Litzendrat wire Lear planned to use on the coils and which he would have to make was no good above one thousand kilocycles, five hundred short of the mark in the range he wanted.

Lear didn't know this, though, not having read Morecroft. He knew that electric current tends to flow on the outside, along the path of least resistance. Therefore, many fine wires woven together, providing more surface, improved the flow of current, which in turn should make for greater selectivity in tuning in the stations.

Lear called on an old friend, Algot Olson, who had gotten rich in the lumber business and was taking life easy at Cedar Lake, Indiana. "I've got an idea I want to do something about," Lear said, "but it's going to take some money. I want to borrow $5000."

Olson rode gently in his swing, looking out over the lake, as he listened to Lear enthusiastically describe how he planned to make the wire he would need. There would be spools and rotating tables, with wire strands being turned and something else going around to wrap silk on the wire. He told how he was going to make a machine to make the coils that used the wire made by the first machine.

When Lear finished, Olson chuckled and burst into laughter.

"Mr. Olson, I don't like to be laughed at," Lear said formally. "I'm serious."

"I'm really not laughing at you," Olson replied. "I'm laughing because I remember when I was your age I was full of vim, vigor, and confidence, too. This thing isn't going to work. I'll bet all the tea in China."

"I know it will!" Lear protested.

"I know you're sure, but it won't come out the way you think," Olson said. "It never does." He paused thoughtfully. "All the same, even though I have no confidence in your scheme, I'm going to loan you the money—because I think you're an honest man and you'll pay me back out of the sweat of your brow."

By the time Lear drew the last of the $5000, which Olson let him have in driblets, he had thirteen wire-making machines going, along with another machine to make the coils, his only helper being Don Mitchell, a trouble shooter on the automatic signals of the Santa Fe Railroad. The basement of his mother's home could have been the headquarters of Rube Goldberg.

Lear installed a set of his new coils in a Zenith receiver and invited Zenith president Gene McDonald out for a demonstration, along with his chief engineer, Carl Hassel.

"But they can't possibly be as good as ours!" objected Hassel, rejecting what his ears told him as they listened first to a standard Zenith set, then to the one with Lear's new coils. These simply had to be inferior, Hassel argued, because the design failed to follow the gospel according to Morecroft.

"Buy 'em!" McDonald ordered. "Buy fifty thousand of 'em!"

For a home basement operation, this wasn't a bad start. Lear changed the name from Lear Radio Laboratories to Radio Coil and Wire Corporation. That had a good ring to it.

Soon he traded his new enterprise for a one-third interest in the Galvin Manufacturing Company, makers of radio chassis. Looking at Lear's diminutive coils one day, visiting Zenith engineer Howard Gates mused, "Gee, these little coils ought to make a nice radio for automobiles."

"I'd like to make an auto radio," Lear answered. "Suppose I design the set and give you the drawings to make up the metal work. Then I'll put in the coils, condensers, and so forth."

They made two sets, one for each man. Lear placed his on Paul Galvin's desk.

"What's that?" Galvin asked.

"An automobile radio," Lear replied.

Galvin looked them over indifferently. "Well, I think it's a bunch of crap," he said. "They'll never be allowed in cars. There'll be laws against it."

Lear bridled. "You know what I think about what you think about automobile radios?" he asked.

"What?"

"Nothing! You're just as wrong as you can be. A radio in the car will be a relaxation to the driver. Instead of bothering him, it'll make him less nervous—give him a chance to listen to his favorite program when he gets caught in a traffic jam. It won't be legislated against."

Lear delivered one set to Howard Gates and installed the other in his own automobile. A couple of weeks later, Galvin sought him out, asking, "Did you run a bill of material on that automobile radio set you made?"

"Yes," Lear replied.

"How much did it run?"

"Twenty-two dollars."

Galvin began figuring. "Let's see—if we sell it for five and a half times $22, that would be approximately $122. Less $50 and 10 per cent discount, that would come to about $50, and we'd be able to make 'em for about $35, so we'd make $15 apiece." He looked at Lear. "Let's make a couple hundred."

On a trip across the country, Lear and Galvin tossed around several names for the new radio, agreeing on one compounded from "motor" and "victrola." They named it "Motorola" and Galvin Manufacturing Company became Motorola Incorporated.

Counting his income from Galvin and that from a sideline venture with Bob Weurfle, building radio chassis, Lear was earning around $35,000 a year, very rare for an honest man in the deep Depression year of 1931. It was enough so he could afford an airplane, and he went to Dearborn, Michigan, to buy a Fleet biplane from a woman who kept the ship in the Ford hangar. She measured him carefully, noting the slicked-back hair, brilliantined and parted in the middle; the pin-stripe suit, the pearl-gray, snap-brim hat. She had heard of types like this in Chicago. One read about them in the papers.

When Lear, grinning genially, brought out $2500 in green money, she all but had him arrested. She sent him home empty-handed while she had him thoroughly investigated, delivering the ship herself in her own good time, weeks later after deciding he wasn't a bootlegger.

Lear tolerated two and half hours' flying instruction, then was off on his own, sneaking in his first solo one afternoon when the instructor was away from the field. He and Madelaine weren't getting along and he had immediate use for the airplane in respect to Miss Nellie Hughes, a trim little blond secretary at Galvin. It wasn't so much that Nellie, reserved and efficient, treated him indifferently, much as he capered and flashed before her. She gave no sign that she even knew he existed. The flying machine got him off the ground in more ways than one.

The little puddle-jumping biplane, buzzing along at ninety miles an hour, would also bear profoundly on the shape of things to come.

He decided early to try the ship out cross-country, not by flying to neighboring Wheaton, or Cedar Lake, or Moline, say, but by flying to New York City. "You can go along," he told instructor F. L. Yeomans, known as "Fly Boy," who had never been on such a trip himself, "but I'm going to do all the flying, all the navigating, and all the landing and everything else. Is that clear? I'm taking you along just in case I do something absolutely wrong."

It soon became clear that the trick in flying across the country was to find where you wanted to go, especially when one was a little hazy on his geography. Lear had always thought that the hogback ridges of the Appalachian Mountains ran north and south rather than northeast and southwest. This gave him a tendency to pull the ship to the right to cross at right angles as he flew over, pointing him southeast toward Philadelphia and Washington rather than east to New York.

Returning to Chicago after three or four days' hobnobbing with other birdmen at Roosevelt Field promised to be easy. By now an experienced cross-country flyer, as cross-country flyers went in 1931, Lear was not surprised to find there was no trouble whatever in keeping the ship on a due west heading. In fact, he realized belatedly, the compass read west no matter which way he pointed the ship. They had used iron screws in replacing his windshield at Roosevelt Field. The compass pointed not to magnetic north but to the windshield screws six inches away. Fortunately, a little weed patch below offered a convenient place to land and find out from the school children next door where they were.

By the time Lear and Fly Boy at last found their way home, it was plain that one needed no faulty compass to get lost. Not knowing where you were seemed the normal human condition aloft. Following the railroad tracks might get you to the next town, all right, but then, which of those grassy fields was the airport?

The *camoufleurs* of wartime should do as well. If it took fifty
gallons of gasoline to get there, it took another fifty to find the
landing field.

It was something to think about as Lear acquired a second
airplane, a Stinson Reliant, and flying more and more took up his
time. This did not escape the notice of Paul Galvin. Lear's timing on
an ultimatum to his employer, after a three-day absence in Fort
Wayne with a balky engine, could have been better.

"Well, Bill, we're going to miss you around here," Galvin said—
and that was that with Motorola. It was 1931, the bottom of the
Depression and not the best time to be cut loose from an income.

Lear moved out to the Curtiss-Reynolds Airport, northwest of
town, renting a large, two-story house to live in and a lean-to in the
hangar for his workshop, all for $90 a month. The furnishings of
his residence, where he kept open house around the clock, included
the usual five-gallon distilled water bottle upended on its stand in
the corner, only this one contained gin, assembled from equal parts
pure alcohol and water with a few drops of juniper juice added for
flavor.

This method of storage for a party staple combined easy access
with effective concealment from Prohibition snoopers. It was good
for laughs, too, as guests hurried to the water cooler for a badly
needed chaser, only to throw down a half glass of raw gin on top
of what already had them on fire. Five bedrooms afforded ample
haven for the wounded.

In the meantime he was keeping Madelaine and their two
youngsters, Patty and Bill, Jr., in high style at the Flamingo, a posh
apartment tower on the lake front in Hyde Park, meeting the nut
with due bills, a form of IOU given by the house to advertising
agencies for advertising in lieu of money and which the ad
agencies sold for thirty cents or so on the dollar. Lear also provided the family with a new Chevrolet.

These details of Lear's *modus vivendi* were high octane fuel to
the clacking tongue of Aunt Minnie, as he learned when he called
on his mother. "You're a source of terrible embarrassment to me,"
his mother said heavily. "Aunt Minnie says you must be in the
bootlegging business, because how else could you afford two airplanes and two automobiles, and have Madelaine and the kids
living at a fine hotel and you living up there in that big house at the
airport and all?" She sighed and shook her head. "I just don't
know what to tell her."

"You can tell her I'm a manufacturer," Lear said defensively. "That's what I am. I'm in the radio business."

She laughed derisively. "What do you mean, you're in the radio business? Why, Mr. Novak up there on the corner with a *radio store,* he's in the radio business and he can't afford anything like that!"

Nothing had changed with Mom through the years. Convincing her of the truth was as difficult as it was to sell the aircraft radio receivers he turned out at the lean-to in the Curtiss-Reynolds hangar, uncowed by occasional threatening letters from his old friends, Western Electric, the Bell Telephone Laboratories, RCA and Westinghouse.

"You want to buy a radio set for your airplane?" Lear would ask a pilot.

"Nah, when I'm flying, I don't want to be entertained."

"This isn't for entertainment. This is for navigation."

"Navigation! How do you navigate with a radio set? You kidding?"

"You use the radio ranges installed by the government for the airlines."

"What's a radio range?"

Patiently, Lear would explain about the broadcast beacons which the pilot followed in his earphones. He described how you received one kind of broken signal flying to the left of the range, another kind to the right, and a continuous signal when you flew down the middle.

"I don't need any fancy stuff like that," the pilot replied scornfully. "I just follow the railroad tracks" (which sometimes ran into a tunnel).

Airplane pilots stood against instruments like old sea captains against steam over sails. Man and boy, by the seat of their pants, they had flown the railroad tracks, and they weren't about to try any of these sissified ways of going across the country.

Bad as things were, they suddenly got worse. With the banks failing right and left, Lear went to his own bank to draw out a couple thousand dollars only to have the doors snap closed in front of him. President Roosevelt's bank holiday had just begun as he arrived.

But God tempers the wind to the shorn lamb. When nobody has any money, it turned out, nobody needs it much; and the Lear household was able to get by for the duration of the bank holiday on a pair of $20 bills Nellie and a girl friend had won from Lear in

a bet. All one needed money for was carfare and phone calls. All
else was on the cuff—with everybody eager to supply the cuff.
The gin bottle was in good shape. Bootlegger, butcher, and grocer
kept delivering as usual.

As 1934 came on, with prospects around Chicago looking no
better, Lear decided to move his operations to New York. He sent
his little crew on ahead to open an office while he detoured to
Florida for a conclave of sportsmen pilots, winning the Miami-to-
Orlando Navigation Race.

He needed the $400 prize money to help pay for the move to
New York.

3: WE'RE GOING TO TAKE NEW YORK BY STORM

Reaching New York in mid-January, Lear found his new quarters through Nellie, on whose address he was better posted. They comprised a single room on the ninth floor at 157 Chambers Street, divided by a partition, with a tiny machine shop on one side, the bookkeeper, secretary, and Lear's office bunched on the other.

While the setup hardly gave promise of becoming an immediate force in the city's economy, Lear was optimistic, as always. "We're going to take New York by storm," he said.

However that might be, something of a blow enveloped him first. To the problems that harried him in Chicago, still with him, he now had to add the disadvantages of being in a strange town where nobody knew him. Fortunes sank to where it was not inconsequential that by investing in a beer downstairs, one could get a London broil sandwich for another dime. Liberally dowsed with catsup and Lea & Perrins, the sandwich wasn't bad.

In his $8-a-week room at the St. George Hotel in Brooklyn, deeply in debt and seeing no way out, Lear considered jumping out the window. But death was so permanent. Pacing the floor, he tried to think of something useful to the world which he could supply. All-wave radio sets, combining a high frequency receiver, which brought in stations up to five thousand miles away, with the regular broadcast band, were becoming popular. The trouble was, no two models of an all-wave set ever came out alike, so that with each new design there was extensive debugging to do.

"Why don't I make a front end that won't be changed for each new model but would stay the same?" Lear asked himself. "It would be a kind of standard front end to fit all models." This would make the production of all-wave radio sets less expensive, making them cheaper to the buyer.

Lear presented the idea to Russ King of RCA at lunch. "How long will it take you to develop such a thing?" King asked.

"Ten days or a couple of weeks."

"You mean six months or a year, don't you?" Nothing went that fast at RCA.

"I'll have it in two weeks," Lear insisted.

He went back to his office with $500 from King to buy materials, and with his arms full of RCA components "to make it easier for RCA to produce the thing after I design it."

Lear and his crew fell to work at once, sketching and making tools to punch out some of the parts they would need. In two weeks Lear was back at RCA with the first radio receiver containing a turret tuner and having five bands—low frequency, broadcast, and three shortwave—made possible by the new tuner. This was the beginning of the "magic brain" for which RCA radio sets became famous.

President E. T. Cunningham of the RCA Victor Division in Camden, New Jersey, was so excited he kept offering Lear a cigarette, not hearing him say he didn't smoke.

They arranged to meet again next day at Cunningham's New York office. On the way there, Lear said to himself, "This is a great idea I've got. It definitely ought to be worth $25,000. I won't take a cent less than $10,000, unless all I can get is $5000. Of course, $2500 would pay a lot of our bills."

When at last he was ushered in to see Cunningham, after nervously cooling his heels for over an hour, Lear had decided not to quote any price at all. "You know a lot more about what the value is to you than I do," he said reasonably. "I would like you to suggest what you would give me for it."

"We'll give you $50,000 cash."

Lear's vocal cords froze. He had the sudden oafish stare of a man hit on the head with a heavy object.

"Wait a minute," Cunningham went on, misreading Lear's silence. "Also, we'll give you $25,000 a year for five years as a retainer to be our consultant."

There still being no sound from Lear, Cunningham piled on some more. "We'll give you $15,000 worth of work a year besides.

That makes a total of $40,000 a year for five years, plus the $50,000 for the patent."

With a check for $50,000 in his pocket, Lear arrived back at the office with the bottoms of his feet sore from slapping at the pavement, trying to find it somewhere below, as he walked. It was Friday the thirteenth, which ever after he would look upon as an auspicious date for special undertakings.

With fresh folding money in hand, Lear moved to better quarters at 123 West 17th Street—at the front of the building instead of the rear, on the fifth floor instead of the ninth. One of the things he developed here, inspired by the memory of his wandering odyssey across country with Fly Boy in 1931, was an aircraft radio direction finder.

This caught the eye of the Air Corps, which invited him to Wright Field at Dayton to assist its "secret weapon," a Swiss named Kruesi whose very name it mentioned only sparingly, work on a direction finder of its own. Thereafter, in any discussion of bureaucracy, Lear would have trouble keeping his voice down.

Kruesi, no engineer but speaking broken English, the way real scientists are supposed to, had first gone to Western Airlines with his idea, which he had filched from a German radio magazine. The airline referred him to the Air Corps which, with pickings slim in the secrecy business, instantly enshrouded the subject with an elaborate huggermugger that could have been a trial run for the Manhattan Project some years later.

Lear's job was to see if he could adapt the "invention" to the radio receivers then in use by the Air Corps. He soon saw, as he studied the contrivance, that it contained a built-in error. The pilot would be better off sticking with the railroad tracks.

"I think I can demonstrate that this equipment will not work," Lear said to Captain Albert F. Hegenberger who, with Captain Lester J. Maitland, had made the first flight to Hawaii in 1927.

Cautiously, they let Lear into the little black-curtained room where Kruesi's direction finder was set up. "Will you take a bearing on any station you want?" Lear invited him.

Kruesi did so and Lear asked, "Now where is the station?"

"The loop points in that direction, so that's where the station is," Kruesi answered.

Lear reached into the set and retuned it slightly, getting a different indication. "*Now* where is the station?"

Reluctantly, Kruesi pointed in the new direction.

"How come the station was coming from that corner of the room a minute ago and now it's coming from the opposite corner?" Lear asked.

The Air Corps' secret weapon Kruesi stared briefly at Lear, then turned on his heel and stalked from the room, without a word.

"You know, Bill," Hegenberger said reproachfully as he and Lear walked away, "the Air Corps is like a club. If you criticize a member of the club, you criticize the whole club. I think you have made yourself *persona non grata* with the Air Corps, and I don't think you can do anything for us."

In the fullness of time, though, as Lear continued to improve his direction finder, the Signal Corps got over its huff. It invited Lear to take part in a direction finder competition at Norfolk, Virginia, the winner to receive an order for two hundred of the instruments. Lear was elated to have this opportunity to demonstrate his Learoscope, hundreds of which he had already sold to civil aviation. The Learoscope, destined to become the standard for the next two decades, was incapable of giving a false reading. In navigating an airplane, Lear believed in the philosophy of Artemus Ward that "It's better to know nothing than to know what ain't so."

At Norfolk, Lear was further encouraged by the stern measures taken to insure the vestal purity of the competition. Each of a dozen Air Corps pilots took up each direction finder, one by one, keeping tight-lipped about how they performed. The pilots spoke to no contenders; the contenders spoke to no pilots. At lunch, contenders and pilots sat at separate tables. If the occasion had been any more aseptic, it seemed, it would have had to be held in another world.

The outcome, therefore, was disillusioning. The restraints invoked on speech during the contest continued after it was over and apparently included not mentioning who won. Six months had passed in silence when Colonel George Holloman confided to Lear, "I guess you know you won that contest, don't you?"

"How in hell would I know?" Lear demanded. "Nobody ever told me. I finally quit trying to find out."

"Oh, yes, you won it hands down," Colonel Holloman said. "There was no comparison between your equipment and the others. Yours was the best on all counts."

The order for the two hundred direction finders, however, had quietly been awarded to Bendix. This recalled for Lear, a small fish, that at about the time of the Norfolk "competition," Vincent Bendix, not yet a whale but more a barracuda at this point, had swiveled a predatory eye in his direction and tried to swallow him.

Bendix operated from a suite of five rooms at the Waldorf, a separate deal cooking in each room. "We'll give you $50,000 for a minority interest in your company—49 per cent," Bendix and his associates offered. "Bring down all the common stock of your company."

"Not all of it," Lear corrected. "You want 49 per cent of it."

"No, bring it all in."

"Why?"

"Because here's the way we want to work it: We're going to issue $100,000 worth of Bendix stock for your company, and we'll give you 51 per cent of that," Bendix explained.

Lear studied them hard, his blue eyes glinting. He rose to his feet. "Gentlemen, it's one thing to try to cheat me," he said. "It's something else to underestimate my intelligence. You're making me a crooked pitch because you think I'm too stupid to understand that I wouldn't own 51 per cent of my company, but rather that I would have a very minute interest in the Bendix Corporation."

Having failed to swallow him, Bendix tried a different tack. They lured Lear's people away with offers of twice the pay and half the hours—nobody worked around the clock at Bendix —the negotiations being conducted by a quisling whom Lear had befriended.

Lear rolled up his sleeves, hired new people, and prepared to play David to Bendix's Goliath. As he continued his ascent in the field of aircraft instrument development, Vincent Bendix once again sent word that he wanted to see him. Bascomb Smith greeted him with pencil and paper as Lear arrived at the Bendix den in the Waldorf. "Mr. Bendix would like you to write down exactly what it is you want," Smith said.

Lear facetiously listed a dirigible, a fleet of airplanes, numerous automobiles, a fat bank account, freedom from responsibilities and expenses. He wrote that he wanted to live five hundred years without getting any older than his present age of thirty-three.

When Lear had finished, Smith picked up the list and disappeared. An anguished shout rang out from another room, and Bendix burst into view, wearing a barber's apron and his face half covered with lather. "Damn it, Bill!" he cried, waving Lear's list. "This is what I want!"

There was another large fish who was annoyed by Lear's activities in aviation electronics. This was RCA. It sent a letter asking Lear to "show cause why we shouldn't prosecute you for violating our patents" in building the Learoscope.

Lear called in a Scripps-Howard reporter, who wrote a few thousand words under the headline, YOUNG INVENTOR BATTLES PATENT POOLS SINGLE-HANDED. Chastened by the publicity, RCA protested and came through with the license to make radio communication equipment, which they had denied Lear for years. At the same time it licensed other manufacturers to do the same.

"How much back royalties do you feel you owe us?" RCA asked Lear.

Lear did some fast figuring in his head. "Five dollars," he said.

Fair enough—that gave RCA their point technically. It took the same question to Freddy Link, who occupied the back half of the same floor Lear was on, sometimes using Lear's tools. Link laboriously counted up all the sales he had ever made and paid RCA several thousand dollars. When he found out about Lear's $5 settlement, he was badly shaken.

And then, in 1940, Lear nearly flew to kingdom come, not for want of faithful instruments but because human hands had faltered. Flying a brand-new Cessna with five people aboard, he was on his way to the 1941 air races in Miami, Florida. After the fuel had lasted a gratifyingly long time he switched to his reserve tank—and in a minute or so the engines stopped. The reserve tank was empty. Somebody at the Cessna factory had installed a fuel selector valve incorrectly.

Below in the darkness lay the Georgia swamplands, studded with scrub pine, whose starved trunks stood up like spear points. Lear radioed Jacksonville. "We have two dead engines. If you don't hear back from us in a little while, send a search party."

As the ship settled with faint whistling sounds in the sudden silence, co-pilot John Osborne of *Time* magazine strained his eyes down through the night. "I don't see a thing—too dark," he said. "But there's a river."

"Where?" Lear asked.

"Right off to your left." Lear preferred drowning to being

skewered by a pine stem and brought the ship down on the river.

The engine nacelles, extending well below the wing, caught the water and wrenched the ship to a stop in less than a dozen feet. Lear jackknifed against the steering wheel, smashing the lower part of his face and losing most of his teeth. By the time a hillbilly doctor got him to Jacksonville's St. Francis Hospital in his Model-T, cold, shivering, and delirious from loss of blood, Lear thought those forms in white were angels. He would carry the marks—like dueling scars—of his first and only air crash the rest of his life. Six weeks later he flew back to New York in a new ship.

As war approached, the Air Corps invited him to help write the specifications for a new direction finder, but things between the two were soon going poorly again. Officers and others in the project wanted to write in that the direction finder should not be subject to mountain effect.

"You might as well write in that an airplane mustn't be affected by gravity," Lear said.

They insisted on no shore line effect and no night effect.

"These are all natural phenomena which must be lived with," Lear explained, hanging onto his patience. "We can't write in specifications that require the direction finder to change or cancel the laws of nature."

The officer in charge had a familiar solution to the impasse. "Since you have a working direction finder, and much more actual experience, it puts us at a tremendous disadvantage in arguing with you. So we would appreciate it if you didn't show up any more."

This substantially remained the Air Defense Services' position on Lear even after the bombs fell on Pearl Harbor and President Roosevelt called for 50,000 airplanes a year, all needing direction finders.

"We still don't need you," they told Lear, in effect.

The Signal Corps, while ordering 100,000 direction finders from Bendix, at length begrudged Lear an order for 390, imposing stiffer requirements than it did for Bendix. But when Lear asked the Signal Corps for information on the Bendix control head so that he could make his direction finders interchangeable with those of Bendix, allowing complete interchangeability, the answer was *no*. They wouldn't permit Lear to see the Bendix equipment because, although the taxpayers had already paid Bendix for it, it still belonged to Bendix, it was explained.

The best the Signal Corps could do was to let a Lear draftsman grab what he could on the fly as they briefly showed him the Bendix device in the Signal Corps hut at Wright Field.

The Signal Corps gave other little signs that they were less than wholeheartedly on Lear's side. Their Air Corps inspector, examining the completed direction finders, found fault not with their performance but with such details as the shade of the paint used. A resourceful fellow, the inspector was able by such means to tie up the acceptance of every one of Lear's instruments, badly needed as they might be to guide our fighting pilots.

Lear took the unprecedented step of complaining directly to the Inspector General's office in Washington, and was assigned a new inspector. The new man asked Lear, "What have you done?"

"Why?" Lear countered suspiciously.

"I can't tell you."

"But you've been ordered to slow us up as much as possible, haven't you?" Lear accused.

"I can't admit that."

The new inspector later confided that he had been instructed to reject Lear's entire output of direction finders. Instead, however, he saw that all requirements were met on each instrument, then passed it—playing the game honestly.

Finished with Lear, the inspector was moved on to the plant of a Bendix subcontractor, the Sparks-Worthington Company, and there, continuing to live dangerously, he made Sparks-Worthington put their direction fingers through the same tests as the Signal Corps had required for Lear's. To the company's extreme embarassment, all instruments failed the humidity test, not one working after it had been in the humidity chamber.

For his impertinence in daring to treat these people the same as Lear, Bendix put the screws on the Signal Corps to get the offending inspector thrown out of the service. This only made the inspector mad; he shut the plant down.

Although he had led in the development of direction finders, Lear got no more orders for them beyond the 390. He thereupon bid on a motor-driven reel needed on Air Corps planes to reel the transmitting antenna in and out. He invested $39,000 developing it, designing a reel that made use of his patented fast stop clutch. He delivered two perfectly functioning motor reels, meeting all specifications, along with complete drawings.

The Signal Corps gave him short shrift for his pains. It chose a company, giving them Lear's drawings, then ruled Lear out because he wasn't listed by the Signal Corp as a reel manufacturer.

"But I'm the one who designed the reels," Lear protested.

"Makes no difference," the civil servant said doggedly. "You've got to be listed as a motor reel manufacturer, and you're not listed."

Makers of fishing reels, makers of barbed wire spools, makers of those big reels telephone cable comes on—yes. These were "reel manufacturers." But Lear, who originated this particular motor reel and alone knew anything about it, and owned the Fast Stop Clutch patent necessary to its success, no—solely because he failed to fit a Yellow Pages' classification. It was bureaucratic boneheadness at its finest.

The Signal Corps did pretty well again, though—in the case of the missile being tested that was guided to its target by impulses sent along a trailing wire by the movement of a pair of binoculars in the hands of a man aboard a helicopter. Unfortunately, the chopper made an unstable platform and the missile connected only once in ten tries.

Finally Lear's auto pilot was installed aboard the chopper, and the score rose to nine in ten tries. "Holy cow!" exclaimed General Dwight Eisenhower as he saw one tank after another disintegrate.

All the same, the Signal Corps turned thumbs down on a contract for Lear to provide stabilization for the missile-firing helicopters. He was not "an approved auto pilot manufacturer" by the Signal Corp.

Whatever discounts Lear might enter against 1942, he would mark it down as a very good year, for that was the year he married Moya Olsen, the dark-eyed daughter of comedian Ole Olsen. They had met in her father's dressing room soon after he and Chic Johnson opened in *Hellzapoppin* on Broadway in 1938.

Moya was out front doing her best to record a "book" on the show for the Library of Congress, not easy since there was no script and not much happened twice the same way. "Honey, come here," her father had said. "I have a friend I want you to meet."

"Ho hum," Moya thought. "Friend No. 4982 he has wanted me to meet."

Nothing more happened for a couple of weeks. Then came a phone call from Lear, who was phasing out his third wife, Margaret. He invited the Olsens to dinner. "Shall we go?" Moya asked her brother, JC (for John Charles). "He'll buy us dinner."

Christmas Eve, Lear phoned again. Would she have a "bite to eat" with him at the Stork Club? A bite to eat had always meant the B/G or White Castle. She had never been to the Stork Club. As they dined, they found a common denominator in life's frustrations. Lear told about his business problems. Moya, who had dreamed of being a famous dancer, in the mold of Pavlova and Nijinsky, only to be told by her teacher she would make a good "jitterbug," talked of her troubles as a secretary.

But it wasn't until one night at the Beachcomber, over shrimp and water chestnuts with a friend, that she knew what the future held. In the rice cake she found a message, "You will marry your present lover and be happy."

"So she put the little fortune away in her heart and tranquillity took over," she would write in *A Little Love Story*, a small, leather-bound book with neatly hand-lettered pages framed in airplanes and four-leaf clovers, "and even though she never believed in Santa Claus or the Easter Bunny, she believed in this."

The happy ending came on the final page, "So one day Bill came and said—"

They were married in Greenwich, Connecticut, on a Sunday in 1942 while *Sons o' Fun* was heading for a record run on Broadway—Sunday because there was no show on the Sabbath and stars Olsen and Johnson could both attend the ceremony. Ella Logan sang an old Gaelic love song, "Moya," for the bride, whose christened name, Moja, is pronounced the same way in the Norse land of her forefathers.

They lived in diverse places from coast to coast and then, in 1946, Lear picked Grand Rapids, Michigan, as a likely site to locate his aircraft instrument business, which by now was flourishing.

His associates were horrified at the informal way he made the choice. "Bill, that's not how you decide to move a business like this!" they protested. "First you hire industrial consultants who make a study of several alternate places. They investigate the labor situation, tax rates, schools, markets, and so forth. Then they make a recommendation. They may find that another location is better for this business than Grand Rapids. You have to know what you're doing, Bill."

Grudgingly, Lear approved and the designated experts were engaged. Ten weeks and $5000 later they came up with the answer. Their recommendation: Grand Rapids.

The Lears lived in a great old frame mansion, turning it into a kind of boardinghouse for their engineers, complete with an ancient hotel register supplied by Ole Olsen from his show business travels. "Grand Rapids was a very important, productive, wonderful time in our lives," Moya remembered.

Grand Rapids could say the same thing, getting a good deal out of having Lear in town. When Lear eventually sold out to the Siegler Corporation, headquartered in Santa Monica, California, the operation he founded, now known as the Instrument Division of Lear-Siegler, Incorporated, went on to become the largest unit in the firm's world-wide complex of fifty-six divisions in twenty-seven states and thirteen foreign countries, dealing in "diversified manufacture, real estate development, construction, electronics, industrial tools, and education," with sales of $566 million in 1970.

"Among all the local aircraft supplier firms to which World War II gave a new vitality, of most lasting benefit to Grand Rapids was Lear-Siegler, Inc.," noted the seven-hundred-page tome *The Story of Grand Rapids*, published in 1966, with a copy inscribed to Lear by Editor Z. Z. Lydens, "in acknowledgement of his contribution to Grand Rapids."

In Grand Rapids, while he went on turning out aircraft instruments, Lear began work on an automatic pilot. Helping him was Nils Eklund, an erudite engineer and physicist with credentials from a half dozen universities, including the University of Dresden, Columbia, and the Massachusetts Institute of Technology.

The two would work on the auto pilot until midnight or later, then drive to the airport and install it in Lear's Twin Beech, flying around until near dawn, dipping and tipping the plane and seeing how well the auto pilot brought it back to even keel. They took turns sleeping, Eklund, no pilot, monitoring the auto pilot while Lear slept.

By the time they arrived home, they were too tired to eat the casserole Moya had prepared. Instead, they fed their spirits by reading the *Rubáiyát of Omar Khayyám,* Moya meanwhile spooning food into them.

They completed the automatic pilot in Santa Monica, California, which succeeded as home base in 1946, and in 1950 it brought Lear aviation's highest award, the Collier Trophy.

The following year, nervously bedecked in cap and gown, he received an honorary doctorate of engineering from the University of Michigan in "appreciation of the advances which your inventive genius has made possible in modern methods of communication and aviation." Other honors followed: the Thulin Award from Sweden, the Great Silver Medal from the City of Paris, and the Horatio Alger Award "for having pulled himself up to the top of his field by his bootstraps."

There was one more, though less formal kudo, which brought a satisfaction all its own to the lad who had been anathema to his teachers. This came from the University of California at Los Angeles where inquisitive students kept him for an extra hour and a half after he had first addressed more than a thousand of them in the Grand Ballroom of the Student Union.

"Mr. Lear," reported Nick Brestoff, science editor of the *Daily Bruin,* "can educate with an excellence not often found in the classroom. . . . You should know that many professors here fail during the whole quarter to elicit as many questions. Mr. Lear can only be termed relevant."

Winning the Collier Trophy upheld Lear's own confidence in his creation. Flying out of New Orleans one morning after an active night, bound for Grand Rapids, he put the ship on auto when he reached altitude and lay down in the cabin, placing himself so that he could see the instrument panel. He "blinked" and saw that the clock hands had moved ahead two hours. He was over Rantoul, Illinois, exactly on course.

Another time, inadvertently intruding on military air space, he hastily switched on the auto pilot, planted three-year-old David in his seat, and hid back in the cabin as an Air Force interceptor came alongside. The bug-eyed AF pilot was still frantically calling the base for instructions on the rescue of infants in runaway airplanes when Lear, grinning fiendishly, materialized in the window.

When Lear had built ten thousand automatic pilots, he was reunited with his old friends, the Air Force, who needed an auto pilot for the F-84. They had given the contract to Westinghouse, but five years and $50 million later the company still hadn't produced an acceptable automatic pilot.

"Try mine in three planes," Lear proposed.

Colonel Al Boyd shook his head. "We can't tie up that many ships," he said.

"Try it in one plane then," Lear countered.

"We have no planes available."

Through the intercession of General Barney Giles, Pacific B-29 commander in World War II, it was reluctantly conceded that one plane could be *briefly* spared, and Lear must have his automatic pilot installed and functioning in three weeks—rather less than the five years Westinghouse had had.

Lear met the deadline, and Colonel Boyd himself took the ship up for the test. "It works fine," he grudgingly conceded as he climbed from the cockpit.

The Westinghouse contract was reluctantly canceled, but "at the convenience of the government." This meant that the company would be fully compensated for the $50 million it had spent, plus being given $32 million more for its trouble—$82 million all told, not bad for producing nothing.

Colonel Boyd later went to work for Westinghouse.

As for Lear, he was blacklisted and threatened with a congressional investigation of his relations with the Air Force to find out how he was able to get a contract with Westinghouse canceled.

"Bring on your investigation!" Lear challenged when he learned of it. "I'd be tickled to death to tell all I know. Now get me off your goddamned blacklist or I'll tell it anyway!"

No investigation ever came.

Lear had no such weapon when he asked to be given the back-up contract on an order for the F-100 automatic pilots given Minneapolis-Honeywell. General Clarence S. "Wild Bill" Irvine, in charge of Air Force procurement, said no, and Lear went to Washington to take it up with Secretary of the Air Force Harold Talbot.

Talbot was all for Lear being given the contract and couldn't understand why he hadn't gotten it. He called in General Irvine and asked him about it.

"I cut orders to give that contract to Lear this morning, before coming here," Irvine replied.

"But yesterday you told me no," Lear said, surprised but pleased.

"I changed my mind," Irvine explained.

Lear made an appointment to meet Irvine the next morning at eleven o'clock. When he had waited outside Irvine's office until three in the afternoon, he could wait no longer and walked in on the general.

"I didn't really cut orders for that contract," Irvine said.

"But you told the Secretary you did!" the astonished Lear exclaimed.

"Okay, so I lied. What are you going to do about it?" Irvine demanded belligerently.

"I think I ought to tell the Secretary you lied to him."

"Go ahead."

Lear knew that once the military-industrial cabal closed ranks on one, whatever the interests might be of the public which supplies the billions the cabal feeds on, for him there was no tomorrow. Combative but also prudent, Lear meant to preserve what he could of tomorrow—and fight another day.

As the fifties slipped away, a daring idea began to form in Lear's mind. The propeller plane was giving ground to Boeing's 707 on the airlines. Why not a private jet that went the same places at the same speed? No such plane existed. Making rough sketches of the ship, Lear spread the designs on the floor and as he studied them on hands and knees, he remarked to Moya, "Some day they're going to be paying a premium for a place in line to get delivery of this airplane."

But the thought of building an airplane—and one of a radical new design at that—brought chills to the board of directors of Lear, Incorporated. It could wreck the company. They voted the idea down.

Lear thereupon sold his interests to the Siegler Corporation for $14,300,000, and set out to build the airplane on his own. The experience would go far to prepare him for Reno.

4: WICHITA HAD SEEN NOTHING LIKE THIS

Wichita hadn't seen so much excitement since Wyatt Earp used to shoot bad men on Douglas Boulevard. For miles in all directions from the airport west of town, automobiles choked the streets and byways. A good part of the city and of surrounding Sedgwick County must have been on hand—thousands more than most had ever seen in one place.

Down a runway, lined a dozen deep with spectators, rolled a small, stubby-winged airplane, rapidly gathering speed. Trailing incongruous thunder from her two jet engines, the ship went howling steeply up into the fading light of a late October day. A half hour later she came back. As the wheels touched down, waves of applause and shouts broke above the sound of the jets. The watching multitude wept and smiled and shook hands.

This was happening in Wichita, "Air Capital of the World," builder of more airplanes than any other place on earth? Why was everybody so stirred up about another flying machine?

Because it wasn't supposed to happen. No man had ever developed a new kind of jet plane on his own. It took a corporate effort, at best. Yet, here he was—Bill Lear had built the airplane and he had flown it, just as he said he would.

And Wichita would never be quite the same again. The big factory built where the cornfield used to be, giving work to two thousand people, pumps a lot more dollars into the local money stream than the cornfield did. That's the bread-and-butter side of it.

There is more. In a place where the heat of summer sets a man to reviewing his past, where the people themselves wryly tell the joke that "if you have six months to live, Wichita is the place to go because it'll seem like six years"—in this place the Lear years left something for the spirit.

"Tell Bill Lear if he wants to come back here and develop his steam engine, we're ready to work with him," City Councilman John Stevens said. Lear had first set up shop at St. Gallen, Switzerland, near Lake Constance, in 1960. An aircraft plant was available there, and labor and talent could be had for less than in the States. But this proved to be as far as the advantages went. Mutual antagonism quickly flared as the hard-driving Lear came up against the leisurely ways of the Swiss engineers whose notion of energetic performance at the drafting board was to make a line, then sit and read while the ink dried. Also in the Swiss scheme of things, there seemed to be more holidays than workdays.

P. Caroni, owner of the plant, thought Lear was crazy. This was nothing new for Lear, who had sport baiting him. "Tell you what I'll do, Mac [for Macaroni]," Lear said one evening as the two were using the indoor driving green. "I'll bet you $1 million. If I lose, you get my airplane and $1 million. If I win, I get your goddamn factory."

Caroni rolled his eyes in despair. "Fantasy!" he exclaimed. "*Verrückt!* [crazy]." Caroni was sure Lear had been "setting him up" by playing poor golf.

Caroni employed an English dish who tutored him in English grammar. "How much is he paying you?" Lear asked one day.

"I don't think that's any of your affair," she retorted primly.

"Whatever it is I'll double it," Lear pursued, grinning wickedly. "You won't have to teach me a thing. I'll teach you something."

That's how it was in Switzerland.

The workers resented being under American engineers and were overheard opprobriously referring to Don Grommesh as "Herr Grommesh." The picture on the wall of Lear in dark glasses changed to the picture of a bull in dark glasses.

Chief Engineer Gordon Israel fought with Dr. Hans Studer, designer of the Swiss P-16 fighter, on which the Lear plane was based. Studer refused to come to the plant when Israel was there; Israel stayed away when Studer was there.

This was getting no airplane built, and Buzz Nanney finally said to Lear, "You don't have a head Indian here in the plant."

"Will you take the job?" Lear asked.

"Look, I'm a policeman," Buzz countered. "I don't know a wing from a tail. Why don't you get one of your good aviation men at home to come over here who knows how to get the job done?"

It was Friday night. Lear phoned a key aviation industry man in the States, generously giving him until Monday morning to be on the job in Switzerland as his new plant manager.

Tied down with a home and family, the fellow said no, somehow feeling he was being crowded.

Buzz then agreed to take the job until Lear could find someone else, and Lear returned home to look for the experienced airplane builder he needed.

Meanwhile, taking a firm hand, Buzz fired Gordon Israel and Lear hired Cessna's Hank Waring in Wichita to take Israel's place. Waring and Buzz soon agreed, as Buzz put it, that Lear "should have a chance to bleed to death in his own backyard where the odds were better," and together they made a list of the reasons Lear should move the enterprise back to the States.

Buzz mailed the list to Lear, who phoned back, "Is it that bad?"

"It's worse," Buzz said. "You better find yourself another hen house. Hank says Wichita is as good as any and I'll back him up."

Delegated by Lear to pull up the pegs, Buzz at length was able to negotiate a severance contract with Caroni which was far from perfect but, a lawyer assured him, not bad either, all things considered. Buzz mailed the contract to Lear, along with a request for fifty thousand Swiss francs to finish closing out the Swiss operation.

Lear objected to several points in the contract with Caroni, arguing that as severance terms they failed to cut deeply enough. His voice rumbling hollowly over the trans-Atlantic telephone, he enumerated a number of things he wanted Buzz to do to "the son of a bitch," the mildest of which was to "sue him for everything he's got."

"Bill, the answer is no, categorically."

"You're fired!"

"Go screw yourself!"

"I would, but I happen to like girls."

The Caroni contract, with Lear's name duly affixed, along with the fifty thousand francs, arrived by return mail, and Buzz was able to get on with the liquidation of the Swiss adventure without further hitch. He wrote his final letter to June Shields, Lear's secretary, on November 29, 1962, sitting on the floor of an empty office, shivering with the cold. "End of report," he signed off. "Assignment complete. No dead bodies but a lot of blood. Mickey Spillane."

Buzz took a restorative vacation with his vivacious German bride, Ursula, then slipped home to Los Angeles, holing up at the Bel-Air Hotel, not sure what he wanted to do about the future. Then the phone rang, and the matter was taken out of his hands. "Ah, we found you!" June Shields exclaimed.

Lear came on the line. "You son of a bitch," he began, indicating Buzz was still in good standing, "you been hiding! Get your ass over to the Santa Monica airport by three o'clock. We're leaving for Wichita."

It was mid-January and a forty-mile wind whistled across the Kansas prairie as Lear set his Learstar down at the Wichita airport. The temperature stood at three above zero. Ursula looked out on this bleak and lonely winter scene of middle America with extreme distaste. "Don't bother to take my bags off the plane," she said to Buzz. "You can stay if you wish. This is stupid."

Buzz wondered inwardly if she might not be right in a wider sense, as he found things in a turmoil, but the groundwork for a fresh start well along, due to Lear's efforts since August. If Lear was going to "bleed to death," it would be through a main artery.

It had been an exhilarating six months for Wichita that began when Mayor Carl Bell, on a sultry morning, received a phone call from the Chamber of Commerce. "There's a man in town named Lear who wants to build an executive aircraft," the Chamber man said. "He's over at the Allis."

"This meant nothing to me," Bell remembered. "I didn't know a thing about airplanes. Especially, I didn't know anything about executive aircraft. I'd never heard of Bill Lear."

But he walked over to meet the stranger, taking his time in the heat. "As mayor I had this responsibility," he said. He found out two things, that Lear was not a man who broke off a telephone conversation just because a VIP was waiting to see him, and when Lear at last finished on the phone after a half hour, what an executive aircraft is. The kind Lear had in mind would have jet engines. This was of particular interest. Wichita, for all its production of airplanes, was still in the propeller age.

Lear spoke of North American's Sabreliner and Lockheed's Jetstar, both delivered to the military. "I'll build a jet that will cost less, operate for less, and outperform them both," Lear said confidently.

It sounded good to Bell, as it did to the Chamber of Commerce. Lear had shown up at a propitious time, as he would do one day in Reno. Boeing was laying off people, bringing unemployment. "We were overly dependent on military contracts," Bell said. "We needed to broaden our economic base."

While not disagreeing that the base could use some broadening, the old-line aircraft builders in town would just as soon find some other way to do it. Lear rankled them. Cessna had built fifty thousand airplanes in its time, Beech fifteen thousand. Boeing hadn't done badly either, among other things having turned out the B-29 which leveled Japan in World War II.

How many airplanes had Lear built? Not one. The most he had ever done in aircraft besides fly one was to buy up a flock of sixty Lockheed Lodestars and by making certain aerodynamic changes in the wings, tail, fuselage, boost the speed from 220 miles an hour to 280. This got him into hot water with his friend Clarence M. (Kelly) Johnson, Lockheed's design genius, who had said there was no way Lear could improve the Lodestar's performance that much.

The feud lasted until Moya, in the powder room at a party one night, saw a familiar face in the mirror. "I'm Mrs. Bill Lear, do I know you?" she asked.

"Hell, yes, I'm Mrs. Kelly Johnson!"

The two men buried the hatchet, and a good friendship was restored. "I only improved what you already had done well," Lear told Johnson conciliatingly. "The state of the art has advanced since 1930."

As the result of the rapprochement, Lear's automatic pilot went into the famous U-2 spy plane, reaffirming an old lesson: that friendship is a more fruitful tree than enmity.

Yet, despite his limited experience, here was this new kid in the block, grabbing headlines with his honking about how he was going to beat the old-timers at their own game. Not only was he going to build an airplane, but he was going to build a radically advanced type which none of them had yet dared to undertake. Moreover, he intended to show them figuratively how not to be all day about it.

"We're going to build and certify this aircraft in record time," Lear declared with galling self-assurance.

Then, making sure he wasn't named Man of the Year, he made snide comments about the local aircraft establishment—as "Beech hasn't contributed a damn thing to aviation in twenty-five years."

This observation in particular fell short of endearing him to Mrs. Olive Ann Beech, head of Beechcraft and "Grand Dame of Wichita," already piqued about Lear because people who had orbited about her socially were going over to the Lears'. "I'll forbid you to mention that man's name around here!" she ordered an executive who had let slip something civil about Lear.

Besides being a major employer, with 6500 people on the payroll, Mrs. Beech was high priestess of the Metropolitan Council, Wichita's more formal equivalent of Reno's round table at the Holiday Hotel. Like other members of the council, she lived in the enclave of Eastborough, where there was not the vexation of paying taxes to the city whose affairs she helped dictate.

Yet, what Olive Ann wanted of the city, Olive Ann usually got, as a member of the City Council told it. She wanted a stretch of Douglas Boulevard improved for the convenience of her plant. Pave it, she said, or she would move part of her facilities to Salina. The city did as it was bidden, redesignating the street a "major thoroughfare" so that it could do so legally, and nicking the protesting property owners along the way to help pay for it. Mrs. Beech holds it as a continuing Damoclean sword over the city that if it ever annexes the territory where her plant is located, she'll pack up and leave town. So this was no person not to mind one's manners about.

But Lear, having committed lese majesty, only had fun with Mrs. Beech's fury, thinking up new ways to needle her. Along with Loel Guinness and the Aga Khan, he bought land on the island of Sardinia, with plans to build a home there—though with a half dozen other homes scattered about the world, he was not excessively unsheltered. He showed a map of the joint Sardinia purchase to Carl Bell. "I want you to notice," he said, "that mine is the only spot with a beach. I'm going to name it Olive Ann Beach," adding that every morning he planned to commit an act of personal defilement on it.

Not long after that, with pilot Hank Beaird, Lear visited his Sardinian holding. One morning, hearing a noise outside their sleeping quarters, Hank looked out the window. There was Lear, hard at work pounding a stake into the sand with a hunk of driftwood, bearing a hand-lettered sign, "Olive Ann Beach." Hank asked what he was doing.

"Just getting a little work done before breakfast," Lear replied, proceeding to carry out the rest of his commitment.

Retribution threatened after the city of Wichita decided to buy the land Lear needed to build on, getting its money back through a lease. Lear was at the Reading, Pennsylvania, air show, and the Metropolitan Council planned to send him a telegram so he could announce the deal at the Reading event, an important annual showcase of aviation: "We cordially invite you to join us in Wichita in building the best airplane in the world," signed by the members of the council. Mrs. Beech was in Williamsburg, Virginia, but Dwane Wallace, president of Cessna, assured all that they could count on Olive Ann. There was talk of signing her name for her.

But Gordon Evans, head of the council, wasn't so sure. He prudently phoned Mrs. Beech in Williamsburg. "She didn't say no —she said, 'Hell, no!'" Carl Bell recalled. She went on to say with some vehemence that she thought it was "a mistake for the city to get involved with that man."

Evans reported the conversation to Bell, indicating he was beginning to sag in his support of Lear. Bell retorted, "If we're going to police industry coming into this town, you'll have my resignation before sundown!"

Things hit another air pocket for Lear when Bell went to see him in Reading, taking along the gray-suited pillar of tradition who headed the Chamber of Commerce. The visit was to be informal, and that it was. Lear was in a bar with his daughter Shanda, being swarmed over by agents from other cities bent on luring Lear and his airplane project to their towns.

Matters were under reasonable control until the man from Grand Rapids inducted all present into the "Turtle Club." The requirements of membership in this organization are simple and undemanding. To the question "Are you a turtle?" the member enthusiastically replies, "You bet your sweet ass I am!" Or he buys the house a round of drinks.

The question was being ringingly affirmed all around when it was put to Bell's starchy friend from the Wichita Chamber: "Are you a turtle?" He barely managed to squeak out the answer, "You bet your sweet ass I am." He didn't enjoy the horseplay.

Next day it looked as if Lear had lost the Chamber of Commerce. So far as its representative in Reading was concerned, Grand Rapids could have him—or anybody else who wanted him. "I don't know what we're doing here," he said to Bell. "This Lear looks like some kind of nut to me."

Nor did it help Lear that all he had to show at Reading was a small, partial mock-up of his plane, contrasted with North American-Rockwell's full-blown model of a Jet Commander. Lear didn't look like much of a threat to anybody.

"But," Carl Bell said, "it was easy to see that the popular sentiment lay with Lear. Flying people were with him. He was the underdog. From there on I was in his corner all the way."

With the city of Wichita providing the place to build, a sixty-four-acre cornfield just west of town, Lear put his money where his mouth was. He borrowed $7 million from the Bank of America, securing it with a note for $10 million. For those wrestling with this dilemma, it's better to keep $10 million and borrow $7 million, earning interest on the larger amount and paying interest on the smaller figure, according to Dean Fran Jabara of the School of Business Administration at Wichita State University, who set up the new Lear organization.

Also, if you're a banker, getting the borrower to put up $10 for $7 is what you do when you're sure the borrower is going to fail at the thing he's borrowing the money for—as all the banks in town had been assured by the aircraft establishment would be Lear's fate. "He can't do it," the veterans in the business knowingly told the bankers. "He's crazy to think he can. If he builds a plane he'll never fly it. If he flies it he'll never sell it."

All chortled at his boast that he would sell $50 million worth the first year.

Carl Bell took Lear around town house hunting, finding him the ten-acre estate of banker Arthur Kinkaid, in the Mandarin country of the east side. Buying it for $175,000, Lear took pictures of the house and grounds and mailed them to Moya in Geneva, Switzerland. He followed up with a telephone call, finding her in Yugoslavia on a motor tour to Greece with her father. "Come quickly!" Lear said. "I just bought you the most beautiful house you ever saw—furnished!"

Moya couldn't believe her ears. Lear was in the States ostensibly to attend the Reading air show, nothing else. They had a beautiful new home near Geneva—just built and barely moved into, it

THE INCREDIBLE STORY OF BILL LEAR

seemed—a show place with roof tile from bars found in the Alps and other such distinctions.

"Oh, no!" Moya cried in dismay. "Not again. And of all places, Wichita, Kansas!—a one-night stand!"

But she had heard such tidings from Lear before. The last time had been when they were living in Pacific Palisades, California. "Is your seat belt fastened?" he asked one evening, out of the blue.

"Yes." She looked at him suspiciously. "I think so."

"We're moving to Switzerland."

"Oh, come now, honey," she said when she was able. "We've had enough of this moving around."

All the same, in three weeks thirty-four pieces of luggage, including eleven trunks, had been packed. The children had been enrolled in school in Switzerland. The house had been rented to Grace Kelly, and they were on their way to Switzerland.

They had returned in a year or so; when their tenant married Prince Rainier, Moya michievously considering putting a sign over the bed, "Bill Lear and Grace Kelly slept here." Then they received a letter from King Michael of Rumania, who with Buzz Nanney had lived in the guest house in Pacific Palisades. Michael wrote that he had visited the mansion they had left abuilding some twelve minutes out of Geneva. It looked like a "Roman ruin" in its incomplete state, and the premises were occupied by gypsies. It was such a magnificent place—they ought to come and live in it, the king wrote.

On a trip around the world in May 1959, Moya rented a car in Geneva and drove out to see the place for herself. Now finished, with the pool brimming, the landscaping and planting done, it was indeed as Michael had described it.

She telephoned Lear. "You should come and see it," she said. "We should live in this house a little while at least. We should light the fires, turn on the sprinklers. . . ."

So back to Switzerland they moved. Now, after "three beautiful years," as Moya called them, during which was born the Lear Jet idea, here was Lear on the phone from Wichita, Kansas, about *another* house—another move! But Moya knew that there could be no protest. If Bill felt they had to live in Wichita—that's where she wanted to be.

As it happened, of the many homes of the Lears spotted about the world, providing insurance against being caught without a roof over their heads, the one in Wichita became the house where her heart was. The summer nights with the fireflies, the scent of clover, the ear-tingling symphony of the locusts in the trees—even the heat—she came to love it all. "They were five wonderful, productive years," she said, smiling at the memory.

In Reno they had planned to build when they found River House, on the banks of the Truckee at Verdi, ten miles west of town. With a barn, fruit trees, pasture and woods, it reminded Lear of the family farm in Illinois that had once given sanctuary from Aunt Minnie. The river sang an endless lullaby as it hurried down from Lake Tahoe to Pyramid Lake, eighty miles away and 3500 feet below.

"I don't care how many houses we have," Lear said. "I want this one."

Besides adaptability, Moya had other things going for her which worked to the benefit of her marriage to Lear. "It's fortunate for me that I have patience," she said. "And I have a very short memory for the bad things. Wives too often keep bringing things up that are past. They have a dirty little string of beads they keep fingering. You can forgive if you really love your husband."

There had been a couple of times, she admitted, when she had thought of leaving him. But each time she asked herself, "Was it really that important? We would be separated—we wouldn't be together any more. No, it wasn't that important."

The ability to laugh, a gift of her father, Ole Olsen, who "loved the whole human race," is another of her assets. "You must have a sense of humor," she stressed.

In a piece of needlepoint on the wall of the family room, amid cartoons on show business themes by her father, a competent cartoonist, she has memorialized the names of the wives and girl friends who have gone before: "Madelaine, Nellie, Charlotte, Mimi, Jill, Irene—some I've forgotten and some I didn't know about."

Moya herself told the story of the girl friend in New York who, when the Lears were living in Grand Rapids, asked Lear when he was going to divorce Moya. "I'd only have to move Moya out of Grand Rapids to make room for you," Lear replied.

"What's wrong with that?" she asked.

"Then who would I get to replace you in New York?"

"I see his faults better than anyone else," Moya said pensively. "But when you've been married to a man twenty-seven years— when you've been through all the stresses and strains and storms we've been through together—all the things that can possibly happen to a marriage—there has to be something very special about a man. I am the happiest woman I know. He is always good to me," she went on, "*always*. Even when he is cross he does not take it out on me."

She knows when this is, although there are no overt signs. She then goes to him, puts her arms around him, and says quietly, "Now settle down—just settle down. Everything is going to be all right."

As for Lear, he administers "big, warm hugs" to her on the street, in elevators, wherever the impulse may strike him. At night as he approaches down the tree-lined drive to River House, he sounds a code on the horn, and embraces her as she comes out to meet him in the darkness.

The Lears have four children—Shanda (the name was Grandfather Ole Olsen's idea), John, David, and Tina, who has shown unusual gifts as a musician. "She has great talent," said Gunnar Johansen, her teacher.

"Come and hear Tina play," her father said on my first visit to River House, leading me into the living room.

At the Bosendorfer, under Peter Paul Rubens' *The Virgin and the Infant*, Tina played a Haydn concerto, but she was not pleased with her performance, displaying her father's penchant for perfection. "I know you think I'm terrible!" she cried with a despairing glance at her parents, playing gin rummy at a little table nearby. Her mother went to the piano bench and clasped the girl in her arms, speaking words of reassurance, "Dad and I both love you."

Moya returned to her game, and Tina declared she was going to try the composition again. "You wait and see," she said. "It will be—it will be 20 per cent better."

And it was, as the proud parents acknowledged in a three-way embrace at the finish.

The four hundred tons of wing jigs, drawings, and other salvage from the Swiss fiasco which Buzz Nanney had crated and shipped to the States at a cost of $81,600, arrived aboard seven freight cars. It was installed in the new plant that came up in the cornfield, after Lear in person, with more symbolism than anyone suspected, piloted the bulldozer that broke the ground.

As operations got under way, a number of engineers from the

old aircraft plants defected to Lear, getting him accused of pirating his help with offers of more money. In fact, except for a few who received another $10 or so, hardly enough to make a man go through the shock of changing jobs, the money was the same. What attracted the defectors was the excitement of working on something new. There was little promise of this with their old employers, who stuck with the tried and true propeller plane, merely altering it a little from time to time, like changing last year's hemline. "Lear gave us a place to go," one engineer said.

"I've always wanted to build a business jet," said Don Grommesh, who came over from Cessna. A trim, compact man, Grommesh didn't meet Lear until after he got back from helping Buzz Nanney liquidate the Swiss enterprise. When finally he did meet his employer, "Lear was handling a long distance telephone call, working a crossword puzzle, and talking to me, all at the same time," Grommesh said. "I was impressed."

After Cessna, he was also struck by Lear's informality. "We would sit and slide a bottle of Winter's Deluxe back and forth across the table as we talked," he said, adding that they "graduated to Canadian Club after the Lear Jet was certified." It was a whole new world.

To Grommesh and his colleagues, Lear was as different as the new airplane they were building. Instead of keeping to the front office, out of sight and above it all, Lear used the office only as a place to leave his coat as he passed through on his way to the shop, rolling up his sleeves as he went. He was everywhere, often seemingly at the same time, looking over shoulders, guiding hands at drawing boards, showing the way with a wrench. He counseled boldness. "Take a big bite—don't nibble at it. Bite all the way to the core." He made decisions on the spot which at the other aircraft plants, one engineer said, would take six months of staff meetings.

There were some who objected to all this, complaining, "This guy's a one-man band. He makes all the decisions."

"I'll make you a deal," Lear replied. "You put up half the money and you can make half the decisions."

By keeping a close eye on the man at the drawing board—"interfacing," Lear calls it—mistakes are caught before they are radiated throughout the project, throwing everything out of kilter, bringing delays and running up costs. Lear likes to tell how North American's Edgar Schmued brought in the P-51 Mustang fighter in a record ninety-three days from the time the first line went on the drafting board in World War II. Schmued did it by rigidly keeping his men on the mark. By the same technique, Lear says, Lockheed could have prevented the $2 billion cost overrun on its big C-5A cargo plane.

Lear has no use for the idea that all it takes to get a job done is to snow it with manpower. More important is to have the right man in charge. "Could five hundred men have painted the Sistine Chapel?" he asks. "Suppose one man wasn't there?"

Aside from mistakes, what Lear watched for mostly was how to make things simpler—which, to him, is another way of saying the same thing. As Lear sees it, most things in this world, whether the works of God or man, are designed wrong. If he were given the job of redesigning the human body, it has been said, he would likely scrap the whole thing as preposterous and start over.

"Two of something is twice as likely to go wrong as one," he says. "Keep it supersimple. If something isn't designed into an airplane," he told his engineers, "it can't go wrong, and it will never require service or replacement."

The doctrine of keeping it simple began with the pieces, and then was carried to the components made from the pieces. Very little on anybody's shelf passed muster. It was too big, too heavy, too complicated, or all three. So Lear made his own. All told, Ed Lenheim's "Lear Jet Laboratories" custom-built and tested eighty different components for the Lear Jet all of which became marketable. Anything they got from suppliers they tore down and drastically re-engineered to Lear's own standards.

The electronics equipment for the plane likewise was original. Helping Lear with this was Sam Auld, an old associate from the mid-fifties who had worked with him on the development of the automatic pilot that won the Collier Trophy. Much of this, too, went into production for the open market.

One item was an "impossible" eight-track stereo tape cartridge system—seven tracks were supposed to be the limit. Lear and Auld worked this out, Sam said, while they were "inventing the plane and the things to go in it," with Lear "running a lathe, handling a soldering iron—making things in the middle of the night. Can you imagine the chairman of the board doing that?"

You could throw it against the wall with no damage except to the wall, and it was "the simplest tape transport system ever devised," Sam said. Since there were no levers or buttons, the driver could slip it into place without taking his eyes off the road. The Lear eight-track stereo tape cartridge system became the standard for automobiles and a mainstay of Lear Stereo, Inc., of Detroit, grossing $2 billion in 1970.

Some things they built from scratch simply because they didn't have them—including the tools to make them with—and contractors wanted six months. They stamped out parts with an old Pacific Hydraulic Brake press. To work on the tail, they used ordinary building scaffolding. "We had one of the items you normally take for granted," Don Grommesh said. "We didn't even have a library."

On top of these handicaps, Lear wanted to do things that "couldn't be done." Being shown by mathematical formula why a thing was impossible only brought a scornful "three times infinity over poop! With my eighth-grade education, I never read that it can't be done." He told the parable of the two frogs trapped in a jar of cream. "They jumped and jumped trying to get out. Pretty soon one frog gave up and was drowned. The other frog kept jumping and after a while he had a pat of butter to sit on."

Lear wanted a door that opened outward. This was sheer heresy. Everybody knows that in a pressurized airplane only "plug" doors will do. They have to open inward so that the pressure inside the ship helps to seal them in place.

"This positively will not work," Lear was assured. Nobody would even try to design such a door, no self-respecting engineer wanting anything to do with it. So Lear designed the door himself. Among other superior features such as being wide enough to admit a stretcher, it weighed 150 pounds less than the usual plug door; the top furnished a canopy and the bottom a step. Lear's door has already been copied several times.

To try things out as the most sophisticated airplane of its kind took shape, "junkman" Ed Lenheim resorted to highly unsophisticated improvisation. Ordinarily, to measure fuel use, costly, exotic flow meters are used. Lenheim brought in a five-gallon bucket, a stop watch, and a set of platform scales. The bucket and the scales told how much fuel you had, the stop watch how long it took to run it through. That was the fuel flow.

On an airplane that lands at 120 miles an hour, it's more than passingly desirable that the nose wheel refrain from shimmying. To test the anti-shimmy device for the nose wheel of the Lear

Jet, the wheel was rigged to the front of Lear's Oldsmobile, about ten feet out, with lead weights piled on to simulate the weight of the airplane, and driven up and down the runway at 100 miles an hour.

"If that son of a bitch had ever broken loose, there would have been Bill Lear, lead weights, and Oldsmobile all over the airport," Ed said, shaking his head reflectively.

The cabin of a high-flying airplane has to be pressurized with near sea-level atmosphere, so the occupants can breathe. Therefore, the cabin must be airtight. To make sure it is, the cabin, filled with air and sealed, is immersed in water—the same way you test an inner tube for leaks. The tank for this purpose, in the case of a tank provided for Cessna at the time, cost $5000. Lenheim had one made for the Lear Jet by Wichita Steel Fabricators from a thirty-minute drawing for $600. It wasn't much more than a big horse trough, but it did the job.

With the cabin in the water, air is pumped in and let out at the rate of one cycle a minute, for twenty-five thousand minutes. Lockheed did it that way. "We don't have twenty-five thousand minutes!" Lear said impatiently. "We got to find some way to cut it down."

"Lockheed has had a lot of experience," Lenheim reminded him.

"I don't care what Lockheed says," Lear replied. "We got to cut those cycles by two thirds."

A well-known hydraulic engineer gave several reasons why faster cycling wouldn't work. "Now, goddammit," Lear exclaimed, "you're not thinking! Go over there and sit down and think!"

Obediently, the expert retired and pondered, grousing admiringly as he began to see the light. "Damn it, he's right! I've got a master's degree. He went to the eighth grade!"

So they put two pumps on the job, one to pump the water in, the other to pump it out, and got the hydrostatic tests done in a third of the time at first thought necessary.

Lear wanted a windshield that was sure to deflect any bird that hit it in flight. Birds coming through airplane windshields have been known to kill people. Lenheim devised a "bird gun," operated by compressed air, and fired live chickens at the windshield at velocities simulating speeds of the plane. The first chicken went clear through the airplane. The last one vanished against the windshield without trace except for part of a claw, leaving not a mark where it hit.

A pilot once dunked a Lear Jet in Lake Michigan as he was coming in for a landing at Chicago's Meigs Field. Firemen threw a hook at the windshield, intending to catch a hold inside. The windshield bounced the hook back. The firemen tried fire axes. Still no luck. They finally had to smash a hole in the fuselage, which was almost as much fun as breaking the windshield. Meanwhile, the Navy, ever interested in things that float, gathered from far and near to ogle the airplane that floated like a boat.

On July 9, 1963, although there was still designing to do and pieces to make, Lear assigned Joe Sevart, who knew his aircraft even though his engineering degree from Kansas State was in agriculture rather than aviation, to start putting the ship together. Sevart set September 15 as roll-out date and made it a hard rule to move the budding ship toward the door twenty feet a week. The push was on. Sunday staff meetings became SOP. Clocks and calendars were forgotten. Many workers punched out at the end of the day, then came back in and worked on through the night for nothing.

Sevart put in thirty-two hours at a stretch, went home for two hours and returned to the plant for another twenty. Ending up in the hospital twenty-five pounds lighter, he received a phone call Sunday morning from Lear. "What in hell are you doing in bed?" Lear asked, disguising his concern with mock reproach. "We need you here at the plant."

Invariably around was Lear himself. "If you were out here ten or fourteen hours a day," Joe said, "he was here fourteen or sixteen." The guard once heard banging in the shop at three in the morning and found Lear at work under the plane.

Coat off, sleeves up, he roamed from group to group, from drawing board to drawing board. "What's your problem?" he would ask over and over, then assist in finding the solution.

"He could help even to the tiniest detail," Joe said. "He worked right along with us as one of the crew, but his great gift was his ability to draw out the best in others."

Lear lost no time at noon by going out for the executive's usual lunch ceremony. He had been careful to include a kitchen in the plant facilities, and at noon he ate hamburger which he cooked himself. If there were guests, what was good enough for Lear was good enough for them. A daily "guest" was Jet, Lear's small black poodle whose broad privileges included riding in the airplane with him.

For supplemental fueling of his energies during his extended hours at the plant, Lear drew on an icebox in the office. Providing the contents for this could entail hazard to the uninitiated. "Whatever you do," June Shields cautioned her newly hired helper, Betty Miller, as she briefed her on the icebox logistics, "under no circumstances allow pickles or tomatoes to come into the plant. These items must never be in the same room with him—better still, not even in the same building." She felt constrained to add, "He has a very strong dislike for pickles and tomatoes."

Lear's aversion for these foods is famous. He won't sit at the table if they are present, if he can help it. "The lowest form of human fodder!" he growls.

Yet, his unrelenting battles to go a separate way in life from pickles and tomatoes are almost unfailingly lost. The story is told of the time he instructed a waitress in meticulous detail that he wanted no pickles or tomatoes with his hamburgers—"not on top of the hamburger, not under the hamburger, not beside the hamburger, not near the hamburger. In fact, I would prefer if there are no pickles or tomatoes even in the kitchen," he said.

"Come now, Bill," chided his companion as the waitress withdrew. "You're overdoing it."

"You want to bet?" Lear demanded. They bet $5.

The waitress reappeared in the doorway from the kitchen. She paused, went back into the kitchen and, re-emerging moments later, put the food on the table—liberally garnished with pickles and tomatoes. "I almost forgot your pickles and tomatoes," she said apologetically.

The strain of the drive at the plant to complete the airplane brought stresses at home. There were separations and divorces. "I became a stranger in my own household," said Jim Greenwood, who came over from Beech as public relations director after holding out for five months, because "I had been buying my own propaganda—the Beech party line—that a pure jet for business would never sell. My own dog would bark at me."

There were strains of another kind when Lear failed to show up as the guest of honor at a welcome-to-Wichita party given by the city's social elite, but stayed at the plant, working. Moya, not unused to cleaning up social disaster areas in the wake of her husband, made repairs with a party of her own for all who had been at the first.

"Everybody loved Moya," said neighbor Pat McEwen, recalling how Moya had taken an active interest in community affairs, involving herself with the Wichita Art Association, the Kansas Historical Society, and a number of other groups. "I think there is only one Moya Lear, just as there's only one Bill Lear," Mrs. McEwen said.

When Lear did attend a party it was on his own terms. For an affair at the big, rustic McEwen home in the woods east of Wichita, Pat once made her husband get into formal clothes, over his anguished protests, only to have Lear show up late in shirt sleeves and an old red sweater. He had come directly from the plant.

Lear made it to enough social functions that he came to enjoy some renown as a maker of Caesar salads. As at the shop, however, he was rigidly exacting in the kitchen. "If I'm going to make Caesar salad," he told Pat McEwen one day as she was planning another party, "I've got to have the right kind of bread."

There was no right kind of bread in Wichita. So Pat, a pilot with three thousand hours in the log and two airplanes, including one built especially for aerobatics, flew two hundred miles to Kansas City to get Lear the bread he needed for his Caesar salad. To make the trip doubly worth-while, she bought an extra loaf or two.

Lear wanted to make Pat McEwen the first woman to go through his Lear Jet ground school. "Now just why would you want to do me this big honor?" Pat asked suspiciously. She answered the question herself. "You want to show if some dumb Kansas housewife can fly the Lear Jet, anybody can."

Lear shook with laughter and confessed that this was what he had in mind.

While Lear had little time for things unrelated to getting his airplane built, when Ken Ferrell dropped by the plant one Sunday after church to show his children "where Daddy works," Lear squatted down to be on eye level with the youngsters, two boys and a girl, five, eight, and eleven years old, and for forty-five minutes talked to them as he would to adults. He told them about his plans, how an airplane flies, what makes it "so pretty."

"When anybody said anything about Bill Lear around the kids after that," said Ferrell, who had been Lear's labor relations man, "it had better be good."

In the Bible belt country of Wichita, where the beer is sold warm and there are no peanuts to go with it, all in helpful restraint of one's trade with the devil once he locates the store with its small identifying sign of shame in a corner of the window —in this place Lear was an unfailing curiosity. "They had never seen a guy who gallivanted around like this," test pilot Hank Beaird said. "One day he'd be seen with a king, the next day with an actor."

He was also an underdog, who brought out the Walter Mitty in people. Like Mayor Carl Bell, the man in the street was in Lear's corner. Knowing where the Establishment stood, he followed Lear's progress in the *Eagle* and *Beacon* was partisan interest.

As Joe Sevart inched the sprouting airplane toward the door for its September debut, there were frequent changes of direction, like the broken-field running of a football player who keeps picking a better way to get there. The changes were ordered by Lear, who then became impatient with the crews for getting behind.

He headed for a showdown one afternoon with the electrical crew. Hank Beaird trotted along by his side, counseling a change of course on Lear's part. "You could end up a lot more behind than you are now," Hank said.

"All right," Lear said finally, turning to Hank. "You're so damn smart. What would you do?"

"I'd be a little more diplomatic," replied Hank, a genial, outgoing Alabamian. "Compliment them on the job they're doing. Then, when you've made them feel better, suggest what it is you'd like them to do."

Lear returned to his office. He took off his tie, opened his shirt, slipped on an old sweater, and went forth again. "Fellows, you're doing a magnificent job," he greeted the electricians with smiling affability. He said words to the effect that it was "because of the conscientious devotion of guys like you that this project is going to succeed." They were so happy they slaved all night to complete the changes he then asked.

"It worked so well he took me to dinner," Hank said, adding, "he's not really impatient. It's just that he's so far ahead of ordinary mortals that he can't understand why they lag behind."

Hank noted that Lear, quick to lose his temper, was equally quick to get it back. It was as if he flipped a switch and nothing had happened. He and Lear one day were going at it hammer and tongs about testing the ship's electrical systems. Lear, as usual, was in a hurry. Hank was being cautious, indiscreetly conveying the impression he thought he knew something about electricity.

"You don't know the first thing about electricity!" Lear yelled. As he reached the door on his way out, he turned and in perfectly normal tones said, "Don't forget—you and Roz are coming to dinner tonight." (Roz was Hank's wife.)

"All rich geniuses are supposed to be eccentric," Lear once remarked to Hank, deadpan. "So I am."

In August there came the biggest change yet. Lear decided that the horizontal stabilizer should be moved to the top of the rudder, well above the slipstream from the wings, for more stability. In forty days and forty nights, working from the building scaffolding Ed Lenheim rustled up, Sevart had the job done.

Lear stood back to admire the new look. "That," he said with *double-entendre*, "is the best-looking piece of tail I ever saw."

On September 15, as scheduled, the ship that critics had said Lear would never build stood outside, in the warm autumn sun. Three weeks later, on October 6, the airplane that they said, if built, he wouldn't fly, was ready to fly except for some last-minute trouble with the nose wheel. It turned sideways— castored—when the brakes were applied.

The entire assembly was taken out and Lear and Sevart fell to work on it together, toiling through the night. "Look here," Lear repeated as he attacked with hammer, punch, and screw driver, "with the combination of Joe Sevart and Bill Lear anything can be done."

When the two had figured out the solution, they called designer Ken Yoman at home. Yoman whistled up a crew of draftsmen and put the design on paper. At 4 P.M. they had the drawings ready and handed them to Sevart. The remedy was built. The nose gear was reassembled, and by 6 P.M. it was back on the plane—just as Lear showed up red-eyed from a little sack time on his cot in the office.

With the sinking sun near the horizon, Bob Hagan climbed into the captain's seat. A former Cessna pilot, Hagan had worked alongside the builders during the final weeks of the ship's assembly. Hank Beaird was in the other seat.

Hank at first had been a reluctant participant. With Lear in Switzerland, he had quit to go to work at Eglin Field, Florida,

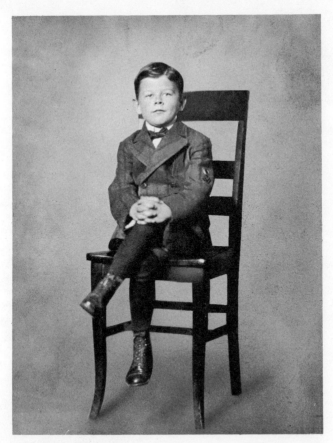

1)   The meeting will come to order! Master William Powell Lear.

2)   Boy Marconi. Lear built his first radio receiver during World War I, using a 25-cent galena crystal. His interest in wireless began when the Cunard liner *Carpathia*, picking up the SOS calls of the stricken *Titanic*, dashed to the rescue in the disaster of 1912.

3)   Lear's first cross-country flight, from Chicago to New York in 1931, was probably his most fateful. He discovered that pilots spent nearly as much time finding out where they were as in getting where they wanted to go. His automatic direction finder, the Learoscope, was the first of myriad aircraft instruments to follow from his drawing board, forming the basis of his fortune.

4)   Young inventor going up in the world. Lear used his own airplane to test instruments he designed.

5) Instruments gave the pilot many advantages over following the railroad tracks. For one thing, with instruments guiding and controlling the airplane, he was free to spend the time aloft in more restful fashion. *(Photo by Hans Groenhoff)*

6) In 1942, after three previous marriages, Lear's romantic course led to the altar with Moya Olsen, daughter of vaudeville comedian Ole Olsen. They have four children: Shanda (the name was Grandfather Ole Olsen's idea), John, David, and Tina.

7) Lear's automatic pilot, setting standards of performance unequaled by any other, earned him aviation's highest honor, the Collier Trophy, and the congratulations of President Harry S Truman. *(Photo by Wide World Photos, Inc.)*

8) A David and Goliath of the electronics industry, Bill Lear and RCA's General Sarnoff, reminisce at a *Forbes* magazine party in 1967.

9)   Like the phoenix bird reborn, the Lear Jet rose anew from the ashes of the first ship, which mushed into a wet field and burned, victim of pilot error.

10)   Wichita, "Air Capital of the World," builder of more airplanes than any other place on earth, maybe 100,000 of them, had never seen one like this. Even in the Kansas rain they came to admire.

11)   While the storm raged below, holding other planes prisoner in its fury, the Lear Jet rode serenely in the sunny solitude of the stratosphere.

12) His people found Lear an unusual chairman of the board. He used his office only as a place to leave his coat as he passed through on the way to the shop.

13) "This guy's a one-man band," some engineers complained. "He makes all the decisions." Lear countered, "You put up half the money and you can make half the decisions." With him here, as he decides about the seats for the Lear Jet, are test pilot Hank Beaird and marketing director Ed Chandler.

14) Not a hanging, but Lear being prepared to receive an honorary doctorate of engineering from the University of Michigan.

15) What a half-billion dollars, give or take a few million, looks like. These knights of the round table, each a multimillionaire, gather daily at five in the lobby of Reno's Holiday Hotel, slake the day's accumulated thirst for one hour, then promptly go home. Reading clockwise around the table from Lear: Norman Biltz, Chet Emmons, Larry Deninsenzia, Bob Helms, John Heizer, Tom Dant and Tom Moore. *(Photo by Michael Bry)*

16) Lear supporting hometown industry. (*Photo by Michael Bry*)

17) Lieutenant General Hewitt T. Wheless, former Assistant Vice Chief of Staff, U. S. Air Force, served as Lear's executive vice-president in Reno until he retired for reasons of health. Standing is former Los Angeles police detective Buzz Nanney, Lear's administrative vice-president. (*Photo by Michael Bry*)

testing fighters. "Lear can be a bear when things aren't going right," Hank explained. "Besides, I didn't think he would build an airplane."

Then Hank had a phone call from Lear. "I have an airplane now," he said.

"I don't believe it," Hank replied.

"It's right outside. Hold the line a minute." In a few moments Hank's ear was being punched with a great roar in the receiver. "Hear that?" Lear asked. "I just opened the door." He persuaded Hank at least to come and look at the ship, sending his Learstar to fetch him.

In Wichita, though, Hank said he wanted no part of flying the ship—he didn't want to get that involved again. It was Moya, a familiar figure in the shop as the plane grew, taking a personal interest in the workers, who settled the matter. Knowing how much Lear wanted it, she fixed Hank with her dark eyes and said, in a tone of quiet command, "You will fly the airplane."

As the pilots taxied the ship across the airport to the take-off point in the fast-lengthening shadows, Lear followed in his Continental. There were a few moments of delay at the head of the runway while Hank gave himself a final sharpening on the controls.

"What the hell's holding you up?" Lear called as he circled in his car.

"We're driving this airplane and it isn't going anywhere until we're ready!" Hank shot back, a little edgy himself. "Go inside and sit down!"

"You know I couldn't do that."

"I know—I just wanted to hear myself say it," Hank said contritely.

Hagan opened the throttle and the moment of truth was at hand. The ship began to roll, picking up speed as if anxious to escape, and as it passed Lear, now standing on the runway with Moya, his shouts could be heard above the screech of the engines. Moya, her arms around him, felt his heart pounding.

"The plane just went straight up into the blue," she remembered. "It was the most exciting moment of my life, and we've had a lot of exciting moments."

Buzz Nanney, standing apart a few feet, and as general manager as well as confidential friend, realizing with a special intimacy the burden that rode on those truncated wings—nearly everything

Lear owned, his reputation, his hopes, the future, was a handi-
capped observer. "It's pretty hard to see when you got tears stream-
ing down your face," he said.

Up and up the ship went until it became a glinting speck amid
the mare's tails being combed by the stratospheric winds of Indian
summer. In all the thousands of airplanes which had tried their
wings from the factories of Wichita, the throngs watching from
the roads and fields had seen nothing like this.

"It was great!" beamed the pilots when they brought the plane
back to earth.

Yet, now that Lear's plane had flown, the wise ones said it
would never meet performance specifications, impressive as the
first flight had been. Lear needed to know about this very soon—
what kind of airplane he had. The creditors were growing restive.
"Make four or five check-out flights and let me know," he told
Hank Beaird.

Hank pointed her nose just south of high noon and zoomed to
forty thousand feet—eight miles—in six minutes and nineteen seconds, half the time it took any other plane to get there. Hank's
fifth time aloft in the Lear Jet, he hit 605 miles an hour.

"I had flown high performance fighters all my life," he said.
"This airplane outperformed nearly all of them up to ten thousand
feet. I told Bill, 'You've got a gold mine.'"

5: NUMBER ONE AIRPLANE JUST CRASHED!

The song of the meadowlark was just beginning across the prairie as the airplane began to roll for its second take-off of the morning.

Since its first flight eight months before, the Lear Jet had been aloft 164 times, enough to get the bugs shaken out and now, at last, she was in the hands of the Federal Aviation Administration, being put through her paces for certification.

Once the airplane was certified, Lear could start getting some desperately needed gold from the mine Hank Beaird said he had —although now that the ship had easily met performance requirements, the skeptics were saying it would never sell. It was too advanced.

The FAA, for its part, had been taking its time. The regional office in Kansas City passed the buck to headquarters in Washington, saying it lacked authority. Washington passed the buck back to Kansas City, saying the regional office did, too, have authority. "They make you do little rain dances," aviation writer John Zimmerman said.

Lear didn't choreograph very well. Sam Auld, a man not given to loose statement, told of overhearing some of Lear's telephone conversations with the FAA from one hundred feet away. In one high decibel exchange with FAA chief Najeeb Halaby in Washington, Lear drew the suggestion from Halaby, "Why don't you hang up and save money? You're screaming so loud I can hear you without the phone."

It wasn't that the FAA was shorthanded. "They have one employe

66 THEY SAID IT COULDN'T BE DONE

for every airplane in their jurisdiction," Lear comments in recurring eruptions over the agency. "If they do the same with cars, we'll have to make friends with Communist China to get enough people to put on the payroll to regulate the auto industry."

As the ship gathered speed on this long-awaited June morning, it seemed to be having trouble getting off the ground. It rolled three thousand feet before it finally managed to break the bond with earth. The ship mushed along at about seventy-five feet, then settled heavily into a rain-sodden wheat field, cutting a swath through the grain as it plowed to a stop. The landing gear was damaged and a wing tank sheared off.

The pilots stepped from the plane and hurried to the nearest farmhouse to telephone the plant. When they came out, the airplane was a column of smoke twisting darkly skyward. The fuel line had broken in the crash, causing fuel to spill on the exhaust pipe and ignite. "She slowly burned herself to death," Sam Auld said.

FAA pilot Don Kuebler had forgotten to retract the spoilers, depriving the wings of lift. It was remarkable that the ship got into the air at all. Also, he had shut off the one engine instead of merely idling it, making it unavailable for the emergency.

At the plant, Ed Lenheim was standing by the hangar door helplessly watching the smoke in the distance as Lear drove up. "Ed, what's going on?" he asked.

"Number One airplane just crashed and is burning."

"Oh, my God! Anybody hurt?"

Even as Lenheim assured him both pilots were safe, Lear backed his car around and raced off toward the scene of the disaster, his first concern the safety of the pilots.

"There were at least 150 people in the building who wanted to sit down and cry," Lenheim said. "It couldn't happen—not when you had that much heart in it."

Returning from the crash, Lear rallied them all by his manner. The irascible one, who flew into Vesuvian furies over little things, was imperturbable now that the sky had fallen. He shook hands with Sam Auld as Sam arrived back at the plant after having worked all night.

"His words told me he was thinking calmly of what to do next," Auld said. "But it wasn't so much what he said as the look in his eye. It was a look that said, 'Okay, fellow, we've had a setback, but we'll not let it slow us down. We'll go right over the top of it.' It told me here was a man who, when the going really gets rough, rises to his finest."

Fifty thousand dollars' worth of test instrumentation, most of it belonging to someone else, had been lost with the airplane, and while the fire was still smoldering, Lear methodically began to make out a list of duplicate instruments on hand, so they would know what new ones to round up. He scheduled a press conference. He called the suppliers, explaining that the crash was no fault of the ship.

Then he phoned Jim Greenwood, heading a group of Lear people at the Reading air show. Lear was scheduled to arrive there the next day in the Number Two airplane. His first words to Greenwood were, "Neither of the pilots was hurt—they weren't even scratched." Then he told what had happened. "It'll only be a matter of minutes before the competition hears about it. So I want you to know exactly what the facts are."

Lear said it would be necessary to cancel Number Two's appearance at Reading so it could be fitted with instruments to carry on the certification tests of Number One. He had no need to remind Greenwood how desperate things were. The very hours counted. Many of the managers were on half salary. The banks were backing off. The suppliers, their own survival often at stake, were threatening to pull out.

Now that his airplane had crashed, the end of Bill Lear was a foregone conclusion. No one lost his prototype and survived—that was axiomatic—because of the money tied up in it, in Lear's case around $8 million. Already Jim Greenwood could visualize the knowing nods and the tongues gleefully cocked to say, "I told you so."

Just as Lear had predicted, the rumors in Reading began within the hour. Both engines had quit on take-off. The controls froze. There was a malfunction in the stabilizers, forcing the nose down. One pilot was killed. Both pilots were killed. . . . The only rumor missing was one that had it right.

Later in the day, Greenwood phoned Lear back. Describing the rumors, he said, "I know it's important to get on with the tests, but at the moment I think there's nothing more important than getting over here with Number Two ship, as scheduled—show them we're still in business."

Lear agreed. Sleeves up, he led a crew through the night to prepare Number Two plane. Earmarked for Justin Dart, head of

68   THEY SAID IT COULDN'T BE DONE

the Rexall Drug chain, it had already been fitted with interior.
They ripped this out and in its place installed test equipment
so some tests could be recorded on the flight to Reading.

There, meanwhile, Jim Greenwood spread the word that Lear
was coming in, especially planting the news among magazine men
and corporation pilots. Nobody believed him. When Jim added the
further tidings that Lear was swinging past Washington to pick up
Wayne Parrish, prominent aviation publisher and one of flying's
most respected spokesmen, they knew poor old Greenwood had
gone to live in dreamland. Why, hell, they knew Wayne Parrish
wouldn't even fly in a Lear Jet that had been fully certificated,
much less one with only a provisional certificate.

But what, then, was this little white airplane with the black
stripe and high tail which streaked in from the west next day
about the time Lear had been due to arrive, exuberantly laying a
couple of thunderbolts low across the field before it skimmed in
for a landing? It was like the arrival on stage of the prima
ballerina. High-tailed and saucy, with speed lines unlike any seen
before, the ship taxied boldly past the stall which had been reserved for Lear but was now filled by someone else, scattered
some ringsiders from their tables, and came to a stop.

A very corporeal William P. Lear appeared in the door, grinning
amiably. The lady was Mrs. Lear and, so help everybody, there
was Wayne Parrish! Moreover, he was saying that everything Lear
had said about the performance of the airplane was true, as was
Lear's explanation of what caused the first ship to crash. "I predict
that this program to build an executive jet will move forward
and be highly successful," Parrish concluded.

His part in the air show having been canceled, Lear got on with
the press conference Greenwood had set up. Some of the newsmen
sounded as if they felt Lear had betrayed them. At dusk he headed
back to Wichita and the job of getting the Lear Jet blessed by the
FAA.

Less than two months later, after another push during which
nobody went home at night but slept on cots at the plant, the
prize was won.

"Boy, what a hot rod!" cried FAA chief Najeeb Halaby as he
stepped from the ship after flying it himself.

"Supermouth" Bill Lear had done just what he said he would do.
FAA approval of his airplane came just ten months after its first

flight. Had it not been for the crash, he would have made it in nine.

"This represents an accomplishment which seasoned veterans of the aerospace industry view as incredible," John Zimmerman wrote in the Wichita *Eagle*.

"The entire city of Wichita extends its heartiest congratulations," wired the Board of City Commissioners. "We are proud to have you in our community."

Lear had earned his personal certification as well as that of his airplane.

As for the quality of the ship, "Man, this Lear Jet is a going Jessie!" exclaimed the Chicago *Tribune*'s Wayne Thomis, after flying the ship.

"No one ever had an airplane like this," said Clyde Martin, who took delivery on Lear Jet No. 6 for Potlatch Forest, Inc., of Lewiston, Idaho, and became Lear's pilot in Reno. "You could go to New York and back in a day and go up out of the weather instead of stumbling along at ten thousand feet. In the old planes we used to just sit there and vibrate and ride that old rough air." He shook his head. "I'll never go through that again."

Like other Lear Jet pilots, Martin was not loathe to needle the pilots of ordinary craft about this advantage. On a flight from Reno to Dallas, he picked up a conversation between the Albuquerque flight control center and a plane which it was routing around a storm. The center asked Martin if he didn't want help as well.

"No, thanks," Martin replied. "Everything's smooth as velvet up here." He added gratuitously, for the benefit of the other pilot, "I sure feel sorry for anybody who has to fly down in that stuff."

When the Albuquerque center repeated the offer at intervals as the storm spread and Martin smugly kept giving the same answer, with further expressions of sympathy for the poor devils who had no option in the matter, the other pilot finally asked to be transferred to the Los Angeles control center; he couldn't take it any more.

As he was flying from Italy once, Lear intercepted an exchange between Bill, Jr., on his way north from Africa in the sunlit smoothness of forty-three thousand feet, and the pilot of another ship helplessly bouncing around in a storm at seventeen thousand feet. "But suppose this weather reaches you?" the other pilot

asked, after hearing a recitation of the Lear Jet's virtues, "what
will you do then?"

"Oh, I suppose we'd turn on the other engine and go higher,"
Bill, Jr., replied.

As for the creator of the plane—"Everything that has happened
in my life—all the things that have gone wrong—flying this airplane makes it all worth-while," Lear confided as he and I had a
predinner drink one night after arching over the Sierra to San
Francisco where he was making a speech. "It's as much thrill now
as the first time."

The Lear Jet, described by Al Higdon as "the only airplane I
know that looks like it's doing six hundred miles an hour sitting
on the ground," was the coaster wagon Lear never had as a boy.
"I could always tell a Lear take-off," Betty Miller said. "He blasted
off—he went straight up." She told of once going along for the ride
to pick up Lear after he had kept a dental appointment in Kansas
City. The plane never really stopped. Lear came aboard while
the ship was still rolling. Hank Beaird slid over to the right-hand
seat. Lear plopped into the left, shoved the throttle forward, and
away they went, back to Wichita.

Woe to anyone going with him who was late. "What're you
trying to do—race me for the left seat?" Lear would demand of
Hank Beaird as the two dashed toward the plane.

"No, sir," Hank would reply. "I only know if I don't get aboard
I'll get left."

Many have learned this lesson the hard way, arriving at the field
only to see the Lear Jet charging down the runway or already
vanishing into the blue. "There are people all over the country
who have watched him take off who were supposed to have been
aboard," said Fran Jabara, reminiscing in his office at Wichita
State University.

The members of the I-Got-Left-Behind-By-Lear Club include retired Lieutenant General Hewitt T. Wheless, former Air Force
assistant vice chief of staff, and for a time Lear's executive vice-
president in Reno. Lear flew to Wichita for a board of directors'
meeting. "Where's Shorty?" someone asked as the meeting was
called to order.

Lear clapped a hand to his forehead and moaned. Shorty was
waiting wistfully out in Reno, twelve hundred miles west. Lear
had forgotten him.

Not even Moya received special treatment when her husband

was ready to go. She was reminded of this each Friday in the
confusion of getting off to Palm Springs for the weekend. Fed
up by dogs, maids, children, and more guests than there were
seats—Lear having invited his guests and Moya hers—the noisy
hubbub of these occasions reached a climax as Lear swung the
tail of the plane toward the lounge and ran up the engines, loosing
a thunderous blast at the door as Moya lingered at the telephone
within. Then he would taxi slowly away, making her run for it,
clasping her hat to the back of her head with one hand as she ran.

"Teach her to be on time," Lear muttered when Hank Beaird
chided him about it.

Moya explained why Lear goes off and leaves people, apart
from now and then absent-mindedly forgetting them. "When he
says wheels in the well at nine and people aren't there, he has no
way of knowing how late they are going to be, or even if they are
coming at all. So he leaves."

Any traveler with Lear in his jet lives recklessly who wanders
away from the plane during stops, for whatever reason. On a
flight to Jamaica, Jim Greenwood went to a telephone in New
Orleans and called Al Higdon back in Wichita on a company
matter, on Lear's instructions. Greenwood had no sooner gotten
Higdon on the line than he saw the plane buttoning up and beginning to roll. "I gotta go!" Greenwood shouted, slamming up the
receiver and bolting from the booth.

The closing top and bottom sections of the door caught him like
pincers as he dived through the opening, getting a helping hand
from co-pilot Rick King. His legs thrashing, Greenwood looked like
something being ingested by a retreating shark as the plane gathered speed.

As the flight progressed, Lear and King fell to jawing. For
King, unemployment was already near and he had lost further
points by helping Greenwood aboard in New Orleans. The two
were going at it so hard that they overshot Jamaica. Apprised of
this detail by Greenwood, sitting in the back of the plane, they
made a high speed letdown. Dumping flaps and spoilers, they
were on the runway in six minutes from forty-three thousand
feet.

"It was like a dive-bombing exercise," Greenwood said.

A customs man came up as the door opened and let fly at the
interior from a spray can. He advised the passengers that they
would have to remain inside the sealed ship for a certain time.

Lear sat on the jump seat, glowering at the closed door opposite. "I'll give him thirty seconds before he kicks it open," Greenwood said to himself, consulting his watch.

He was close. At twenty-eight seconds Lear planted his feet against the door and sent it flying open. As he strolled disdainfully away from the ship, other customs men came down on Greenwood with demands for entry papers. Greenwood appealed to Lear. "Look," he said, "these guys aren't kidding. They want papers."

Lear paused. "They want papers?" he asked. "Give them a brochure."

This did nothing to improve Lear's disposition. He fired King and wanted to abandon him in Jamaica, but was talked out of it by Greenwood, who felt it was a little strong to strand a man that far from home. That evening King had his revenge. Lear had given permission for a couple of low-level passes over the set of a movie, and as Lear rested in a nearby motel, King went over in the jet at house-top level as near Mach 1 as he could manage.

Lear rushed out on the balcony with nothing on except his shirt, which wasn't as long as he might have wished. "What in hell was that?" he demanded of Greenwood, who appeared on a neighboring balcony.

"That was Rick King," Greenwood replied.

"Who authorized this?"

"You did—don't you remember? Get set now because he's coming around again."

King laid down a second wallop. Lear now remembered, but King was almost back to getting stranded in Jamaica again.

Besides those who have been left behind by Lear, there is another group, made up of those who wished they had. The membership of this group derives from Lear's habit of attacking the instrument panel with a set of pocket tools in mid-flight, with disquieting results to the flight pattern. "Is he fixing it?" an uninitiated passenger once asked nervously as Lear fell to with his screwdriver. "No," replied his seat mate, "he's building it."

Sometimes it gets a little trying even for the sophisticates.

John Zimmerman, on a flight from Montreal, watched with little more than passing interest as Lear traded seats with pilot Bill Darling and began to dismantle the automatic pilot. Zimmerman had seen this before, and he maintained a reasonable equanimity as the ship began to pitch and roll like a playful porpoise, all accompanied by raised voices and harsh tones from up front.

But the sight of loose parts suddenly rolling down the aisle cracked him. "I was sure he'd never get the thing back together again," Zimmerman said.

Another time, as Hank Beaird told it, Lear had the automatic pilot out and lying in his lap in several pieces. He was working on the altitude-hold part. This is the part that keeps the airplane at the altitude the pilot wants to fly and generally is the part that falls short in performance—as it was doing now. The plane was going up and down like a roller coaster.

All at once Lear threw the offending piece over his shoulder, attached wires and all. "The hell with it!" he cried.

Lying on the floor in the back of the plane, it did its job perfectly, the ship settling down to smoothly level flight. "Don't touch it!" Lear cried as Hank moved to retrieve the piece—and there it stayed until the end of the flight.

"If I was caught in a lightning storm—couldn't see a thing—and the electrical system went out," Hank said, "I'd rather be flying with Bill Lear than anybody else I know, because he'd fix it."

Something like that happened as Lear was dodging thunderstorms in his Learstar above the rocky peaks of Mormon Mesa, Utah, one midnight in the fifties. A rheostat went bad in the radio and Lear told his co-pilot to turn the radio off. The co-pilot, with seventeen thousand hours' flying time, hit the wrong switch and turned off the instruments. The ship began to drop. In moments it had gone from nineteen thousand feet to fifteen thousand. The peaks spearing up from the darkness began at thirteen thousand. There were about thirty seconds to go.

The co-pilot desperately pulled back on the stick, struggling to level the ship off. It was going one hundred miles an hour faster than its maximum safe speed, pulling two Gs. At 2½ Gs, the wings would come off. The plunge continued.

Lear took over. He suspected the ship was in a vertical spiral. This would explain why it wasn't responding to the co-pilot's efforts on the stick; as he pulled back, he simply tightened the spiral, accounting for the G-loads they were getting. The ball on the turn and bank indicator floated in the middle position, indicating level flight, but Lear knew this was also where the ball would be in a loop. A vertical spiral was a loop in a different plane.

There was only one question: Was the turn and bank indicator working? Lear waggled the stick. The ball floated off center. He straightened the ship—about ten seconds from joining the Great Majority.

Lear began flying instruments after he hired an "instrument" pilot to fly him and Walter Beech to the 1935 Cleveland air races. As the weather closed in, the pilot kept flying lower and lower. When he was down to about one hundred feet from the ground, barely skimming the trees, Lear told him to go higher.

The pilot climbed into the soup and was soon traveling in circles; Lear could tell from the oscillations of the Learoscope. "You better give me the wheel," Lear said.

The pilot refused, and Lear appealed to Walter Beech, working on a quart of corn product in the back seat. "Give him the wheel!" Beech ordered, making it two against one.

The pilot obeyed, later admitting he had neither flown instruments nor cross-country before, and Lear became an instrument pilot. "If you ever get caught in instrument conditions and you don't know instruments," he says, "you have to fly instruments the rest of your life—about a minute and a half."

The Lear Jet "gold mine" yielded $52 million in sales the first year, $2 million over the mark Lear had told scoffing bankers he would reach. The plane which the kibitzers had said would never sell, seen on more than forty magazine covers in a dozen countries, took the lead in sales the first year after it was certificated and has held it ever since. This occurred despite three fatal crashes in seven months. Those shook Lear as nothing else had shaken him, because men were killed. "If only we had a little more contact with the hereafter!" he cried wearily one late night as he led his engineers in a search for the answer. "Then maybe we could find out what happened."

"Bill," Ed Lenheim replied, wiping the sweat from his forehead, "we'll start on that division in the morning."

The cause of the crashes was found without recourse to celestial communications, but there came other turbulence. There were management mistakes. Planes were being built faster than they were being sold. At one point, the "production genius" in charge of the shop, who had once built eight hundred warplanes a month, was seventeen ships up on the sales department, bringing the sneering comment in an ad by another builder, "We don't shell them out like peas in a pod."

As things worsened, Lear threw in everything he still owned to stave off disaster. At the board meeting where he was brought the papers turning over the last of his possessions, including his two Peter Paul Rubens' paintings, board member Joe Walsh advised him not to sign. "Close up for a while," Walsh said. "Don't fold, but suspend operations temporarily. Stop the drain on your resources." Given the water time to come back up in the spring, Walsh was saying.

"Get out of here!" Lear roared and put his name on the documents.

The chiefs went down to half pay. Some volunteered to do without pay altogether for a while. Many of the hourly workers offered to clock out, then stay on a few more hours on their own time. When the boss himself had maybe $10 million in the project, he must believe in it, all felt. "I didn't think it was such a big gamble," said George Dean, the plant engineer, who went ninety-two days without a paycheck.

This was more than Lear expected of anyone—as was the time he found Dean, supposedly on vacation, cutting grass on the six-acre Lear estate. "I thought you were on vacation," Lear asked.

"I was," Dean acknowledged, "but I wasn't doing much and the place needed a little trimming here and there."

Lear stared uncomprehendingly, his eyes slowly beginning to swim. "I don't understand," he said slowly. "I don't understand."

Dean was cutting the grass out of the same impulse which had moved him and his wife, caretakers in the after years, to set up two beds in the big empty room upstairs which the Lear family had favored. This was in case the Lears might want to spend the night in their old home sometime when they were passing through town.

Dean, a low-spoken, kindly man, noted that so far the Lears hadn't come, always staying at the Diamond Motel out at the airport. "But I understand," he said gently. "The emotional shock of coming back to a house filled with so many memories is too much for them."

So the neatly made beds waited, somehow reminding one of Little Boy Blue's toy soldiers.

For the rest, the Deans kept away from that part of the house. "We feel this belongs to them," Dean said softly, tiptoeing from the room.

Besides the pay cuts, another step to help keep the enterprise afloat was to send a Lear Jet on a record-seeking dash around the world. Lear personally bought the supplies for the crew, among them a clothesline "to hang yourselves with if you don't get back on time."

John Zimmerman, included in the crew after he got nosy at finding Lear and Hank Beaird on the floor poring over maps of the world, was delegated to write the story at the finish of the flight. Meanwhile, Lear ordered, there would be nothing said about it. As the flight neared the halfway mark, Lear complained to Jim Greenwood about the lack of publicity attending it. "This is the best-kept secret since the atom bomb," he rumbled acidly.

"So I changed from an exclusive reporter to a pool reporter," Zimmerman said.

Before the take-off, Lear told Hank Beaird he would give him a dollar for each minute he beat the estimated time back. When the flight reached Osaka, Japan, Lear was on the telephone to Hank. "Make that $5," he said.

When the plane swooped home back in Wichita, after fifty hours and twenty minutes flying time, Lear was on hand with a roll of bills. He peeled them off at the Osaka-quoted rate not only for Hank Beaird but co-pilot John Lear and the rest of the crew as well.

The ship hung up eighteen world records on the flight, but the money crisis at the plant deepened and as it did so, a friend appeared on the scene from an unlikely quarter. Kenneth E. Johnson, new president and chairman of the board of the Kansas State Bank and Trust Company, late of Phoenix, Arizona, had the notion, "You're not a banker if you're just going to be custodian of the money and keep it in the vault."

A trim, distinguished man with full gray hair and a cosmopolitan manner, Johnson nostalgically recalled his adventures in Lear Land as a thunderstorm was breaking in a windy fury on the water outside the window of his club in Twin Lakes.

Repeatedly he let money out of custody to meet the Lear payroll, each time successfully betting on Lear to have the money back to the bank from the sale of an airplane before the next payday. "I felt it would be catastrophic to let them go down," Johnson said, adding that he thought time had vindicated him. "I was able to save an industry for Wichita."

It was Johnson who came to Lear's rescue when the Bank of America cut him off. "We'll save this money for you and you'll thank us when you go broke," the bank told Lear.

Johnson phoned them. "It's a perfectly good loan," the Bank of

America admitted, "but we're just tired of Bill Lear out here at arm's length, tweaking our nose. He doesn't like our interest rates. He won't renew." The complaint ran on.

Johnson advised Lear to go to the Bank of America "on your hands and knees if necessary." He said, "We don't need any more trouble."

Lear listed a number of things he would rather do first, mostly of an unprintable nature, before he went to the Bank of America on his hands and knees. Johnson, whose own lending limit was only $350,000, struck out in other directions and got Lear the $6 million he needed from the Union Bank in Los Angeles.

Finding such sums for Lear was not easy. "You're not exactly popular with bankers," Johnson reminded Lear.

"They think I'm a son of a bitch?"

"You are a son of a bitch."

As he traveled the banking circuit around the country on Lear's behalf, Johnson often found more clinical interest in Lear, the man, than in lending him money. "He was one of the greatest door openers I had," Johnson said. "They would see his name on papers, then say, 'We're not going to give you the loan, but tell us about Lear.'"

Besides perseverance and unusual persuasive powers, being banker for Lear called for patience, too. Johnson had a call from Lear one evening at six o'clock. "Can you get me $5 million?"

"I'll try," Johnson replied, pointing out that it was after hours and that he therefore was under a certain handicap.

At nine the next morning, Lear was back on the line. "How're you coming?" he asked.

"Look," Johnson said, "when you called last night the banks were closed. They're still not open this morning."

This only brought a critical dissertation from Lear on the working hours of banks, who stand with Lear about where he stands with them.

But Johnson was able to come through, as he again came through when Lear put another kind of stress on banking orthodoxy by writing a check for what used to be a fortune, on a piece of foolscap in payment for some stocks.

"For Christ's sake, that's no good!" exclaimed Dick Millar of the William R. Staats Company, who had asked him for the money. "But don't throw it away!" he added hastily.

June Shields wrote to Johnson, forewarning him. "William R.

Staats Company tells me that Mr. Lear made history at the office by sending them a check written on a piece of paper in the amount of $104,294.89." she wrote. "I mention this in the earnest hope that it will not make further history by bouncing. He simply didn't have a blank check with him at the moment he wanted to write one, and so put into application his famous maxim, 'use what you've got. . . .'"

Lear called Johnson "my kind of banker," writing the words, much cherished by Johnson, in a book which he inscribed to him; and when Lear Jet was sold, Lear told the new owners, "I want you to do business with Ken Johnson as long as you can. If it hadn't been for him there would have been no Lear Jet."

Lear went on seeking Johnson's advice long after Wichita, phoning him from all points at all hours.

"He run a lot of deals by me," Johnson said, using the colloquial present tense.

One of the deals Lear run by him was the proposal to buy his present site in Nevada. "I'm buying the Stead Air Force Base," he said.

"What are you trying to do?" Johnson asked. "Outdo Howard Hughes?"

"Yes," Lear replied. "Hughes is buying up southern Nevada. I'm buying up the north half."

If Lear esteemed Ken Johnson, so was it true the other way around. "I'd go to hell for him," Johnson said with grim intensity, expressing a quality of partisanship not uncommon among Lear loyalists.

The end came in Wichita after Justin Dart, who had bought the second ship, paying for it in advance so Lear would have the use of the money, advised Lear that selling was the only thing to do under the circumstances. There was no more free board. While the Lear Jets were selling, the money wasn't coming in fast enough to mollify the creditors. Coming from Dart, whose judgment Lear greatly respected, the advice struck home.

He approached the sale to the Gates Rubber Company like a man selling his child. Through the night before the fateful event he paced the floor, pausing to make notes of conditions he wanted included in the deal. In the morning Moya typed them up, then drove him to the office. "Well, darling," she said, trying to ease his gloom, "we've had a wonderful time. We have wonderful memories. Nobody can buy those—and there will be other challenges."

"I know it," Lear muttered unconvincingly.

Arriving at the plant, Lear handed the Gates people his list of conditions and settled down to wait for their decision. Moya drove home. Late in the afternoon she received a call from the representative of the company which was handling the deal. "Bill says to tell you he's all right," Miller said.

"Of course he's all right," Moya replied, curious. "Why not?"

"He has decided he doesn't want to sell."

"Then that's the way it should be," Moya said firmly. "Don't try to stop him. That's what would be right for him. He's a very special kind of person."

Lear's voice came over the line. "Mom, I'm going to tell them to go to hell."

"That's fine with me," Moya assured him. "The steaks are ready to put on. I picked some fresh mint from the yard. You come on home."

Hours later, Lear was back on the line. "Mom," he said buoyantly, "I want you to meet your new partner." He introduced the new owner over the telephone.

When he reached home shortly, he filled her in on what had taken place between the first and second call. As the hours dragged by, he had finally gone into the room where the buyers were meeting and told them, "If you're thinking of taking away even $1000 from my proposal, forget it—the deal's off. Now get on the ball!"

Minutes later, Gates bought the company for substantially more than Lear had asked.

Lear spared Moya the fact that before this happy ending came the negotiations had really turned into a cliff-hanger, which any moment could have climaxed in disaster. During the six hours they were in progress, two lawsuits were filed against the company in Michigan. If one more had been filed in Michigan there would have been nothing to sell. Under the law the company would have to be declared in involuntary bankruptcy.

It impressed Carl Bell, who sat in on the proceedings as Lear's legal counsel, that Lear acted as if nothing unusual was going on. He spent the fore part of the evening with Edgar Bergen, emceeing a show for the Society of Test Pilots.

"Most men would have been climbing the wall," Bell said.

The epilogue to Wichita came a couple of years later, when Lear resigned as chairman of the board. Now he no longer held even a ceremonial function in the firm's affairs. Al Higdon went with him for a farewell look around the scenes which had claimed most of each day for five years. Higdon had been on hand for three of those years. "They were the three best years of my life," he said, in the faraway tones of a man who had been at Balaklava. "But I wouldn't want to go through them again."

Walking in front, Higdon realized that he was getting no responses as he talked over his shoulder. He looked back. Lear was standing on the catwalk, staring down at the water tank they had used for hydrostatic tests of the ship. He stood with head bent, his big shoulders drooping, lost in the privacy of his own thoughts.

Higdon faced back the other way and swallowed.

6: WE'RE GOING INTO THE STEAM BUSINESS

Having sold Lear Jet, Lear wanted to leave for Los Angeles at once. "Characteristically," Moya said, "he wanted to get out and never look back."

She persuaded him to wait until Friday, when Tina got out of school. There were five days to go. Lear paced the floor, worked crossword puzzles, played the organ, paced some more.

"I couldn't stand it until Friday," Moya said.

Fortuitously, she saw in the *Beacon* that Walter Hickel, then Governor of Alaska, was in town. "Why don't we call him up and offer to fly him home to Alaska in the Lear Jet?" she craftily suggested, having in mind this would give Lear something to do. Lear was at the phone getting Hickel on the line almost before she had the words out.

Next day, with a police escort to the airport, they flew from Wichita to Seattle. That took care of Tuesday. Wednesday they flew to Anchorage and Juneau, and Thursday to Nome. Friday, hearing about the Alaska Centennial at Fairbanks, they went there instead of home. Saturday they were back in Wichita to pick up Tina, and Sunday they flew to Los Angeles. It had been a fairly busy six days.

They found a new home in Beverly Hills, the wooded estate of Leonard Firestone, in the hills above Sunset Boulevard. What now? "Now we were fat in the bank and nothing to do," Moya said.

While being a multimillionaire with no work to do is a condition most men feel they could learn to live with, for Lear it was a poverty worse than being broke.

On the night of his sixty-fifth birthday, with Moya in Europe, Buzz and Ursula Nanney dropped by with champagne and a half dozen bottles of Löwenbrau. They were through the champagne and well into the Löwenbrau when Lear said woefully, "The problem is, what the hell do I do now? Life is slipping away. What can I do?"

"Bill, I feel awfully sorry for you," Buzz replied with irony. "You got your pockets full of money. You have the world in your lap. You can move around. With that fertile mind, you'll find something to do."

Giving minor thought to Buzz's words, Lear halfheartedly tried the life of the rich idler while he looked for something new to turn up. With the family, he spent the summer in Europe, taking in the Salzburg Festival and other such traditional cultural events —all the time sourly wondering how they survived long enough to become traditional. Bill Lear in the role of the American tourist, camera slung from his neck, was a gross piece of miscasting.

Back home in Beverly Hills, the Lears had dinner one rainy night with Bob Prescott of Flying Tigers fame. As Lear turned to say good night, he slipped on the wet terrazzo and fell, breaking his leg at the ankle. Apparently on the theory that if a little cast is good, a bigger one is better, the doctors encased the entire leg in plaster, toes to hip, pretty well immobilizing the patient.

Not for long. At St. John's Hospital in Santa Monica, with Lear more or less directing the proceedings, the long cast was removed. The bone was reset, and a cast of more local extent applied.

Although it was not a walking cast, Lear walked. He also danced. He conducted himself as if training for an endurance championship. He wanted to go to Geneva for daughter Shanda's wedding December 16 to Gian Carlo Bertelli, Fulbright scholar and vice-president in charge of European operations for Hill and Knowlton, the public relations firm, but settled for a trip to New York on December 17 instead. On December 18 he attended a reception at the 21 Club, and on December 19 he flew back to Los Angeles for a reception in Beverly Hills on December 20.

For some reason, his leg failed to heal, and early in January

1968 it was necessary to break and reset the bone once more, a metal pin being added to hold things in place. Not long after this, his nose began to bleed intractably. Repeatedly the doctors cauterized and packed his nose with gauze. The bleeding went on. It continued all through February, finally getting so bad he was bleeding into a pan.

"It was driving him up the wall," Moya said. "Nobody thought to ask what was causing it. They just kept packing and cauterizing!"

Along with the pain came depression. Late one Saturday night, no longer willing to accept life on these terms, Lear decided to get rid of the packing in his nose, come what may. He was just starting to pull when the telephone rang. It was Dr. Dick Barton, returning Moya's call of some hours earlier. In another moment Lear would have had the packing out, and he probably would have hemorrhaged to death.

"Get him to the hospital right away!" Barton told Moya.

At St. John's minutes later, taking one look at the patient, Barton sent Moya home to fetch a spray Lear had been using —to get her out of the way, she suspected. When she returned to the hospital, Lear was already in surgery, giving her a few bad moments as she found the room empty in which she had left him; there was another place than surgery they might have taken him, she knew, in the basement.

Lear's trouble was that a blood vessel back of his nose, the anterior ethmoid branch of the ophthalmic artery, had ruptured, spilling blood into the nasal passages. There was awe and gratitude in Moya's voice as she told how Barton, displacing an eye for access through the socket, tied off the broken artery, working four tense hours in the middle of the night. "He was the right doctor at the right time," she said.

Outside the saloons, Palm Springs is probably a better place than most to recover from an illness, what with the desert peace and quiet all about—but it was no good for Bill Lear. Instead of getting better, he lost ground. He went down like an unwatered plant in the sun, and soon fled for his life, spending more time in Reno and mulling over what he might do there.

He reflected on the things he had told a Reno dinner audience one night after he bought land at the defunct Stead Air Force Base, with nothing in mind at the time except investment. Getting slightly carried away, he tantalized his eager listeners with hints of big plans for Reno, hard hit by the closing of Stead. What his plans were exactly, he didn't say—he didn't know.

Back home in Beverly Hills, Moya scolded him for "misleading all those people—making them think you were going to start an industry in Reno."

"But if we get something going up there I can commute back and forth," Lear replied. "After all, that's what we have the Lear Jet for. We can go on living here in Beverly Hills."

Moya knew that wouldn't work. "Any woman who thinks she can live in one place when her husband has to work in another might as well forget her marriage," she said.

So the work in Reno, whatever form it took, would entail yet another resettlement of the family. They would move to Reno as they had moved to Wichita, to Geneva, Pacific Palisades, and so on back through the years, making the home where the action was.

It wasn't long before Lear had a number of things going in Reno. There was Titanium West, a project to make titanium ingots from titanium sponge. A second project involved development of an improved jet engine, which used titanium, the immediate incentive being greater range for the Lear Jet. The Lear-Stead Development Company had to do with real estate, and the William P. Lear Enterprises were a group of miscellaneous undertakings.

Headquarters for all this were in two adjoining residential apartments on the twentieth floor of the Arlington Towers, leased by Buzz Nanney after a short stay in even tighter quarters at the First National Bank. Apartment J somewhat resembled a command post for military assault. A tangle of telephone lines lay on the floor, connecting the outside world with four phones in Apartment J and one phone in each room of adjoining Apartment K, reserved for residential use. One closet bulged with equipment operating the push buttons for the telephones, the other with filing cabinets.

There were three desks in the living room. A conference table spanned the dining area. A rollaway bed did little rolling as it accommodated the spillover from K or contained Lear Jet pilot Morgan Hetrick. Against the north picture window, looking out on ten-thousand-foot Peavine Mountain, stood Hugh Carson's drafting board.

Carson, like Lear, a man who heard a different drum, was a

solid, quiet-spoken Southerner, born in Cloverport, Kentucky, who had defected from the South the day after he graduated from Alabama's Auburn University, degrees in science and mechanical engineering in his pocket. Carson left home in haste because, having read a thousand books before he was twenty, he "held ideas that didn't fit in with the Southern way of life," such as having black, Jewish, and Catholic friends and going with a Methodist girl.

As a boy, Carson built and raced model airplanes, habitually walking away with the prizes. He built four hundred airplanes in a seven-year span, financing his production with income as a laborer in a textile mill, custodian at the post office, and proprietor of a $12 lawn mower.

"I would prepare at least one aircraft for every event, giving me maybe twelve planes in each contest," he said. "I'd come away with as many as three first places."

Carson served as the townsmen's Mr. Fixit. He repaired their automobiles long before he received his driver's license at fifteen. He kept their clocks running, their radios, TV sets, washing machines. "Any kind of mechanical problem—they came to me for the answers."

A year after he left town, Carson was in Santa Monica, California helping Bill Lear find the answers on a number of projects. And again, as at home, he was the guy who unofficially kept everybody's car going. Then Lear went to Switzerland and Carson, publicly finding his new boss an "idiot," soon was in Santa Ana working with Sam Auld, his former associate from Santa Monica.

One day Lear turned up in Santa Ana. "What's Carson doing here?" he demanded.

"I hired him," Sam replied.

"Like hell you did!" Lear growled. He told of the operations he was starting in Reno. He hardly looked like a man beginning new enterprises. He was on crutches. His face was gray. His blue eyes were sunken and wore the dull patina of death.

So Carson, out of compassion as well as loyalty to his old employer, joined the bustling scene high in Reno's Arlington Towers.

In the midst of the chaos and having much to do with making it functional, sat blond Ginny Hamilton, Lear's secretary, with an expression of amused incredulity and as coolly unflappable as an Englishman in wartime, which it pretty much was. It had been awfully dull working at the bank. It was dull no more.

But Lear's condition was worrisome. "That first week in Reno nobody knew if he would make it or not," Carson said. "Each time he took a pill he sneezed till we thought he'd break a blood vessel. We didn't know if it was to be the beginning or the end of something here in Reno."

During a presentation by Neil Plath, president of the Sierra-Pacific Power Company, regarding power for Lear's works at the Stead Base, Lear passed out from the medication in his system. Plath politely said he would be glad to come back another time, probably feeling there wouldn't be another time.

"How do you feel, boss?" Buzz asked one evening.

Lear's halting answer made everybody heartsick. "Terrible. I'm so tired. I ache all over."

Yet he sat up till all hours of the night, making and receiving telephone calls. Carson finally took the phone away from him, carrying it into the back bedroom. The crew matched their schedules to Lear's, working, eating, and sleeping when he did.

Gradually, as he began working at the drawing board himself, Lear looked better. The color returned to his face. The glazed blue eyes returned to their old glint. He grew stronger.

Perhaps it was the Chinese food. Lear sent out for it ten days in a row—until Buzz, heading out on the eleventh day, said, "I ain't coming back with any goddamned Chinese food!"

"You will or don't bother to come back!" Lear called after him, as good a sign as any that the boss was improving.

Lear's fondness for the fodder of the Celestial Empire was equaled by his addiction to Kellogg's Special K. This he undeviatingly consumed for breakfast, putting it away with accelerating gusto as he recited the good things it did for you.

He also liked the bread Moya made from an Old World recipe, using whole wheat flour with brown sugar and molasses, a staple of the household since Switzerland days. To make sure Lear got it, Moya, coming up from Beverly Hills, became a part-time resident of Apartment K until their first house was ready at Lakeside.

After they moved in, and for all the improvement Lear was showing, he still suffered fits of depression. One night, coming home from a frolic at the Holiday round table, he mysteriously refused to have dinner, eating only popcorn. What was on his mind Moya, in her wisdom, deferred asking until another time.

After dinner that night she and her mother went to church. On their way home after the services, they planned to stop and buy ice cream, but Moya suddenly felt a strange need to get home as quickly as possible, and the ice cream was canceled. They reached the house just as Lear was coming out the door with a bag in hand.

"Where do you think you're going?" Moya asked.

Lear mumbled something to the effect that he was "going away." He seemed confused and undecided.

"You march right back into that house!" Moya ordered.

Lear silently obeyed. Pressed by Moya, he muttered that he had planned to rent an airplane and fly it out to sea until the fuel was gone. He showed her the note he had left.

"Get into your pajamas and get to bed!" Moya commanded.

Not long before, it had been the timely phone call from Dr. Barton that saved Lear's life. Moya felt her extrasensory decision to forego the ice cream purchase had done it again. "Believe in God or not," she said reflectively, "somebody looks after him."

As Lear's health grew, so did his interest in steam. The Senate hearings in Washington on air and water pollution, at which the steam automobile was dusted off as a possible answer to exhaust pipe poison, were much in the news. Sam Auld, who had been keeping Lear abreast of technical developments in various fields, sent him a prepublication copy of the Washington proceedings.

Auld phoned around the country to see what was doing in steam car development. He talked to the Williams brothers at Ambler, Pennsylvania—Charles and Calvin—making the connection through the sheriff's office since the brothers hadn't yet adopted the telephone. While the brothers, twins like the famed Stanleys, belonged to the Stanley age of steam, they clearly were intelligent, and Auld recommended to Lear that he go and see what they had.

Auld, Scotch for "old," included this in a letter to Lear on June 28, 1968, saying he was "impressed with the potential of steam-powered automobiles," and that he felt the time had come to apply the new technology to this purpose.

He listed the reasons. Steam power gave off practically no

pollution, because combustion was out in the open and therefore complete, rather than confined to a cylinder, with a third of the fuel wasted. There was no maintenance to speak of for the first hundred thousand miles. It cost at least a third less to operate. It gave the performance of automatic transmission without its complexity. Steam was far more powerful. It was silent. It was compatible with the interests of the petroleum industry as now set up, precluding resistance from that quarter.

"When do we start?" Auld ended his letter.

He followed it with assorted magazine pieces, among them one from *Life* liberally underscored, and a clipping from the *Wall Street Journal.*

"It was such a good match—putting a basic need of the country and Bill Lear's capabilities together," said Auld, a native of southern California, who remembers the Los Angeles basin before it became a gas chamber where at least one person in five has a breathing impairment. "We all recognize that it was a difficult technical problem, but this was good for him. He isn't happy unless he has a tiger by the tail."

Lear did visit the steam car works of the Williams brothers. He took in the Harrah collection of automobiles in Reno, personally driving the old nine-thousand-pound Doble steamer. The two visits only confirmed for Lear that there had been no basic advance in steam since the clock stopped on its development back in the twenties.

Lear phoned Hugh Carson, at the moment in Monterey, California, working with Professor Michael Vavra on the new jet engine. "How would you like to work on a steam auto project?" Lear asked Hugh.

"That would be great—at last to be doing something I've studied and trained for all my life," Carson replied.

A week later Lear phoned again, saying he had definitely decided to go ahead. "We're going to build a steam engine to take the place of the internal combustion engine and get rid of air pollution," he said.

"Good! Count me in!" Carson said happily.

"You can start by outlining the problems we are going to have and how to lick them," Lear said, not to seem stingy about giving Carson something to start on.

Lear phoned Art Linkletter, a member of his board of directors, in Los Angeles. "We're out of the titanium business," he announced.

THE INCREDIBLE STORY OF BILL LEAR

"We're going into the steam business. We're going to build a steam car."

"Fine," Linkletter said, having heard the news for the first time.

"I'm going to commit $10 million."

"How much you got?"

"Oh, $15 or $20 million."

"Just so you don't get down to running on the rim again, like you did with the Lear Jet."

Lear had previously let Linkletter know he didn't think much of the titanium business. "That's just plain old money-making," he complained. "Let's get into something we have to worry about day and night."

Building a steam automobile would do it.

7: WHO CARES? EVERYBODY!

The star of the New York Auto Show in 1917 was easily Abner Doble's new steam automobile, causing far more excitement than anything else on the floor. "The internal combustion engine—the type used in cars consuming gasoline for fuel—has about reached the limits of its possibilities," Doble wrote confidently. "On the other hand, the day of the steam-propelled vehicle—the ultimate car—is just dawning."

Compared to the steam cars that had gone before, Doble's new steamer was well into the dawn he spoke of. It overcame all the old drawbacks: the deep thirst for water every few miles, scale in the boiler, slow starting time, high cost of operation, and the concentrated attention it took to drive a steamer without the risk of being blown up.

The display brought Doble more than fifty thousand letters from the general public, and seven hundred telegrams from dealers who wanted to handle the car. In three months he booked 11,320 orders—$27 million worth.

Then the dawn Doble had heralded faded as materials to build the car were diverted to the needs of making the world safe for democracy. By the time World War I ended, Henry Ford's assembly lines were spilling out Model-Ts. These sold for a few hundred dollars. The Doble steamer cost thousands. Relative quality had nothing to do with it. The internal combustion engine was in command. The dream of steam vanished like the vapor at the steamer's whistle.

Now, a half century later, the vision formed again, and this time it was William P. Lear who caused the excitement. The mail pouring in at his Reno plant came from all parts of the world, ebbing and flowing with Lear's presence in the news. He personally read each letter, marking those calling for reply, usually by Doug Hardy, or marketing director Kenneth Nall, after which receptionist Bernie Eppinger committed the letters to the glassine pages of large black albums.

More than six thousand engineers sent resumés on their backgrounds in the first few months after Lear opened shop. Like those who flocked to him in Wichita to have a hand in pioneering a new airplane, these wanted to be in on the taming of the steam frontier for automobiles.

Most had rather more to offer than the man whose father, tooling around Washington in the family Stanley, scared the horse being ridden by President Theodore Roosevelt. By way of further certifying his qualifications, he would be "happy to send a picture of the old steamer and me."

Mostly, though, the mail was from people who only wanted to applaud this St. George who had thrown down the gauntlet to Detroit. It was as if they had given probationary status to the internal combustion engine all these years while they waited for something better to come along. "You are doing the public a great service," wrote George W. King of Volcano, California, an "old pensioner with fond memories" of the early steamers. "Only a fool will laugh."

On stationery festooned with hearts, Jeannette Kaplan wrote from Brooklyn, "This is a love letter from a city dweller who dreams of a clean, quiet automobile, who had read with considerable excitement . . . that Lear Motors is busy working to make my dream come true. Please accept my personal encouragement. . . . I for one will buy stock in your corporation, urge my senators and congressmen to help finance your enterprise, and ultimately I will buy one of your cars. . . ."

"With joy and profound respect," Albert E. Anderson, seventy-eight, inventor and mechanic of Quincy, Illinois, wrote as "one of those folks who wept when they took the steam car off the market sixty years ago. If we had spent a mere fraction of the billions of dollars wasted on the internal combustion engine we would not now be gasping for air. . . . May God forgive them! . . . some day soon I expect to see Learmobiles in sales rooms all over the nation. . . . This will, and should, become your monument to fame."

An Iowan "skimping along on my rocking chair money" hoped to live long enough to ride in the Lear Steamer. "Sock it to them!" There was a gracious letter from a man who remembered when "you were first starting out in Piqua, Ohio. You have certainly put a lot of stars in your crown since that time. I believe this most recent unit may be the highlight of your whole career, and I congratulate you on the courage to undertake it in the face of a good many of these big institutions—General Motors, Ford, etc., who will, of course, resist any major change. . . ."

For a young Virginian, the son of a doctor, Lear had brought an apocalypse. He would now return to college "with a wiser countenance" after having been suspended for "academic deficiencies. . . ." Lear had "helped me decide how to tackle life head-on and with a great deal of vigor. . . . I wish you long life, health and happiness, and I hope that I may find success in your example."

"We are waiting to greet your new steam car," wrote a California woman in a long, chatty letter filled with nostalgic recollections of the early steamers. "There is an old British expression which we have adopted in our private life: 'Illegitimus non carborundum.' Freely translated: 'Don't let the bastards grind you down!'"

The cheers ran on:

"Hip, hip hooray for your well-aimed frontal attack. May your follow-through flatten the opposition"—"So many of us have been grinding our teeth over the gassy and overcomplicated monsters Detroit produces. Great success to you!"—"I'm fascinated—good luck!"—"Your work might just become one of the most important items in the history of mankind."—"[You] deserve the respect and admiration of us all."—"Keep those 'crazy ideas' coming. The world will be the better for them."—"I can only admire the David who takes on the Goliath."

They came from far away. "I wish you success," wrote an Australian. "Keep up the steam!"—"Godspeed to make this project a grand success!" cheered a man in Bombay, India.

Many writers wanted to be helpful. A Salt Lake City man urged Lear to write to Ruthven H. Packard, an old family friend in Massachusetts "who has been telling the world that the steam car is the car of the future, but all laugh at him. He could give you immeasurable help." After all, he had been using steam at the sawmill every day for sixty-five years. Lear must be patient, however. Besides the sawmill, he was also running the farm, and might take a while to hear back from him. "Open up the throttle and away we go!"

A retired Chicago policeman in Arkansas who had "seen more than my share of traffic accidents caused from these tin automobiles" saw a way to put a stop to them. He would buy these tin automobiles, beef them up with oak timbers all around, and equip them with the Lear steam motor. (Perhaps he could have Mr. Packard up in Massachusetts saw out the timbers at his sawmill.) In passing, he warned about those people in Detroit, saying they had "spent $50 million to beat" Preston Tucker, the last man to come up with something new in automobiles.

Detroit repeatedly received a hiding. J. Howard Barnett of Austin, Texas, let fly with hard words both for the auto makers and all others who were "trying to glut themselves at the expense of the American citizenry's well-being. The oil industry, the pharmaceutical industry, and the appliance industry, to name a few, have demonstrated similar 'to hell with them' attitudes which anyone interested in the perpetuation of the free enterprise system would find not only repugnant but dangerous as well," he wrote hotly. "Since it seems now that you won't be able to get car bodies for your engines, why couldn't you market them as replacements for the Detroit catastrophies . . . ?"

A retired Army engineer in San Gabriel, California, who had "bought a pile of crap called a Buick," included garage owners and "repair men of all kinds" among the villains who would oppose Lear. "I do not say they are crooks," he wrote, "but believe [them to be] controlled from Detroit." He listed "oil stockholders and undertakers" as others who might make trouble. "Yet," he concluded, "I urge you to stay right in there and pitch. We'll back you."

"I'm just a middle-aged housewife with limited education," wrote a woman in Redlands, California, but she would like "a chance to drive one of your cars if you ever use the general public to test-drive them." C. W. Trump of St. Louis had a Mercury which "in its eight months of life has been at the dealer seventeen days." He had several free ideas for Lear which "will keep you from being trodden on. . . ." Biochemist William M. Grogan, Jr., at Purdue University, knowing the hazards of air pollution, "would be delighted to contribute to the project in any way." A man in Hudson, Massachusetts, was so "impressed, so intensely interested" in what Lear was doing that he planned to ask for his pension early and help tell the world about it.

But it was hard to match the spirit of a booster in St. Louis, whose father was a locomotive engineer and who had been building steam engines as a hobby since he was six. "I have been worried because you have spent so much money hiring engineers whose salaries are so high," he wrote, "and spending also for your plant upkeep and materials that cost so much these days. I have nearly 10,000 dollars saved up that my wife does not know about, that I could lend you and your company without any strings attached and no interest rates. . . . Let me know if you need the money."

Many letter writers were anxious to buy the new steam car, often stripping some more hide from Detroit by way of preface. "The Detroit jackals will do nothing until they're forced to," wrote a Hoosier. He owned a Corvair and a Rambler, which he kept "running with the help of several barnyard mechanic friends. I will try to keep these old *internal explosive* klinkers going until your car is on the market."

A Reno man sent what he hoped would be the first purchase order for a Lear steamer. "Note our preference in body styles. . . . We may want to make multiple purchases, possibly converting our entire fleet to steam." An "automobile instructor" in Ohio who did "not believe in the gas piston engine in any form" had promised his wife a steam car and wanted to know when he could deliver on his promise. "If it rides as well as your jet flies," came word from a New Yorker, referring to the Lear Jet, "please put me down for two of them."

J. D. Paddock of Encinitas, California, who made two hundred stops and starts a day on an egg route, looked "forward to the day your product is on the market." A man in Natal, South Africa, awaited "the moment when your product will be marketed in South Africa, and I will be, for sure, one of the first customers." Another South African wanted "to get your first or one of the first few automobiles with a vapordyne engine" for the Connoisseur Taxi Company which he was starting.

"Thank God, America still has a few men with not only the ability but the money and willingness to really pioneer a new field," penciled a man in Santa Ana, California. "I want to be put on your waiting list for new cars." A Coloradan "wouldn't give a damn for the best Cadillac in Colorado, but will sacrifice to own a good steamer."

There was demand for more information. ". . . We have been besieged with letters from our subscribers inquiring as to how much fuel your proposed new automotive steam engines will use," wrote the *Dow Digest* magazine, "the best of the month's stock market reports." They asked to be put on the mailing list.

A Berliner offered to send "some old German publications on steam" in return for further knowledge on the Lear steam development. Krupp International in New York, sounding as if working through an undercover man, had "information which would indicate that you may be involved in the development of a steam engine for automotive propulsion" and asked for a copy of any press release on the subject.

From New South Wales, Australia, the *Automotive News* sent word of "considerable interest in this country" in steam engines and asked to be put on the mailing list for news releases. Fisher and Hornaday in Kenai, Alaska, wanted to know if the steam motor would work in the cold of the Alaska coast. An Irishman in Kilkenny asked, "How long do you have to wait to start?" A Brooklynite sent a self-addressed envelope for further details. "Three cheers for Lear!"

Chemistry teacher Charles A. Edwards of the American River Junior College in Sacramento wanted film on the Lear motor and anything else informative he could have. The topic evidently had proved to be a cure for snoring by his students. "Usually the response from the class in a large lecture hall is not overwhelming," he wrote, "but in this case it was—so much so that the subject took up the entire period. . . ." Accordingly, he planned to devote a good part of the semester to "your steam engine."

Visitors included a deputation from the Toyo Kogyo Company, Ltd., in Hiroshima, Japan. The three had been all over the United States, and they said Lear was the only one they had found who had anything to show them in steam. The matter was of more than academic interest to them, since the good things of the Western world which have come to the Japanese since Perry's time now included smog, and they were eagerly looking forward to telling the Japanese Government about Lear's steam work.

But the interest in Lear's steam power extended well beyond its use in automobiles. "We operate a fleet of approximately 400 Diesel-powered 'off the road' tractors," wrote the Arkansas Fast Freight System, Incorporated. "We have been designated by the Ford Motor Company as one of the first motor carriers to place their turbine engine into practical application. The Lear steam engine sounds much more interesting. . . ."

The Varied Engineering Products Company of Appleton, Wisconsin, described a huge, self-propelled harvester to cost $40,000 which it was building. "We are interested in knowing whether you have any potential interest in a program where your steam engine could be applied to this forage harvester," they wrote. A firm in South Africa asked about "steam engines in the 45 to 120 horsepower range" for similar uses.

Timberland Ellicott, Limited, Ontario, Canada, had in mind steam for winches and other construction equipment. A company in Arcadia, California, inquiring by telegram, wanted a steam motor "to replace the cumbersome electric motor and storage battery system now being used in most golf carts." The Plymouth Locomotive Works, Plymouth, Ohio, was interested in the low pollution aspect of steam for its mine engines.

The Goodyear Aerospace Company was excited about steam for its blimps. "The general information we obtained about your steam propulsion system confirms our opinion that this may be the optimum propulsion system" for airships. Richard George of Downers Grove, Illinois, thought steam was just the ticket for an airplane he was building. "My preference for steam is based on the quietness of operation and on the ease of making a cold start without help," he explained.

Likewise with quiet in mind, Lieutenant Wayne Miller in Vietnam sent word to Lear in care of "Round Table, Holiday Inn" asking "if you have given any consideration to developing a steam package for a helicopter. We do not ask for any trade secrets which we could sell to Ford Motor" but "we implore you to lend us advice on the possibility of the steam-driven rotary wing." He enclosed specifications on the chopper they were using.

Brad Mayfield of the Universal Franchise Exchange, Newport Beach, California, offered to buy ten thousand steam motors a year for five years, to be used in dune buggies. Chief Engineer G. Donald Dyne of Minicar, Incorporated, in Goleta, California, came to see if Lear could build a fifty-horsepower steam motor for a small car which his company was building for the Department of Transportation.

The International Paper Company mused that Lear's steam system "should have good application in the logging and material handling equipment used in the paper and lumber industry." The Clark Equipment Company of Battle Creek, Michigan, sent specifications for its fork truck requirements. With steam, the firm noted, there could be power on the trailing wheels, which is happiness in the fork-lift world.

Could they apply steam to its crawler tractors, asked the J. I. Case Company's Ronald A. Steen, telephoning from Racine, Wisconsin? J. A. Hasten of the Caterpillar Tractor Company came by in person. At this point he was chiefly interested in steam power for small bucket-type loaders which his firm made by the hundreds of thousands. "[We] were very impressed with what we saw and heard," Hasten wrote to Lear when he returned home. "My impression is that your organization is indeed quite dynamic and that you, as an individual, are quite a man of action."

Mack Trucks, building eighteen thousand trucks a year, sent executive vice-president Walter M. May out to see if they might take a hand in developing a steam system for its trucks.

The United States Army was keeping in touch. Colonel Edward B. Kitchens, Jr., director of the Army Combat Development Command, observed during a visit that steam seemed only half as complicated as the internal combustion engine. The FMC Corporation of San José, California, which made a lot of the Army's equipment—combat vehicles, troop carriers, amphibious craft—called at the plant to see about fitting steam to these machines.

The Aerojet General Corporation asked about steam power for Surface Effect Machines—those things that ride on a cushion of air—of one thousand to fifteen thousand horsepower. Dr. Michael Waters of the Institute of Defense Analysis asked about the same thing, scaling the horsepower up to sixty thousand. An Oregon firm sent information on its five-hundred-ton crawler transporter, which is what they use to move moon rockets around, wanting to know if steam could be applied to this.

Captain Don Dragonette of Brooklyn could "hardly write this letter to you since upon reading about your steam engine I've been actually trembling with excitement." He was building a new fishing boat, the *Vixen,* "which will not only be the very finest of her type in the world but will be the largest privately built fiberglass vessel in this country." He had been depressed at the need to use a pair of monstrous Caterpillar engines, weighing nineteen tons between them and gulping one hundred gallons of fuel an hour.

Captain Don was thinking along sound lines. Nowhere does steam make more sense than in boats. With water all around, there is no condenser problem. At least ten boat-building outfits were heard from. Chris-Craft and Larson Industries of Minneapolis each sent a boat to be fitted with steam; the United States Navy offered to supply two boats.

All of which should have a calming effect on a man in Huntington, New York, who was worried that this use of steam power was being overlooked. "With no pun intended," he wrote, "you would be missing the boat if this application is not actively explored."

The bus industry was quick to contact Reno. The Greyhound Corporation sent a telegram. "As builders of inter-city coaches for the domestic market and Canada, we feel we should thoroughly investigate the steam power unit. . . ." Thor Haggloff, president of Hagglunds of Sweden, "the greatest workshop industry in Norrland," asked during a visit to be notified when a steam bus was running.

And the operators of buses: General Manager Alan L. Bingham of the Alameda-Contra Costa Transit District in California referred to a piece in the Los Angeles *Times* which "contained a provocative reference to steam-driven buses" and wrote, "We are prepared to place into scheduled service and test under controlled conditions any bus equipment which may be developed experimentally with or without federal assistance. . . ."

The oil industry, whose products would be needed the same as before, was sending messages and emissaries to Reno, anticipating the change from internal to external combustion. "The practically omniscient (sic) publicity on your venture into the production of steam cars has aroused a great deal of interest here at White and Bagley," wrote company president H. P. Bagley II from Worcester, Massachusetts. ". . . We are interested in your steam engine from two standpoints. First, as businessmen, we would like to be ready with the proper type of lubricant, and second, we'd like to know more simply from the standpoint of laymen."

The American Oil Company's T. O. Wagner came to see for himself, then followed up with an urgent letter asking for "a complete steam system as soon as possible for experimental work on fuel and lubricant requirements. Please place us on your production priority list." Visiting engineers from Shell hoped to persuade their superiors to buy a Lear vapor system to carry on similar researches, and Continental said it would like to join hands with Lear in developing it.

Finally, Detroit, which for a time had treated Lear like a country cousin, barely deigning to speak to him, stopped this. For one thing, if Lear didn't make it now that he had the whole world steamed up about steam and with everybody believing the worst about Detroit to begin with, the industry would never live down the suspicion that it was responsible for his failure. Also, it could just be that what Lear was onto really could set them on their ears. Detroit became good neighbors.

The Chrysler Corporation gave him a brand new Dodge Polara, complete even to the Nevada license plates. American Motors presented an Ambassador. General Motors offered the use of its best men, its techniques, its facilities. "We'll help you," President Ed Cole said. "Whatever we can do, we'll do it."

The last word from those who cared what Lear was doing belonged to Dr. Morly J. Slote of Los Angeles' Kaiser Foundation Hospital. Dr. Slote was "concerned about the day when thousands will fall with severe pulmonary and cardiac reactions." Therefore, "Your work might just become one of the most important items in the history of mankind."

8: THE NEWS IS NOT ALWAYS AS GOOD AS IT COULD BE

The challenges Lear longed for were off to a good start with the problem of rounding up a team to help him. Not many auto engineers knew about steam. Those who did, for the most part, took the view that steam had long since been tried and found impractical. Else Detroit, ever seeking a more perfect engine, would be using it. Right?

Lear had one man who didn't think so and whose mind wasn't wedded to the past. This was Hugh Carson. Where did he find others?

He thought he had a good prospect in Ken Wallis, who called on him one morning in Beverly Hills—not looking for a job but financing for a sailboat. Wallis, with an air of restrained contempt, was the son of William Wallis, the English authority on steam, and had been closely involved in Andy Granatelli's turbine racer project at Indianapolis.

Lear persuaded Wallis to see Hugh Carson in Reno, sending him up on the jet that afternoon.

Wallis went to work for Lear, and his boat, the 72-foot racing sloop *Soliloquy*, ended up belonging to Lear because Wallis had caught him in the midst of his annual boat-buying seizure. "It comes on him like hayfever," Moya said. She explained that this time she had been too late with the antidote, which consisted of patiently explaining to Lear that if they wanted to go someplace on a boat they were better off to charter one. Then when

they got where they were going they could get off and have no
further bother with the boat.

Hugh Carson and Ken Wallis. That made two for the steam team.

Wallis knew a third steam expert. This was Ken Rudolph, with
whom he had worked on the transmission for Carroll Shelby's
Indianapolis racer. Wallis also knew of a stronger recommendation
for Rudolph—that he had worked with old Mr. Steam himself,
Abner Doble, during the years when Doble presided over Bob
McCulloch's steam car project after World War II. Sitting on an
apple crate, Rudolph drove the experimental steamer five thousand
miles around the streets of Los Angeles before McCulloch gave up.
Rudolph was a man to have. Wallis phoned Rudolph in Los
Angeles. "If I can get you an appointment with Lear, would you
come up and talk to him?" Wallis asked.

Would a Tommy care to talk to the Coldstream Guards? Would
a law student be interested in clerking for Mr. Justice Holmes?
But there were also more utilitarian reasons for Rudolph's interest.
He was with a small consulting firm at the time which wasn't doing much consulting. His wife had just asked, pointedly, "How
long are you going to ride that dead horse you're on?"

Rudolph was writing a book on planetary gear ratios, the de-
finitive work in that field, but, while one could not wish his worst
enemy to be without planetary gears for the day, it was not the
sort of book that got banned in Boston, assuring a good sale.

Yes, Rudolph was interested.

On the job within the week, his sandy hair freshly crew-cut,
Rudolph promptly got some matters of nomenclature straightened
out with his colleagues. "I don't think we should say steam system," he said. "We should say vapor system, because we may not
be using water. If you use anything but water, it's not steam. It's
vapor."

The fourth man added to the crew was Dick Moser, a former
Chrysler engineer and another associate of Ken Wallis at Indianapolis.

By now operations had been moved from the Arlington Towers
to the new site at the Stead Air Force Base, ten miles north of
Reno, in Lemmon Valley. There, Carson and Wallis spent the
first weeks investigating what had gone before in steam systems
for automobiles, from that of the famous Stanley on through all
the rest and finding out what was wrong with them. If you're

going to build something better, you first have to know what was wrong with the old.

"All were sadly lacking," Hugh Carson said. "We easily faulted every one."

On the whole, the clock had stopped on steam car development decades ago. None of the old steamers' basic shortcomings, beginning with the Stanley, had ever really been licked; they had only been minimized.

To begin with, steam cars were hard to start. Preparing to get the Stanley going was something like the countdown for a rocket shot. For a half hour the driver was busier than a one-armed tramp picking up dollar bills in a high wind—opening and closing valves, pumping, checking gauges, opening the throttle, closing the throttle, jacking up a wheel, jacking down the wheel, and so on and on, being careful that he did it all in the right sequence.

Once under way, the early Stanley motorist was wise to program himself past a horse trough or stream no more than ten miles out, for by then he would be out of water. The forty miles he was later able to go between boiler fills still made the Stanley steamer less than the ideal vehicle for safaris in the Sahara. As he drove, while he had no clutch to worry about, the power being applied directly to the rear wheels, the motorist kept one eye on the water gauge, knowing that the penalty for inattention could be disaster.

In stopping, it was critically important (everything he did was critically important) not to step on the reverse pedal. There were times when the driver of the Stanley steamer, making this mistake, found himself continuing on down the road while the car went back the other way in a clean separation of man and machine.

Once, in a race, finding the road blocked by spectators, a driver hit the reverse pedal as a brake, as experienced drivers often did. His technique was faulty, however, and he landed amid the crowd still seated in the body of the car while the chassis charged to the rear, breaking through a fence, crossing a field, and finally coming to rest against an oak tree.

Also, the steamer was strictly a warm weather conveyance. As cool weather came on in autumn, the owner drained the boiler, put the car on blocks, and went back to the horse and buggy. You put the steamer away for the winter the same as other things that belonged to the summer.

Still, for all their shortcomings, the old steam cars were capable of astonishing performance, generally outdoing their gasoline counterparts. In 1906, Fred Marriott drove a thirty-horsepower Stanley, the Rocket, 127.6 miles an hour at Ormond Beach, Florida. The next year he is alleged to have got the same machine up to around two hundred before he sailed skyward on a rise and crashed in one of the more comprehensive totaling jobs on record.

Nobody hit two hundred miles an hour officially, with steam or otherwise, until British Major H. O. D. Seagrave did it in 1927, propelled not by a thirty-horsepower steam engine but a pair of mighty twelve-cylinder aircraft engines.

Unlike the gasoline car, which was noisy, smelly, rough running, and wont to break the arm of him who cranked it, the steamer engendered fierce partisanship. Nobody cussed the steam car—except horse drivers who shared the water troughs with it. Of more than four thousand automobiles built in 1900, nearly half were steamers. Besides the Stanley twins, Francis E. and Freelan O., who opened the Stanley Motor Carriage Company in an old bicycle factory at Newton, Massachusetts, in 1899 after they had seen a steam car at the Brockton fair they didn't think much of, there were nearly a hundred others who built steamers. Few machines have got off to such a good start with their creators.

One speculates what the steam story might have been if the Stanley brothers had been a little less conservative. They refused to advertise, holding that if your product was any good it shouldn't be necessary to parade its praises in vulgar public print.

Merchandising was not the Stanleys' strong point. The customer paid everything down in advance, and if he had the crudity to wonder about some sort of written guarantee that he would get his car, the deal was off. Moreover, if the customer showed serious character flaws during the period he was waiting for his machine, such as going into a saloon, he again was out of luck.

The Stanley cars were built by hand—650 a year at the peak— and the brothers disdained to do it any other way. Labor-saving devices? Short cuts? More efficient procedures? Good day, sir!

Pander to the customer—please him with an accessory like a coiled hose conveniently at hand to draw water from the trough? The twins would have none of this until Freelan O.'s wife got after them about it.

More fatefully, what was good enough technologically today was good enough tomorrow, the Stanleys seemed to feel. Instead of going to the quick-starting flash boiler, for example, they stuck with the old fire tube type, so that the long rigmarole of getting started went on as before, never taking less than twenty minutes. They had little time for this problem even after Cadillac came out with the self-starter, removing a major objection to the gasoline car. It was 1914 before the Stanleys added a condenser. This turned the steam back to water—not all of it, but enough that it substantially reduced those stops at the water trough. The presidential limousine in Washington, a White, had a condenser and it could go five times as far as the Stanley without needing more water, even though it was much larger and heavier than the Stanley.

Yet the Stanley brothers added the improvement of the condenser only after a couple of things happened which made it a matter of immediate self-interest. One was that Boston and Chicago threatened to ban the Stanley steamer from the streets because of the clouds of steam they rolled out on damp, cold days, making navigation hazardous to those following. The other prod was an epidemic of hoof and mouth disease. This caused water troughs to be removed, which in turn hit steam-car sales. The condenser, allowing more range, made a lot of the troughs unnecessary.

But the Stanley brothers were not the only steam-car builders who were in no panic to try something new. Carson and Wallis, probing the work of steam-car men in general through the years, found that this could be said of all of them. Making due allowance for the lack of technology, they had made no break-throughs. They had taken no "big bites" out of the problem, words familiar to Lear men. They had only "nibbled at it."

The steam automobile had stalled by the roadside of history. In a world where the only permanence is change, as Heraclitus said, it remained unchanged.

It still took too long to start the car. It still used too much water. Abner Doble's last steamer, said by connoisseurs to have been the finest steamer ever built, started in forty-five seconds from stone cold and would do hundreds of miles on seventeen gallons of water. Forty years later, Calvin and Charles Williams could tell a United States Senate committee, after thirty years' work in their shop at Ambler, Pennsylvania, that their best was a car that would start in less than a minute and go five hundred miles on ten gallons of water, about the same as Doble had done.

Not good enough.

How did one do better? The heart of the problem was that the steam car had too much in common with the teakettle. Despite condensers, too much steam drifted off into the atmosphere. Clearly, as Carson and Wallis well knew, if all the steam could be trapped and sent back to work—if the spout could be turned back into the teakettle—one would have a more efficient car. The water would be locked up and sealed away. Passing from liquid into steam and back to liquid again, which is what distinguishes the Rankine cycle, the same water would be circulated indefinitely, like the Freon in the household refrigerator.

But this was much easier said than done. Before the water can be locked away in a sealed loop, there must be *complete* condensation after each cycle. Any steam left is going to cause mischief at the pump which whips the water back into the boiler for another go-around. Cavitation is the word for it—the same as the slippage that occurs at a boat propeller when it's spun too fast.

Attaining high efficiency calls for very high pressures and temperatures—more than were available to steam auto men in the past, even if they had bothered to try for it with the limited technologies at their disposal. The best they could do was 600 degrees and 750 pounds of pressure. Attaining high pressures and temperatures is how the power generating stations overcame the inherent inefficiency of the Rankine cycle. They went for 1000 degrees or more, and supercritical pressures as high as 4000 pounds per square inch.

But these are the power stations. They stand in one place. In automobiles, jiggling about the streets and roads, crashing into one another, bouncing off assorted impediments, these readings on the steam in their systems could be a hazard in themselves.

"Steam under those pressures could go off like an atom bomb," Hugh Carson said. "Dynamite explodes with a pressure of only 800 to 1400 pounds to the square inch, far less than superheated steam. A pinhole leak in a power station would cut a man in two as he walked past fifteen feet away. Bullets go only 3000 feet a second. Steam goes 4000. This is too damn much power to handle safely in a car."

Along with raising the heat and pressure to improve the efficiency of the Rankine cycle in a car, without going to the levels of the power stations, there was the parallel problem of doing it with less: with fewer and smaller pieces, linked together with less complexity.

For want of modern electronic controls, the old steamers were as packed with equipment under the hood and in the trunk as a Nevada warehouse at California tax time. The old boilers were the size of beer barrels, hogging most of the space under the hood. The condensers, nothing more than the standard car radiator on a larger scale, took up most of what was left. Both boilers and condensers must be greatly reduced while at the same time being made to do far more work—the boiler at least four times more.

This was the mark, then—a steam power plant for an automobile which was smaller, lighter, and simpler than any steam-car engine made before, which was more efficient and powerful than the old and cost no more to build than the internal combustion engine, starting that ingenious device on its way to the Smithsonian Institution.

This was Lear's goal in Reno.

In achieving it, there would be many times when one of Lear's favorite stories would apply. An Indian chief called his people together at the end of the harvest season and told them he had some good news and some bad news. "I'll give you the bad news first," the chief said. "The harvest was poor and we didn't gather enough to see us through the winter. We'll have to piece out with buffalo chips. Now I'll give you the good news. We got plenty of buffalo chips."

And so it went with the steam project. The good news often wasn't as good as it could be.

9: TAKE A BIG BITE—DON'T NIBBLE AT IT

As Carson and Wallis completed their researches on the old steamers, Wallis promoted a small office for the two in a separate building. He put a sign on the door, "Keep the Hell Out," and in the next month or so they worked out a steam cycle that looked good enough to start with, along with an engine design to go with it. Meanwhile, the staff grew, reaching 133 by Christmas.

One of the new hands was James Wimsatt, a young electrical expert from General Electric. He made the change to Lear because, besides liking the frontier country of research and development, the prospects at GE were intolerable. "I would be forty-six before I made vice-president," he said. At that rate he probably wouldn't make chairman of the board at all.

Although his field was electricity, Wimsatt knew something about steam as well. His thesis for his master's degree in mechanical engineering at Penn State had been on heat transfer, the science of getting heat from here to there with as little loss as possible along the way.

Before they took to their drawing boards, Wimsatt and Carson put in weeks at the libraries of half a dozen Western universities, boning up on what had been done in steam. Wimsatt devoted a week alone to the lifetime of notes kept by Abner Doble, at the University of California at Berkeley. They consulted with Cal Tinkham, keeper of the steam cars at the famous Harrah collection of automobiles, who treated them to rides in the old steamers.

Then they divided their work. Carson had ideas on the configuration of the boiler, Wimsatt concentrated on the combustor, better known to laymen as the burner. The art, they had learned, lay in getting the best combustion possible, with the flame homogeneous and well distributed.

Their respective designs done, they brought in metal tubing, nozzles, and other materials they would need, and began to fabricate. In a month they had a "clean-looking burner and boiler that operated." A first big step forward from the past had been accomplished.

At the same time, chief engineer Wallis was progressing with an engine, an involved delta design which looked suspiciously more like a racing engine than an engine for the ordinary automobile. Carson especially viewed Wallis' design with distaste.

"I've worked with piston engines all my life and don't like them," he said. "This one had complexity just for the hell of it."

Besides being intricate, the delta engine called for a fluid which expanded like steam, which was lubricating, and which stood up under extremes of temperature—from 1200 degrees Fahrenheit above zero to 40 below—without in the least changing form. It must be non-toxic, non-flammable, and non-corrosive.

This was not something you could get at Sears Roebuck. As it was put by a new man in the Lear organization, Englishman Peter Scott-Brown, who had worked with Ken Rudolph on the McCulloch steam car and was "head cook and bottle washer" on a steam-car project in England, "The search for a better fluid leads you into some interesting mare's nests."

Scott-Brown mentioned one such mare's nest. This was a well-known refrigerant which, at high temperature, turned into phosgene, the infamous World War I gas. Yet, the Urban Mass Transportation Administration had contracted with a firm in Dallas, Texas, to develop a steam bus using this refrigerant as the "steam" producing agent, committing $309,789 to the project.

"This hardly seems to be the ideal fluid to circulate inside anybody's steam engine," Lear protested in a letter to Secretary of Transportation John Volpe. With Lear, safety was the first criteria.

As the search for a fluid continued, the subject came to be uppermost in the minds of everyone, including members of the Lear household. At the dinner table one evening the talk was about polymerized water, in which four water molecules have been tied together. Lear had just returned from Washington where he had rocked Dr. Glenn Seaborg, Nobel prize winner and chairman of the Atomic Energy Commission, with the news that he was producing "poly water" at his Reno facilities. The federal government's position was that no poly water was being made in the United States.

Poly water stays liquid until the temperature reaches around 50 below zero, and it has four times the density of water, which could make it lubricating.

Could this be the fluid needed for the steam system? It could, Lear replied as he left the table.

"That's the key to the whole situation, isn't it?" observed Moya's mother, seventy-nine-year-old Mrs. Ole Olsen, who had driven up alone from Los Angeles, covering the five hundred miles in ten hours. It was indeed.

By the spring of 1969, the dimensions of what he was setting out to do were in sharper focus for Lear. Accordingly, he had a number of things to pass on when Senator Warren G. Magnuson sent him a copy of the testimony at the 1968 hearings before Magnuson's Commerce Committee on alternatives to the internal combustion engine, inviting Lear's comments.

Lear responded with a 3500-word letter, copies of which he found on the desks of all senators he called on in a later visit to Washington. The report of the 1968 hearings, he wrote critically, gave no hint that the committee understood "the magnitude of the problem and the extent of the research and development necessary to develop a low emission vehicle . . ."

Then he brought the club down. "Your committee is trying to prevent a national calamity due to air pollution on a penny ante basis. The amount of money appropriated for its accomplishment and the way in which the money is being spent is literally akin to trying to perfect the splitting of the atom and the development of the A-bomb for peanuts and distributing the problem to garage type operations on the basis of the low bidder. If the Manhattan Project had been attempted on the same basis, we would still be working on it. . . .

"Developing a steam power plant for automobiles cannot be done on a shoestring, nor can it be done by shade tree steam experts, backyard steam buffs or greedy individuals that would like to get their hands on government money for meaningless studies and worthless devices. A successful low-emission steam vehicle cannot be developed by such operators any more than the Manhattan Project could have been similarly accomplished. . . ."

As to the costs once the steam motor is developed, Lear wrote, "If an engine is going to be designed and built for the automobile, then, obviously, to compete in cost with the internal combustion engine, it must be produced in the same quantities, and at the same rate. . . . In my opinion, the actual conversion of the automobile industry to steam, not including the trucks, buses, motor boats, fixed power plants and airplanes, but just for the automobile, could cost almost $1,000,000,000.

"I cannot attempt to evaluate the necessity for all this. I can, however, feel sure that the net result would be an early reduction in pollution, based on such a massive approach. . . ."

Soon after Lear wrote his letter, the penny ante thinking he complained of was borne out in a proposition which came up in California. The state Assembly Rules Committee had been awarded a munificent $450,000 by the Urban Mass Transportation Administration to develop a steam bus for city use. Other sources kicked in with $160,000 more, including $2000 which the California Air Resources Board was able to scrape up, making $610,000 all told.

But even of this paltry sum, $460,000 was allocated for expenses—$275,000 to a pair of research firms to oversee the project, $25,000 to a film maker to produce a documentary record of the proceedings, and so forth, leaving only $150,000 for the main event.

Lear Motors of Reno was among the half hundred or so vendors whom the committee invited to an open hearing in San Francisco, all but two or three of them backyard operators. On the morning of the meeting, Lear was airborne and setting course for San Francisco at eight-fifteen. With him were Buzz Nanney, sartorially sharp as usual, a little plastic hat like Wheless' perched on his head, marketing director Kenneth Nall, and myself.

At twenty-five-thousand feet over the Sierra Nevada, still white with snow in May, Lear leveled off briefly, then slid down to San Francisco, hidden under a heavy fog. He dropped into the pea soup. The ship shook a bit, like a car on cobblestone, and suddenly there was the runway, dead ahead.

Packing himself into the back seat of a waiting car, Lear squirmed elaborately as he found and fastened the seat belt. "Now begins the unsafe part of the trip," he commented.

On the drive into town Lear told his men of having written a letter the day before to General Motors' president Ed Cole, taking Cole up on his invitation to let Cole know, frankly, what he thought of the big GM press conference and Progress of Power show which Lear had attended in Detroit a few days before.

"I spent all day Sunday on the letter, but the harder I tried the worse it got," Lear said. "Finally I tore the letter up. It would only have caused offense."

Lear didn't think much of the Detroit affair. He called it a "propaganda exercise, designed to discredit steam and protect the internal combustion engine." He found nothing new in the two steam cars GM showed. Their Progress of Power display showed him no progress at all in steam.

At the hearing room in the California state building, an NBC man sidled up to Lear. "I wonder if I may catch you for a few moments on tape?" he asked. As always, it was Lear the press headed for.

Reading the specifications while he waited for the meeting to start, Lear scowled as he flipped the pages. What galled him most was that so little of the money for the project was being spared for the actual development of a steam system, the rest going for costs.

"Most of the money," he muttered, "is going to end up in the pockets of politicians."

In the corridor when the meeting broke for lunch, Lear said, "They're living in another world. We're spending $350,000 a month and they want to spend peanuts against a nine months' deadline. How you do dat?" he asked humorously.

At Kan's Chinese restaurant things soon looked better. "M-m-m, my god, that's good!" Lear murmured as he took aboard the first mouthful. The food primed him for the next session. The morning meeting had been quiet. It would be different after lunch. "I'm going to let them have it," Lear said.

The afternoon session was not long under way when Lear rose and went to the microphone. "I think this brings us to the crux of the situation," he began. "The money you're talking about is ridiculous. A more realistic figure would be $250,000 a month—for ten months. We're spending $350,000 a month—have been for some time—and we still don't have what we're looking for."

Lear gripped the rostrum and looked from one end to the other of the seated line-up on the stage before him, thrusting his jaw forward. "Just where do you expect to find so charitable a vendor," he demanded sarcastically, "who will give you all this for what you're offering? It looks like you're trying to build an atom bomb for a nickel. Then you add insult to injury by requiring the return of the bus to its original condition by the vendor. This is a phony anti-smog effort!"

As Lear returned to his seat, quiet reigned for several moments. Then the man from Aerojet stood up and endorsed Lear's words. "No responsible corporate management could enter into such an open-ended contract," he declared. "Their lawyers wouldn't allow it." Ony by one the others followed suit.

It was a new ball game. Chairman Mike Wenstrom, looking sorrowfully out on the assemblage, seemed stunned. His speech returning, he reversed the approach to the issue. In place of the state saying what it would pay, he proposed that everyone spell out what he would undertake the project for, submitting an estimate of his costs. These figures would be forwarded to Washington, and perhaps some more money would be forthcoming. All agreed this was more like it.

Flying back to Reno, Lear snaked the plane down through Verdi Canyon, roaring low over River House to "alert Moya to put the beans on." Keeping under thickening storm clouds, he worked his way around Peavine Mountain and landed. He taxied the ship into the hangar and turned off the engines just as the first raindrops began.

But the workday was far from over. Lear climbed into his Cadillac and wheeled down to the plant. "Give me a three-sentence report on the auto pilot," he said as he entered the electronics section. Barely waiting for the answer, he moved on to the easel-filled area where design modifications to adapt a bus for steam were going forward. The bus, donated by Flxible, had arrived from Cleveland not long before.

"Everyone in connection with this bus—I want to see you!" Lear said, waving them over to a corner. He told them what they were to do, in line with the San Francisco meeting. "Take all the things that can make heat and put them on top," he instructed. Released on top, the heat would drift off into the atmosphere rather than infiltrate the next car in line.

He gave directions to Bill Moore who, as head of the industrial design department, had the job of figuring out where topside to put the things Lear referred to. Moore must think not only of aesthetics, but must keep engineering considerations in mind as well.

"I want everything insulated within an inch of its life," Lear stressed, adding other requirements. "This is the way it has to be done. We want to make this the finest bus in the world, built so that we never need to do anything over and people will say there goes a Lear bus."

He charged them to be bold. "The only way you can solve a problem is to take a bite out of it—you don't nibble at it."

He told again of his ride in the General Motors steam car.

"It was unbelievably bad," he said. "It was hot, noisy, and smelly."

In the next room Lear found Ken Rudolph who, as design engineer, was in charge of "making practical what artist Bill Moore makes pretty" down in the art department. "How're you coming?" Lear asked.

Rudy told what he could, talking from behind as Lear led the way to the office of Ken Wallis, who was home sick. Sitting astride Wallis' chair, resting his elbows on the back, Lear repeated for his key people what had gone on in San Francisco.

"We have to be outstandingly successful," he said. "I'm not talking about being an also-ran. I'm talking about leading the pack."

Lear told of the emphasis on safety and noiselessness, and of the need to get the heat to flow out on top. "We want it so it won't bother the guy in the Cadillac or the Volkswagen behind," he said. He turned to Carson, "What about the pumps?"

"I've already ordered them," Carson answered.

"Good!" Lear directed Carson to help Ken Nall draw up the proposal agreed to in San Francisco whereby some more money might be made to flow from Washington.

His attention next went to Dick Moser, a gaunt, quiet type. "When are we going to see some performance out of that delta engine?" he asked. "One hundred horsepower out of a nine-hundred-horsepower engine isn't very much power."

Carson spoke up. He had received a letter from the Eastman

Kodak Company offering a lubricating chemical to try out for the fluid. "There's a gold-plated guarantee on it to withstand 750 degrees, minimum," Carson said. "There are eight quarts in existence. We can have one for nothing."

Carson disappeared into his office next door, returning with the letter from Kodak. Lear read it through with quiet concentration. "I'll buy this 100 per cent," he said. "Why haven't we had something like this before?"

Carson reminded Lear of his habitual insistence on perfection. "You never settle for maybe 10 per cent short of it."

"Nothing will bite you as hard as unreliability," Lear countered. He told of once making a direction finder, using the very finest materials available and exercising the most painstaking care in the assembly, hoping thereby to achieve the best instrument of its kind in the world. Instead, to his baffled dismay, it performed erratically. By the time he found the cause of the mystery, he had been badly hurt. The moral was: Materials and workmanship mean little without dependability, which is not necessarily achieved with high cost.

Getting back to the compound from Kodak, Lear went on, "Let's go this direction now. Let everything you've done up to now go down the drain and go this way. Yes, this is the way to go—and do it *now!*"

"Yes, sir!" Carson replied.

Lear ordered that copies of the Kodak letter be made and passed around. "This is all we got?" he asked.

"It's the best this week." Carson answered.

Gunnar Johansen spoke. "Beel," he said, "have you ever considered ultrasonics as a possible solution to the fluid problem? It's available in a terrific spectrum—from 100,000 cycles upward."

Applied to water, the vibrations could keep it from freezing at the bottom of the temperature range needed, Johansen commented, and help it absorb more heat at the top. As a pianist who had recorded the complete works of Bach and Liszt, taking ten years for each, Johansen should know about sound waves.

Lear acknowledged the interpolation and spoke to Dick Kutz. "How're you coming with the boiler?"

"In two weeks we should have a boiler doing what it should be doing," Kutz replied.

"What should it be doing?" Lear asked.

There was a problem of bleeding off the heat, Kutz said,

but he was sure that in two weeks they would have the problem under control.

"If you say in two weeks," Lear pressed, "what did you do today to bring that about?"

"I ordered more tubing."

Carson explained that the new tubing would be seam-welded rather than spot-welded. Seam welding was better and cheaper.

"What can you do on 1000 psi (pounds per square inch) and 750 degrees?" Lear asked, referring to the critical twin factors of pressure and temperature in the boiler.

There were several answers, none in agreement.

"Look, fellows," Lear said impatiently, "let's get together. There are a lot of things we can be doing besides making a steam engine. Tomorrow I want you to come up with some precise figures."

He thanked them and dismissed the meeting. It was seven o'clock.

10: WE'RE NOT THINKING RIGHT

Hugh Carson's jaundiced view of Ken Wallis' delta engine, coupled with the doubts about it held by other Lear men, including Lear himself, set poorly with Wallis. It stimulated him to get on with a scheme he had pursued more or less covertly from the start. This was to get rid of the Lear men and replace them with more of the old Granatelli crowd he had known at Indianapolis —in short, build his own empire.

For that matter, one had the feeling Wallis would as soon be rid of Lear, if it were at all practical. "He's a bully," Wallis said a few moments after we met. He described how he had to go about the shop setting things right again each time Lear passed through. "He's not the least bit interested in clerical or managerial problems—only the drawing board. It's the same bloody thing I went through with Granatelli, a thoroughly unpleasant character."

Wallis complained that while "we're working at a pace which by any other standards would be ridiculous," Lear said it was too slow—"any slower and we'd be moving backwards."

Wallis was soon reminded, though, that empire builders sometimes end up on Elba. "That's a good way to get rid of your useless people," he ventured to reply when Lear spoke of sending Carson on a mission to Japan.

"Mr. Carson is not useless," Lear rejoined coldly. "In fact, your own utility has not yet been proved. Carson has been with me a long time."

But Wallis' subtle mischief began to tell on Lear, who started to behave strangely. He left the plant promptly at five each evening, going home by way of the Holiday bar and crap tables. He seemed to lose all interest in what he was doing. "He was way out of character," Moya said.

He told her he wanted to "go away for a while" and was priming Ken Wallis to "lean over the drawing boards."

"Why don't you lean over the drawing boards?" Moya asked pointedly.

"I don't want to take away their incentive," he muttered.

"Baloney!" Moya exclaimed. "It wasn't that way with the Lear Jet! Nobody lost his incentive."

Moya called Dr. Douglas R. Collier, Lear's physician, in Carson City. "You're destroying yourself," Collier told his patient bluntly. "This is of concern to me, your wife, and your business associates. Stop it!"

This having no effect, Moya took Wallis into her confidence, meeting with him in Lear's office. "Don't leave him out but involve him more," she said. "Ask his opinion. Show you have some respect for his knowledge, even though steam is new to him. Things will go a lot better."

Wallis did, and it worked.

Then came a Saturday morning in May. The delta engine was on the dynamometer being load-tested. Suddenly the hum of a smoothly running machine came to a grinding, crunching stop—like a garbage disposal overcome by bones. Smoke drifted up and there was the smell of burned oil. The engine had "frozen." There had been a lubrication failure.

Carson felt a little sick. That was an awful sound to an engineer. Should he tell Wallis, his boss, or go over his head to Lear? He walked slowly to Lear's office where Wallis and Lear were talking. From the open door, Carson motioned Wallis outside.

"Take off!" Wallis ordered when he heard the news.

Carson hesitated.

"Buzz off!" Wallis repeated. "You're not needed. Get the hell out of here. I'll handle it."

Wallis "handled" it by going bowling, and Lear got the word elsewhere. He thereupon fired not only everybody involved in the affair, but all those on the periphery as well, such as Bea, Carson's wife and secretary.

What happened to the delta engine and the $2 million it

represented upset Lear a great deal less than the disloyalty his people had shown. "He insisted on making a point," he said of Wallis. "All he had to do was say we had tough luck."

But with Lear it's a rare anger that survives the night. Sunday morning, by which time Hugh Carson had indicated in a phone talk with Buzz Nanney that he had no thought of staying fired, Lear phoned Carson. "Can't I fire a man when I want to?" he asked.

"Yes," Carson conceded, "but you can't fire me, Mr. Lear." (Carson always used the formal address to Lear, saying "Mr." or "sir.")

"Why can't I?"

"Because I'll work for you for nothing. I'll be in in the morning at the usual time."

There was a pause at Lear's end. "Make it Wednesday. We'll be reorganizing—give things a chance to settle down.

Carson rejoiced in the thought that he would have two days off—Monday and Tuesday—a rare event in Lear Land. He planned to use the time equipping his car with the new Lear stereo, which he had bought three months before, and drive to Los Angeles to visit his friend Sam Auld. Sam had told him if things ever looked murky in Reno to let him know.

Monday morning Lear phoned Carson's home, catching Carson in the middle of his stereo installation work. Lear talked for a half hour. "Hell," Lear said finally, "we can't stay on the phone all day. Come on in to work."

Carson arrived in time to join in a meeting which consisted mostly of knocking the delta engine and getting things off their chest they had been wanting to say for a long time.

When the meeting ended at six o'clock, Lear and Carson assuaged recent abrasions with a bottle of scotch. Then they drove to Carson's apartment to pick up Bea, tarrying there until eleven, and then going on to the Rice Bowl for a Chinese dinner.

By Wednesday there had been a regrouping of Saturday's survivors, and everyone understood that it was all over with the delta engine. Lear made it clear that "not another nickel will be spent on it. I heard him say so myself," Peter Scott-Brown said with puckish humor. "I think I was three blocks away at the time."

A new steam system "we could live with," in Carson's words, had been decided on, and the movement once again was forward.

As Ken Rudolph put it, "We changed plans and kept going. Normally, when you pick up a man's desk and move it, it's two days before he accomplishes anything. These guys were still working while the desks were being moved."

In the reordering of things, Lear moved into Ken Wallis' office, placing him directly on the firing line, with Hugh Carson, the new chief engineer, next door. Lear's old, much larger office out in front went to Joe Walsh, the new company president. Walsh had been with Lear in Grand Rapids and received much of the credit for a sales increase there from $15 million to $60 million annually in the eight years before Lear sold out to Siegler.

Nobody mourned Wallis' departure. "He was the most frustrating man I ever worked for," Bill Moore said, expressing the general view. "He would never say what he was up to, so we could find out what to do."

But more would be heard from Wallis, who landed on his feet in San Diego, California, involved in another steam enterprise. Promptly at nine o'clock one morning, as if on cue, four members of the vapor dynamics section rose from their desks and gathered around Redford McDougall, the only man still seated. "Goodbye," they said as McDougall looked up in astonishment. "We're leaving, you know. We're going with Ken Wallis."

One by one, they shook McDougall's hand and left.

To British Columbian Red McDougall, holder of a master's degree in chemical engineering and star player on the local ice hockey team, the Reno Aces, Wallis' lure of more money seemed a squalid reason to go. "I don't understand," said McDougall, who wears the wide-eyed look of a man brought erect in his bed by the sound of a gunshot in the night.

"With all this excitement—the chance to be in on something historical . . ." He looked around at the empty chairs. "The only way I'll leave here will be if Lear fires me."

He bent back to his work. Now that he was alone, there was no time to waste.

While Lear had lost $2 million on the delta engine, he was delighted at the way things turned out. "The little revolution over the weekend was a godsend," he said. "It solved so many problems. The worst thing that could have happened would have been to build an engine that was halfway successful."

Now they could speed things up. It was possible they could have something running in days.

One of the problems solved by the delta debacle was that of lubrication, for the new engine selected to work with was the steam turbine, which wouldn't need oil in the steam. Since it had no cylinders to get the steam into and out of, there was no spinning valve needing lubrication, so ordinary water would do. It would be fairly easy to rig a pilot light to keep the water from freezing in cold weather.

The steam turbine had other merits as well over the piston engine. It was far simpler, comprising no more than two or three moving parts, and for that reason much more reliable. And it was smaller; in a turbine the size of a shoebox could be packed three hundred horsepower!

To get started on the new direction, Lear ordered a couple of turbine starter motors for jet aircraft, run by compressed air, flown up from AiResearch in Los Angeles. The wheels from one and the gear box of the other would be mated, giving them something to work with while they designed their own turbine from the ground up. To build such an original, Lear arranged with big Charlie Hill of Ann Arbor, Michigan, a free-thinking turbine man of solid reputation. Charlie had visited the Reno operation, spending a night as Lear's house guest and an afternoon sitting with him in the shade of the old apple tree in the yard.

With a new direction set and lost time to make up, activities were quickened. Peter Scott-Brown, who normally spent Saturdays with his boat at Lake Almanor, was at his drawing board busily making a schematic outline of the new power system. "The key document that holds the system together as an egg holds the entire chicken," he paused to explain, cupping his hands. "Getting the thing boxed in within the confines of a drawing leaves no loose ends lying about."

He turned back to his work. "Let us press on," he said to his assistant, Kelly Moore.

By Tuesday Scott-Brown had progressed to the final form of the schematic outline. It was all there now, each part numbered— the foot pedal, which operated the main control valve of the turbine, which drove the transmission, which drove the wheels —all linked together. The final number would be near two hundred. They were within 95 per cent of that mark now, that close to identifying and placing each mechanical item in the first new steam system of the modern era.

Over doorways throughout the plant appeared black-on-white signs counting down the days until the bus for the California competition was ready—"63 days to bus ride, 62 days to bus ride . . ." This was the idea of Ev Alford, the plant manager. A former Air Force captain, with a couple of aeronautical engineering degrees from Oregon State and the University of Texas, Alford had handled countdowns before, namely on the Minuteman intercontinental ballistics missile. He joined Lear because he thought it would be more exciting. "You've seen one ICBM, you've seen them all," he said.

Ev began the countdown for the bus on the day the decision was made to go ahead with the steam turbine. He fixed August 23 as the target date.

"On that day," he said, chomping his chewing gum, "we will pull the bus around to the front and say, Mr. Lear, put your reporters aboard and go for a bus ride."

A California Highway Patrol car, likewise to be fitted with steam, would follow on September 13, all ready to take after malefactors.

The prospects of triumph at last were tonic to Lear's spirit. At his birthday party in Joe Walsh's office, highlighted by Moya's gift of his 135 patents, *William Lear Versus Inertia,* in two leather-bound volumes, he recalled that he had once estimated the business they would be doing in Reno at $250 million a year. This was a mistake, he said. It was more like $1 billion. He spoke of the new hangar going up, seen from the windows. There would be many more buildings.

"You'll remember this occasion," he concluded, "when you have to go through three secretaries to get in."

At sixty-seven, he was a young Alexander at the Granicus, with the world still before him to conquer.

11: A BUS THAT'S REALLY MODERN

Word came that Lear, on his way home from seeing Charlie Hill at Ann Arbor and another call at Detroit, was forced down at Las Vegas with a dead engine. A Howard Hughes plane was bringing him on to Reno, due at two o'clock. General Wheless hurried to meet him. Converging with Wheless as he arrived at the north end of the airport, where a state police car waited, was Moya in her white Mercedes roadster and Buzz Nanney in his Cadillac.

A twin De Havilland taxied up and out came a smiling Lear, in gray shirt, white suspenders, dark tie and gray trousers, coat slung over his arm. He was followed by Nevada's governor, Paul Laxalt—which would account for the police car. Someone asked Lear if that was a good airplane he arrived in.

"Any airplane is good when you don't have one of your own," Lear answered, passing on.

Getting into Wheless' car, Lear took the wheel. As he slipped along back-street short cuts, he told what happened. The starboard engine went out as he passed over Kingman, Arizona, at forty-five thousand feet, after he had spent the night in Phoenix. All the fuel was on that side, and a stiff cross-wind blew from the left. It was touch and go if he would be able to keep the ship from spiraling down out of control.

"I had the wheel all the way over to the left," Lear said. "If I had needed any more, I wouldn't have had it."

At the plant Lear immediately called a meeting of his key men

in Joe Walsh's office. Ginny provided a pitcher of ice water.
"Anybody who's been to Phoenix always drinks a lot of water,"
someone observed.

"General Motors is devoting full effort to applying our system
to locomotives," Lear began. "They said the Diesel was fine,
but that this is now obsolete."

GM would drive their turbine with gas. "Otherwise, their system
is the same as ours."

Lear instructed that they were to go all out on the new turbo-
electric system. He addressed himself especially to Jim Wimsatt,
who said he was shorthanded. He told of a man "down south" recommended by Sam Auld, who was willing to help with the design
for $20 an hour—$3500 to $4000 all told. "Peevers [Al Peevers, the
personnel man] was on the phone all day yesterday." They had
also run an ad. "This fellow can start Monday. He can do both
thermal and electrical design—both turbine and generator."

"Get him up here for the weekend so we can talk to him," Lear
directed.

The immediate application of the turbo-electric system was to a
new style bus wanted by Santa Clara County, California. The bus
was to be very different from the lumbering, smelly stereotype
now on the streets of the country. It must be clean, spewing no
pollution, lightweight, quiet, and much smaller than present buses.
The Californians would take 325 of them—$20 million worth—pro-
vided the voters said yes to a half cent tax on gasoline on September 15 to pay for the buses.

Lear said he was willing to put a motor on each wheel. "What
would be the penalty for four motors?" They discussed it, Wimsatt
making marks on a big pad of engineering paper. He mentioned
motors of fifty pounds at each of the four wheels.

Lear asked, "Can we put two motors back to back with a flexible
shaft to each wheel?"

"No problem," Wimsatt and Hugh Carson agreed.

Lear sat in heavy-lidded thought, the slits of his eyes barely
showing the blue. "Well, we don't have to decide that one now."

There was talk of speeds and horsepower—what you get for how
much. "Give us 180 horsepower for the bus," Lear said. "I'll take
that."

Receptionist Bernie Eppinger appeared in the doorway. "Mr.
Hill is on the line."

Lear lifted his phone. It was Charlie Hill back in Ann Arbor. "I made it non-stop from Chicago to Phoenix against a hundred-mile head wind and landed in Phoenix with a thousand pounds of fuel left," Lear said, going on to describe his forced landing. They talked about the turbine Hill was designing. Lear gave him his new private telephone number. "Call me collect," he said.

The question of cost came up as the bus discussion resumed. "That's what scares me," Wimsatt said.

"Nothing should scare you," Lear replied with faint humor. "It's like being in the Army. Either you come out alive or you come out dead."

There was some laughter.

White-maned Joe Frost came in. "Mr. Myers is on 111. Your airplane is ready, sir."

This was good news; there was a Washington trip coming up Monday. Lear spoke to Myers, who had gotten the balky engine going again. "You want to fly it up yourself?" Lear hung up the phone and turned back to his audience. "Loose V-nut." He looked puzzled.

Hugh Carson told how a motor at the wheels might be mounted. "Show me on paper," Lear said. Carson made a sketch on his pad. Bill Moore was worried about the weight of the wheel with the weight of the motor added.

"The motor won't be on the wheel but on the frame," Jim Wimsatt reassured him.

The issue came down to whether there should be a motor at each of the four wheels or two motors mounted back to back with axles to the wheels, one in front and one aft. Lear rocked gently in his chair. There was protracted speculation about torques. Ken Rudolph mused that one thousand foot-pounds of torque at the wheels "will burn rubber"—it was all determined by horsepower and diameters.

"Why can't we get these goddamn things laid out so we'll know the answers?" Lear demanded.

Wimsatt mentioned something that wouldn't work. "I don't want to know all the things that *won't* work!" Lear chided. "All I want is *one* that *will* work!"

Lear poured a glass of water from Ginny's pitcher. "It seems to me we could steal a hell of a march on these guys by coming up with a wheel motor. I don't give a damn what it costs to develop the best wheel motor in the world." He paused. "We come up with the lightest weight, strongest bus in the world, but it's got to be beautiful."

Kenny Nall put in, "So people will look at it and say there goes a Lear bus."

There was agreement all around on forty horsepower at each wheel. Lear dismissed Wimsatt to get on with his designing work on the motors. He was to concentrate on this. "Don't worry about anything else," Lear said.

Another phone call came in. It was from Louis Reynolds of Reynolds Metals, in Richmond, Virginia. Lear enthusiastically told him about the plans to build a new bus—"a bus that's really modern"—for Santa Clara County.

"Everybody who has designed a bus up to now has either been in the furniture business or a trucker," he said scornfully.

He described the main features of the bus, adding, "You know, it'll use a couple pounds of Reynolds aluminum. Have your people doodle and I'll have my people doodle. I'll see you on the afternoon of July 9."

Back to the business at hand, Lear pointed at Bill Moore. "Bill, I think you better start doodling. You go." He swung the finger to Wimsatt, who had delayed leaving. "You go." And then it was LeVell Tippetts, who was finishing up the new automatic pilot, which would be so much better than Lear's old one as the old one was better than all the rest. "And your work is cut out for you."

Moore, Wimsatt, and Tippetts left the room to pick up at four-thirty where they had left off to come to the meeting.

There had been trouble with the feed water pump, whose function was critical to the steam system. "They better come up with that water pump or there's going to be an awful lot of hell raised around here," Lear rumbled, rising from his chair.

He headed for the shop, his people falling in behind like the children of Hamelin after the piper. In the fabricating section he stopped to inspect the nearly completed new boiler, essentially a tightly coiled mass of tubes. Near it on the bench lay a heavy metal flange. Lear hefted it, frowning. "We've been working our asses off to save weight and somebody comes up with a thing like this!" he growled. He flung the ring resoundingly back onto the bench and stalked off, muttering obscenities.

At a drawing board in the drafting room on the second floor, Lear asked, "When are we going to see a pump work?"

The situation was briefly described, with some nervousness. "Let's make it up and try it," Lear ordered.

At the Dodge Polara being fitted with steam for the California Highway Patrol, Lear looked long and scowlingly at the mocked-up parts fitted in place under the hood. "It's a no-go," he said. He shook his head. "It's a no-go."

Hugh Carson admitted there were too many captive belts—belts in behind belts. For one thing, under the perverse workings of Murphy's Law (If anything can go wrong, it will), these would be first to go wrong, entailing removal of the others in order to get at them.

Moving on, Lear stopped to study the schematic for the CHP car on a drawing board, saying nothing. The final form of things was yet to come.

Over the weekend, Lear was concerned to see that his airplane was ready for Monday's flying. He had his midweek appointment with Louis Reynolds in Richmond, Virginia, along with others in Washington. He still wondered why the engine had failed, suspecting there was more to it than pilot Myers had found. He was unable to locate Myers. At home, from his favorite seat at the end of the couch nearest the fireplace, he set up a three-way telephone conference among himself, General Electric, and his two keepers of the Lear Jet at the Stead hangar, Kenneth Beers and Norvie Ennis. The mystery of why the engine quit remained.

Hugh Carson phoned. He had heard from pilot Myers, to the effect that Myers intended to keep out of reach and refused to fly the airplane again except eastward to Wichita for an overhaul. (Hearing this from Myers, Carson had wryly remarked to me earlier at his office that there was "historical precedent" for the belief that Myers' tenure as Lear's pilot was coming to a close.)

"That did it!" Wheless remarked, cocking his head reflectively. "Maybe we can help him along."

Lear phoned Clyde Martin at his home in Lewiston, Idaho. Martin agreed to take the job. "Meet me at the Flying Tigers hangar in Los Angeles Monday," Lear said. "You can fly back to Reno with me."

Lear drove out to the hangar at Stead and took personal charge of repairs to the airplane. He found the problem: a loose $1.65 circuit breaker. All it needed was to be pushed back into place.

On to Washington.

12: WE'RE RUNNING OUT OF TIME

The space-age family surrey with the fringe on top was a white Pegasus which traveled far above the clouds, near the speed of sound. Lear, in the captain's seat, was working a crossword puzzle, using his customary fountain pen. Moya was doing needlepoint. Her mother was reading.

Eight miles below, the internal combustion engine was getting huge support in its work of making the upper sky the only safe place to breathe. A band of cadaver brown hung to the south, toward the copper mines at Ely. Near Salt Lake City, four dark plumes were seen simultaneously, the Wasatch Mountains showing dimly through the filth. Just beyond, a flat-topped cloud, miles wide, spread from an enormous trunk, a frozen image of the hydrogen explosion at Bikini. Moments later a second cloud loomed. The universe was ringed with a backdrop of mud-colored poison.

General Wheless, on the jump seat, called for sandwich orders. Hamburgers or cheeseburgers? The order was radioed ahead to Lincoln, Nebraska, to be ready when we landed for fuel.

Lear, his puzzle finished, began writing on a sheet of manuscript-size paper. He handed the completed page to Moya. When she had read it, she passed it to me. "Dear Family," the message began, expressing regret that they couldn't be all together under the apple tree at home so he could tell them in person about his plans and activities.

"Besides the joy of a healthy, happy family, my work has been a blessing to me," Lear wrote. "It's like a game which is played every day, every hour, with exacting rules that change daily with odds that vary from good to impossible and back to good. The hoped-for jackpot is not nearly as exciting as the challenge, the gamble . . . the matching of wits, the trials, the errors and the runs brought in. . . .

"Jack Entratter says you can't win money if you keep it in your pockets. . . . So mine is on the table, but the difference between craps and the game I play is that in my game I can change the odds by the English I put on the dice—i.e., effort, intelligence and common sense. I . . . adjust according to my inputs and calculations. . . . So I start out to make a steam power plant but it might end up something else—especially if I find steam isn't the way to go. I never care what the other guy does or thinks of what I do. . . .

"Right now I see something which might make it worth-while to develop a different kind of power plant. . . . I wish I could detail the reasons here but it is premature to write them down. However, within a month I'll be sure and within a year I think you'll witness another major accomplishment by your old dad. . . .

"Mom will try to explain it but you won't get it because she doesn't know all about it yet. She just knows her man is thinking. . . . All my love, Dad."

If heat and humidity make the corn grow, then it should be making good time as Lear brought the ship down at Lincoln, two and a half hours and 1400 miles from Reno. The sandwiches were waiting in the lounge. The gas tanks were filled, and in thirty minutes we were on our way again. A southern California-style yellow stain blotted out the earth to the north. East of the Mississippi, smudges of pollution drifted near the ground like mustard gas.

Indiana vanished under a weather cover that resembled a field of tumbled pack ice piled up by the wind. Thunderheads in hourglass and anvil shapes towered from below. Only one intruded into the sunlit solitude where the Lear Jet flew. As Lear napped, head back on his pillow, Clyde Martin steered around it.

Lear awakened and took the wheel as we approached Washington's Dulles airport in weather that nearly hid the wing tips. "These are times when I'm glad I'm with a pro," Moya said, looking out the window.

We left Moya and her mother in TWA's VIP lounge to await

their plane to Europe. We loaded three hundred gallons of fuel into the wing tanks and took off through the fog for Richmond, Virginia. Besides the weather to obscure the way, a pair of giant stacks were rolling out pollution like the Navy laying down a smoke screen for the Battle of Midway.

It was only a ten-minute hop to Richmond, one hundred miles away, and Lear flew by visual flight rules, keeping sight of the ground. Forty miles out, he heard from the Richmond tower, "You're now cleared to go to fifteen thousand feet."

"I don't want to go to fifteen thousand feet. I'm ready to land."

"Well, you'll have to go to nine thousand," the tower insisted.

Lear jammed the throttle forward and shot up to nine thousand feet, as prescribed. "Okay, you're cleared to land," the tower said.

It had been the same up-and-down procedure coming in to Dulles, evoking maledictions from Lear on his favorite bureaucracy, the FAA. "The procedures were probably thought up by the Pentagon," Wheless offered as the flight ended, having taken a half hour instead of ten minutes.

We were met by a chauffeur in a Cadillac version of the stretched Douglas DC-8 and driven to the white-colonnaded antebellum home of Louis Reynolds, head of Reynolds Metals. Reynolds was a Pickwickian cherub with forward-brushed sideburns, who sat in his high-backed chair with his right leg doubled under his body as he sipped a before-dinner mint julep with his guests. He was talkative, knowledgeable, and intelligent. The conversation was topical, business talk awaiting the new day.

At the motel next morning, Lear was in the dining room for breakfast at seven-thirty, an hour early. He had been driven from his bed by a bad dream. "I thought to myself, 'To hell with this' and got up," he said. His face was ruddy, his blue eyes clear. He looked even healthier than smokers of those cigarettes you can't take the country out of.

At the Reynolds plant two hours later, Lear got down to business. The audience of a dozen or so, gathered around a great oval table, listened closely as he described the new pollution-free bus he and his people were planning for Santa Clara County in California. Driven by a turbine-electric system, with a motor at each wheel, the bus would be low to the ground and little more than half the weight and size of the standard bus. It would carry only thirty passengers, but would make up the difference in capacity with more of them on the street, the theory being that a small bus every few minutes was better than a big bus every hour.

Mr. Pickwick arrived, walking briskly. He took a seat near Lear and listened thoughtfully, chewing a pencil, as Lear described the advantages of a motor at each wheel. "You haven't really enjoyed driving an automobile until you've driven a four-wheel drive like this," he said enthusiastically. He condemned the present four-wheel drive vehicle with its multiple differentials as a monstrosity.

Lear spread a number of drawings on the table. They discussed the feasibility of using aluminum for the radiator—that is, the condenser. Reynolds did not make the size radiator needed, but they were quite able to do so, Lear was assured. A pair of radiators were brought in and put on the table.

Would Lear be willing to consider some radical new idea, like spreading the radiator out over the top of the bus, where there was plenty of room? he was asked. Lear grinned. "I like radical new ideas," he reminded them.

At twelve-forty the meeting ended and all adjourned to a private dining room for lunch of filet mignon, seated at a single large round table. The talk, led by Lear, was relaxed and discursive. He drew a good laugh when he told of the time he signed himself in at Lockheed Aircraft as being from the USSR, the topic at the moment having to do with security folderol. He was inside the plant two hours before the alarm was sounded. "Oh, no!" groaned his escort, taking the call from the front desk. "Oh, no!"

Lear told about the time he and Moya impulsively flew to Moscow during a tour of Europe in the family Cessna 310, causing an enormous flap back home, with Lear employes in Santa Monica threatening to quit because they didn't want to work for a firm which dealt with the Russians, thanks largely to the enterprise of a Baltimore *Sun* reporter. "Aren't you concerned over what he's done?" the reporter badgered General Nathan F. Twining, Air Force chief of staff.

"Not particularly," Twining replied.

"Doesn't he have a lot of secret stuff on his plane?"

"Nah," said Twining indifferently. To mollify the persistent front-page type, Twining turned to Colonel Pete Everest and said, "Find out what he's got."

On the television news next evening, back where the press was free, the announcer intoned, "And now to Moscow and the Lear-

18)   Telephone conference call with consulting engineers Barber-Nichols, vapor turbine designers, in Denver. Clockwise from Lear: Byron Hanchett, Dick Kudlicki, Ev Alford, Hugh Carson, Max Winkler.

19)   Lear stresses a point with Pete Lewis (left) and Ken Rudolph. Bill Moore listens in doorway.

20)   Old Wichita hand Ed Lenheim has a word with the boss in Reno. Ed's job was to see that components for the Lear Jet were better than anything on anybody's shelf, which meant custom building and testing of more than eighty parts for the plane.

21) Getting ready to run another test on the boiler, or in the Space Age, "vapor generator." This one is a fraction the size of the old Stanley boiler and far more powerful. Lee Blodgett talks from the control booth to Red McDougall inside.

22) The first automobile to be fitted with a steam power system of the new era, a Chevrolet Monte Carlo donated to the cause at the personal direction of President Edward Cole of General Motors. With Buzz Nanney looking over his shoulder, Lear shows installation progress to W. A. (Red) Martin (far left) and Dr. John B. Saunders of the University of California (far right).

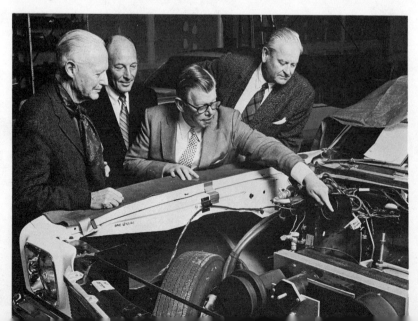

23) Red McDougall and Pete Lewis look over the racer which may one day take on Indianapolis.

24) Tina, youngest of the Lears' four children, is a concert performer at fifteen. She is a pupil of Professor Gunnar Johansen, artist in residence at the University of Wisconsin.

25) Lear travels some 200,000 miles a year, most of them at the controls of his own jet. This leaves little time for woolgathering at transfer points. Here he had the use of a helicopter provided by County Supervisor Warren Dorn in getting from the airport to the Occidental Tower in downtown Los Angeles for a press conference.

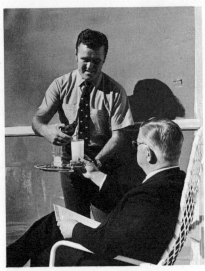

26) Gunnar Christensen, a machinist by trade in his native Denmark, is a man-of-all-roles for the Lear family: cook, bartender, grounds keeper, herdsman, orchardist, Lear Jet co-pilot. He lives upstairs in River House with his blond Swedish-born wife, Elsie, and little John, five.

27) Lear goes over details of lightweight bus with designer Bob Davids, honor graduate of Los Angeles Art Center School of Design, who joined Lear from General Motors.

28) "A mock-up is much better than just having pictures," Davids told Lear. Helping him build it are two students from his alma mater, Paul Morris and Leif Chapman.

29) The completed mock-up of tomorrow's bus—with windows three feet square, a one-foot step, and seats for eighteen, riding in limousine comfort, with no sound from the turbine engine but a low hiss.

30) West Pointer Joe Frost and Jim Sweger (at desk) at work on "Leareno," a balanced community of 20,000, "designed for the enjoyment and employment of people," covering 2500 acres of Lear's Lemmon Valley holdings. Made up of independent clusters, each with its own shops and recreation areas, the layout reflects the advanced thinking of such planners as William Pereira and Victor Gruen.

31) First "breadboard" for new automatic pilot—one that does more things, does them better, and is far smaller—about the size of a small loaf of bread—than the one that won him the Collier Trophy. Lear checks progress with LeVell Tippetts, "the best circuitry man in the world." *(Photo by Michael Bry)*

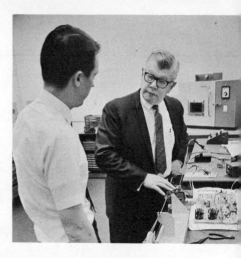

32) "Now, here's what we're going to do . . ." The model of the turbine, hopefully opening the way to a new era in automotive power, lies in its wig box in the foreground. The pump, without which none of the rest would have mattered and no near equivalent of which was to be found anywhere in the world, rests on Lear's desk in front of Max Winkler, its chief designer. Lyn Davis listens at the left and Buzz Nanney stands pensively at the window.

33) Buzz Nanney, just back from Europe, hears from Lear what's been going on while he was away. The wheel, Lear explains, is the heart of the system. Spinning at 45,000 rpm under the impulse of the vapor jets striking the vanes, the wheel will deliver the power to drive an automobile—or a bus, a truck, a tractor, anything now driven by the internal combustion engine.

34) Lear Jet owners and others bring their planes to Lear's new hangar for servicing. Two aircraft here, by their contrasting lines, sharply limn the progress of forty years—the Ford Trimotor, airways pioneer of the 1920s, on the left, and the Lear Jet on the right. Completed in 1969, the hangar is large enough to accommodate a DC-9.

35) The Internal Revenue Service wins the argument—and Lear, knowing something of what will make the newspapers, turns the occasion to account by writing the check on the turbine wheel.

36) General Motors President Edward Cole came to see for himself, bringing along Paul F. Chenea, his research chief. Cole pledged to give Lear whatever he needed, stationing a GM liaison man in Reno.

37)   A breather on the sun porch at River House. Well, not too much of a breather—there's a telephone. . . .

38)   Here comes steam! Two years and $8 million later, Lear makes the announcement everyone has been waiting for: He has a steam propulsion system for the Age of Space.

Twining incident," making it out that there had been a big scene between the two men and that Twining had ordered an "investigation" of the Lear flight by Colonel Everest.

As Lear told it, he flew down the corridor into Berlin, becoming the first private flyer to do so.

The colonel in charge of international traffic, an old friend, was impressed. "Bill, I'm supposed to dress you down for not following procedures," he said.

"What are the procedures?"

"There aren't any. I'm supposed to draw up some."

Having come this far, Lear decided to try for Moscow but the Russian Consulate official in East Berlin smilingly said this might take a while to arrange. How much time did Lear have?

"Oh, I could wait till tomorrow afternoon," Lear replied solemnly.

The Russian laughed outright. "We can't do anything but try," he said gamely. "Could you come back tomorrow at two o'clock?"

He could, and did, and the visas were waiting.

A U. S. Government agency had asked Lear to get some information about the radio equipment aboard the Tupolov-104 if he was ever in Russia. But Lear had refused. As it happened, Lear found out the things the agency was curious about anyway—though by means which were quite prosaic. His Russian hosts eagerly showed him all he asked to see, including the Tupolov-104. When he indicated a special interest in the antenna, pleased and flattered that he was interested, they took him aboard and proudly showed him the rest of it—a highly advanced piece of equipment on which they had done a fine job of design. A girl photographer for *Life* who tagged along took all the pictures she wanted without hindrance. As cloak-and-dagger stuff, it was a bust.

The Russians wanted to show their American visitor more—factories, laboratories, anything he named, but the Baltimore *Sun* reporter took care of that. So Lear missed what could have been a rare, informative tour by a visiting Yank.

General Wheless looked at his watch. "Boss, you got a couple of appointments in Washington," he reminded Lear.

As the table broke up, Lear got in another swipe at the FAA. "They'll probably route us by way of Chicago," he muttered.

At the Reynolds hangar, Clyde Martin came running from the hangar, where he had been keeping out of the drizzle. In seven minutes we were off, skirting a storm. Lear first kept under the weather, then zoomed above it. He approached the Dulles runway at right angles. Nearly over it, he flipped the ship into a vertical bank and dived, as if peeling out of formation to attack—a symbolic diving attack on Washington.

Old airman Wheless smiled. "That's what's known as a 360-overhead," he said, eyes alight. "It's a carrier approach."

Lear's mission in Washington kept him on familiar ground: He was fighting inertia. He wanted to get the Grand Bureaucracy off the dime and make it do something about air pollution from automobiles. He was the irresistible force from Reno colliding with the immovable object on the Potomac.

The very air of the place seemed to get his hackles up. He reminded one of a dog sensing an enemy as he cursed under his breath at the slow-moving routine of checking into the Washington Hilton.

The first caller at the three-room suite was S. Lynn Sutcliffe, counsel to Senator Warren G. Magnuson's Committee on Commerce. Sutcliffe was a young man of serious mien with sideburns and red hair, who seemed deeply reflective as Lear talked.

Lear pointed out that the automobile industry was not fighting him but, on the contrary, co-operating with him. He told of having driven all five generations of Chrysler's gas turbine cars, and said the performance of the latest was all one could ask. The gas turbine had advantages over the steam turbine. It needed no boiler, no condenser, no blowers, saving space and complexity. It did use a lot of fuel in traffic, since it idled at half speed, but this drawback could probably be overcome.

The industry admitted, Lear went on, that it could build the gas turbine car for the same money as the car with the internal combustion engine—once they retooled. That was the sticking point. It would cost $5 billion to get new tooling set up. Then it would take another $300 million to turn out enough gas turbine cars to get the price per car down to a competitive level with the price of the IC car. All this would set poorly with the stockholders. If the government forced the companies to take action, then they would have an out with the stockholders who would object.

Congressman John Tunney of California and Senator Howard Cannon of Nevada phoned the room, saying they were sorry they couldn't come. Lear talked to each at length. He told Cannon he had spent $4 million of his own money to develop a clean automobile engine. "If you want us to go ahead with steam," he said, "we'll give it a yeoman's try."

Congressman Tom Foley of Washington arrived. He took a seat and bartender Wheless poured him a drink. Like Sutcliffe, Foley gave an impression of sincere concern, listening intently to the man from Reno. He was a big meaty man with black, straight hair and heavy features.

Wheless said there should be no more money appropriated for research but only to *produce*. No product, no pay. The time for study was past. Foley took him up. "Why should the government put out money for studies when we have the technical problems solved?" he asked rhetorically.

Sutcliffe suggested that the General Services Administration, which operated thirty thousand vehicles, offered a way to start. To get things off dead center, it could be stipulated that a certain amount of money from GSA's next appropriation be set aside for either a gas or a steam turbine car. The first thing was to have a meeting and decide which it was to be. Lear would bring his experts, Detroit theirs.

Sutcliffe pursued the point at dinner downstairs. He said he had prepared legislation to procure pollution-free cars for the government, which bought sixty thousand cars a year. It could be specified that half of one year's purchases be pollution free, the next year all of them. A rider could be attached to an appropriation bill for cars for the Navy, for example, saying the cars they bought with this money must be emission free. The attraction of this procedure, Sutcliffe pointed out, was that the money would come from regular appropriation funds; nothing additional would be needed. And it should be salutary that the government was taking this step, ordering cars that were clean.

The conversation was impeded by the dining room piano. Lear called the waiter. "Ask them to cut the volume down or I'll cut the goddamn wire!" he said.

The waiter mumbled that there was nothing he could do, and the piano went on.

For Lear the situation recalled the time he had dealt with a similar problem more productively when the offender was a juke box. He simply severed the wire to the machine, using a pair of insulated pliers from his pocket kit.

He handled the problem in similar fashion on three subsequent occasions at the same place, a Chinese restaurant in Santa Monica.

The fourth time, as he approached the machine, the proprietor intercepted him, pleading, "Please, no cut! I have switch now!"

Lear's habit of carrying pocket tools, he reminisced, went back to his boyhood. He started his business life as a sort of wandering Mr. Fixit in short pants, outfitted with hacksaw, pliers, file, screwdriver, and a hunk of battery carbon, looking for stalled motorists with distributor trouble. Usually the problem was that the brush had worn out. For $2 Lear would saw a new one from his battery carbon, install it, and send the man on his way.

For a while the rescued motorist was prone to forget about the $2, saying thanks and driving off—until Lear learned to take back the new part. He had it on his side that the driver was anxious to avoid the taunt "Get a horse!"

From this early service to the cause of the engine which he now sought to retire, these fifty-plus years later, young Lear moved up a rung in the world of entrepreneurship. He went into the business of renovating batteries, making new ones out of old ones. This enterprise left a lasting taste in his mouth of the sulphuric acid in the sandwich he carried in his pocket for lunch. But the returns were good. "A rebuilt battery was worth $35, a lot of money then," he said.

After dinner, I found the lobby drugstore closed—too late to buy sleeping pills. "I got loads of sleeping pills," Lear said.

I had heard about the miniature apothecary he packed in his luggage. Contained in a black box, besides sleeping pills the stocks included pep pills, vitamin pills, assorted pain killers, and whatnot. "You never know if he's giving you cyanide or what," Hank Beaird had said.

Upstairs, Lear extended his palm with two tablets, one round, the other oblong. "Take both," he said in sepulchral tones.

Feeling a fleeting kinship with Socrates, I did as told. Next morning the matutinal chores were reduced by the need to comb. Every hair was in place. Lear's pills worked like his airplane.

The first caller of the day was Dr. Fred Singer, deputy assistant secretary of the Department of the Interior, house guest of Lear's in Reno some weeks before. Lear told him about the bus which he hoped to build for Santa Clara County in California.

Bob Norton of Congressman Tunney's office came in, followed by Senator Howard H. Baker, Jr., of Tennessee. Lear told both men about the work in Reno. "We don't want just a dime-store invention that only won't make smog," he emphasized. "It has to be something that can challenge the internal combustion engine on a competitive economic basis."

Lear criticized the government's approach to the problem of air pollution. It isn't taking any "big bites. It's only nibbling." There were 90 million automobiles on the road. There would be 180 million in ten years. Soon the situation would be irreversible. He said the present anti-smog devices being forced on the public have many flaws. They cut power by over 25 per cent. They add weight. They can't handle leaded gasoline. They are hard to maintain and don't last long. On top of all this, while they reduce hydrocarbon emissions, they increase the production of nitric oxides. He accused the auto companies of doing too little too late. His voice rose slightly. "What's the good of controlling one problem if you amplify another?"

Referring to the lead in the atmosphere, put there by automobiles burning leaded gasoline, Lear declared, "The public health department has been bamboozled into saying that 99 per cent of the lead passes through the body," he said. "What they don't mention is that about 40 per cent of lead taken into the lungs passes into the blood stream. England has banned the use of lead in gasoline. Why don't we?"

"The long-term answer to air pollution by automobiles, of course, lay in a new kind of engine," Lear went on. "We have spent $4 million, not one dime of it from the government, which has kept throwing money down a rat hole for studies. It's like studies on how to make a ham sandwich."

Lear urged that there be new hearings like those before the Senate Commerce and Public Works committees in the spring of 1968. At the new hearings all the alternatives should be explored. Then, some outsider should be given a contract to go ahead with development of the engine that had the best promise.

"Quit the studies," Norton agreed, nodding.

"No more studies are needed!" Lear exclaimed. "Come out to our lab in Reno and we'll measure the emissions for you! You don't need a car to do that. We're running out of time."

For the meeting in the afternoon with Secretary of Transportation John Volpe, at his office, Volpe sent word that he wanted no reporters present. Wheless filled me in on the meeting afterward. Volpe was on the defensive because of Lear's letter to him in March indicating displeasure with his department for letting a Dallas corporation "get their paws into the pork barrel" for

$309,789 to build a "steam" bus using the lethal refrigerant as the vapor fluid.

Lear repeated for Volpe the things he had been saying for two days—namely, that the federal government must get off its bottom and do something about air pollution. The response was a reminder of inertia's place as a controlling force on the Potomac. "The law says the solution has to be economically feasible," one of the Volpe men replied.

Volpe asked what it would cost Detroit to retool. He cautioned that this expense must be borne by the customers. The auto makers, he said, could not be forced into an action which would cause them to lose money.

In the contest between the dollar and public health, the dollar came first.

There was yet some of the day left as Wheless finished his account of the Volpe meeting. Lear, with nothing more to do, paced the floor. He looked at his watch. "We could start back," he said tentatively, pursuing it no further as Wheless demurred.

At the airport next morning, one of the Reynolds men going with us west was late. The poor devil knew not what disaster he courted. The Lear jet was buttoned up and moving when he appeared at the door from the building in the distance, semaphoring frantically. Lear passengers left behind would ever hear his story with skepticism as he told how the plane stopped for him.

In the sun-washed world of eight miles up, with thunderheads knotting the sky below, Lear read my *Newsweek*. He handed the magazine back, asking me to read a piece about anti-pollution devices on automobiles. "Then pass it to the general," he said. He put his head back in the pillow he had bought in Washington, and went to sleep.

The *Newsweek* article told about spark plugs wearing out prematurely in cars with exhaust control devices. The engines idled poorly. Performance was off. Thousands of drivers were taking the gimmicks out.

At ten-thirty, just over two hours out of Washington, we landed in Wichita. Lear refueled at the plant he founded and was off to Reno, leaving me behind in Carry Nation country.

He would make many more trips to Washington.

13: THE POSSIBILITIES OF SUCCESS ARE OVERWHELMING

The steam turbine, which had looked so promising at first, had begun to develop problems. Daily it became more expensive and complicated, growing from a single turbine wheel to five in series.

Ideally, because of steam's low density, it should turn at 100,000 rpm. But at that speed the turbine sets up an ear-piercing screech. A blade tip flying off packs the wallop of a large naval shell. This is a lot of fire power for everybody to be carrying around under the hood of his car.

Reduction gearing was noisy, expensive, and unreliable. "It would sound like a helicopter taking off," Hugh Carson said. "Just to get things to hang together is extremely difficult. When they push against each other, it's worse."

The gas turbine came in for consideration. Lear, just back from Detroit, had driven Chrysler's fifth generation gas turbine car and was impressed. Hugh Carson, though, was suspicious of the mileage claimed for it. It is the nature of the gas turbine that it idles like the wings of a humming bird, racing on at a half speed of 35,000 rpm. "You would get about four miles to the gallon at low speeds," Carson estimated.

Also, the gas turbine operates at 1500 degrees Fahrenheit. "Cherry red begins at 1200," Carson said significantly.

Materials that stand up under such extremes of heat are scarce and costly. There is constant fire danger. Stainless steel burns. Nickel survives, but nickel costs so much there is hardly any in nickels any more, and it would take five pounds for each turbine.

No, the answer still seemed to lie in the steam turbine, but using a different kind of fluid from water—something that was denser than water. Then the turbine could be slowed down, for the vapor driving the turbine, being denser, would impinge on the blades with more force. The reduced speed made the turbine compatible with ordinary gear boxes.

Back on the front burner went the search for the new fluid, to be known as Learium. Lear and Carson began the search by first designing a reasonable turbine, then finding a fluid that fitted it, matching the turbine's speed, instead of going at it the other way around. The criteria called for getting the answers to more than a hundred questions, some involving long, complex equations. With the help of the computer in Palo Alto, California, Carson finally got the standard pinned down.

Then for six 12-hour days he drove himself to find the mix that fitted the standard. Lear dropped by every hour for a briefing and to offer advice and encouragement. Together they studied probably a thousand existing compounds, two hundred from DuPont alone.

On the sixth day the riddle began to break. Two days later, "All the answers came up right," Carson said. In three more days, a whole family of compounds came within the range formulated.

Lear was doubtful. "Hugh, we've been at this too long," he said. "Something is wrong."

"I think so too," Carson agreed, "but I can't find it."

Carson checked his figures again. It was true—they had Learium!

All the components had been used before, but never in combination. As with a good salad dressing, it was the blend that counted.

The ideal of a closed vapor system, with the fluid sealed away like the coolant in a refrigerator and good for fifteen or twenty years, a car which used 30 per cent less fuel and went one hundred thousand miles before needing a wrench put to it—all this was no longer visionary.

With Learium at last in hand, the many subsidiary problems fell away or were diminished. The condenser, four times as big as the usual car radiator, came down to half that size. The boiler became smaller. In short, with Learium things could either be eliminated from the system altogether or made smaller, simpler, more reliable, and less expensive. It was a great leap forward. It was the big bite Lear likes to take.

"It means there's going to be a new world around here," Carson said. "The possibility of success is overwhelming."

14: CAN WE GET THROUGH THAT STONE WALL?

As the engineers made themselves better acquainted with the family of organic compounds Lear and Carson had uncovered, the automobile industry staged an exercise for President Nixon and his cabinet at the summer White House in San Clemente, California, from which it appeared that Lear's efforts in Reno didn't really matter.

Detroit was on top of the dirty exhaust problem and in just a few more years the skies would be back to the salubrity of 1940. There was no cause for alarm, no need to develop a new kind of engine—these words being spoken as the air poison at nearby Los Angeles reached the first stage alert level three days running for the first time in the twenty-three-year history of the county's Air Pollution Control District.

Lear was not invited to the San Clemente meeting or to the further program which followed at the Newporter Inn at Newport Beach. This was because he had no "hardware," it was explained. He sent a telegram to the President, saying that while there might be some value in looking at hardware when it represented the past—in some cases even the horrible examples of the past—rather than anything new, he felt that hardware did more harm than good.

This brought him a pass, but with no part in the program. Officially, on Olympus, there was no interest in hearing what Lear had learned about steam. It was strictly a Detroit show. In a letter to Nixon afterward, Lear let him know that he considered the whole performance a snow job, pulled off in line with the auto industry's habit of spending more to improve its image than its product.

The participants—Chrysler, Ford, and General Motors—mounted elaborate charts with curves to show that by 1975 the pollution from cars would be ended and the air clean and shining bright once again. Already you could almost smell the orange blossoms in southern California.

These happy prospects depended chiefly on a labyrinthine tangle of exhaust-consuming gadgetry which made the bottoms of the cars, shown with the help of mirrors, resemble an oil refinery, as Lear described it in his letter to Nixon. Up to now no exhaust control system, introduced in California in 1966 and nationwide in 1968, had worked. All began to fail at about four thousand miles and then went down fast. Man had opened up the moon to rock-hounds, but there seemed no way to keep a tailpipe from smoking.

As for General Motors' two steam cars, these vehicles made it difficult to put down the suspicion that they had been built as horrible examples, to demonstrate the hopelessness of steam. One sounded like Jack Benny's old Maxwell. Smoking copiously, it presently gave off an explosion which levitated the dignitaries a foot off the floor and sent them scattering in alarm.

From under the other steamer, built for GM by William Besler of Oakland, California, for its "Progress of Power" at Detroit some months before, rolled enough steam for a Turkish bath showing that you wouldn't get far in that one without stopping for water, just as with the old Stanley long ago.

Besler, who had been Abner Doble's chief engineer, spent much time knocking steam to Lear, trying hard to convince him there was no future in it for automobiles. "I don't believe it," he said. "I never have believed in it."

Didn't believe in steam? It was an interesting admission, coming from the man who had been selected to build one of the steam car examples. Was this the reason he was chosen?

Dr. Lee DuBridge, Nixon's science adviser, pridefully told the gathering how the government had already spent $2 million or $3 million in the search for a clean engine (Vietnam was costing that much with each passing hour), and in the next couple of years planned to double this amount. That would put the nation with a gross national product near the one trillion mark only slightly ahead of what private citizen Lear alone had spent to alleviate a calamity which in one scientist's opinion had brought emphysema to every big city dweller in the country over twelve years old. That was how the toll read on the lung-destroying disease from which there is no recovery, by the estimate of Dr. Russell P. Sherwin, professor of pathology at the University of Southern California School of Medicine.

Whatever automobiles might be contributing to the catastrophe, DuBridge had previously told a San Francisco audience that the auto builders ought not be put to any inconvenience about it. "The responsibility for air pollution from auto exhaust rests on drivers, not on car manufacturers," he said. "[They] just couldn't pay dividends if profits went too low."

In brief, at Newport Beach the auto industry gave the government a booster shot of the propaganda heard for years; that all was well and getting better still, keeping the government from waking up to the scope of the problem and doing what Lear was convinced it must do. This was either to underwrite the development of a clean engine or force Detroit by law to do it. We are spending billions to explore space. It ought to be worth a little of that to clean up the small space close to home, no higher than fifty thousand feet, which most men will never leave, Lear wrote to the White House.

A week or so after the Newport Beach affair, Bill Besler invited Lear to visit his plant in Oakland, Abner Doble's old place, to see for himself why steam was no use.

"I wanted to save you $20 million," Besler said.

Lear flew up on Labor Day, taking Hugh Carson and Gunnar Johansen along. With a couple of model airplane propellers rigged to help the condenser change the steam back into water, Besler's steam engine could only be a parody, it seemed.

"It was hard to see how the man could be in the steam business so long and learn so little," Hugh Carson summed up.

Flagging spirits picked up on the flight home as Lear buzzed his house at two hundred feet. Arriving at the hangar, he phoned home, getting Tina on the line. "Did you see us?" her father asked.

"Daddy, everybody in Verdi saw you," Tina replied delightedly.

The buoyant mood induced by discovery of the new fluid suddenly collapsed as California turned thumbs down on its use in the bus as too dangerous. Only water steam would do. In this crisis, Lear called a meeting of his key engineers to review what they had accomplished and decide whether to keep going with steam or switch course to the gas turbine.

"The pollution problem is very serious," Lear said, "and I feel our basic dedication is toward its solution. We are of course interested in making a buck, but not without, at the same time, making a contribution toward solving this problem. We so far have spent $4½ million.

"Now every man in this room," Lear went on, "has to take the position that he is sixty-eight years old, has earned a certain amount of money in his life, and so far has spent, let's say, half of it. Now he faces the decision whether to go on and spend the other half. You are now acting as the Board of Directors, each with the same interest financially in the company as I have. And, of course, I have had the good fortune to make many people rich from riding along with me. So there is a good chance that if we do the right thing we can be quite well off.

"The basic decision I'm going to ask you to make today is, which way we should go."

Lear dropped back to beginnings and restated the objective: the development of a non-polluting propulsion system for all applications now served by the internal combustion engine.

"I have felt for a long time that our destiny so far as the automobile industry is concerned is tied first of all to having the satisfactory device," Lear said. "That means an engine that can compete in price, size, and efficiency with what they already have."

To make it cheaply called for tooling and this was expensive. George Huebner of Chrysler had confirmed for him at Newport Beach that it cost $300 million on the average to tool a new automobile engine. "Now if there's one thing we don't have right now it's $300 million," Lear said.

They did, however, have one thing to offer the auto industry after all their efforts which made sense. This was the turbo-electric system, which eliminated the differential and other trouble-making contrivances devised by the auto men in dealing with the old problem of hitching the engine to the wheels to make the car go. It was the electric car without the problem of batteries.

"I feel the money we have put into that has been worth-while," Lear said. He felt there was something to be salvaged from their boiler developments, and from the pump they had been working on.

He struck an old theme. "I'm sure of one thing: We've got to treat anything we make from here on out as something that's going to operate in space. The quality of the service available today in the automotive field is so bad you almost hesitate to take your car in. Any device we put on the market has to run continuously without service."

The first requisite of reliability was simplicity, and this was something the steam car did not have, Lear said. "It involves a much greater number of systems than the internal combustion engine or the gas turbine."

The condenser still hogged space, keeping horsepower down, and while they had greatly reduced the boiler and improved its efficiency, there were other things about the boiler to consider. It had to be carefully controlled. Too much heat caused the tubes to burn out; too much pressure caused them to burst. So there must be safety devices, to detect trouble in advance and do something about it.

"Worse, if we use organic fluids we must have a completely enclosed system, because we don't want to spew organic fluids into the atmosphere," Lear said.

There remained much to learn about fluids. "We know that if we get the temperature above 800 degrees, it automatically ignites from the heat," Lear went on. "We know that certain combinations of air and fluids at certain temperatures will burn. Now, whether this band of combinations that burn is wide or narrow makes very little difference when you have someone like Mr. Nader take out after you," he added, referring to Ralph Nader, the safety crusader.

"Along comes a steam car and he looks at it and says, 'Aah, they've got not one thing that can burn but they've got two things to burn: the fuel and also the fluid!' And his position, I think, would be well taken and certainly it would be difficult to offset. You could present all the curves you wanted to about how you have to have special conditions. I don't think it would prevail over his argument that two are more than one."

If they used water instead of organic fluid, they would be up against another obstacle. This was the code of the American Society of Mechanical Engineers. Although written thirty or forty years ago, there was little doubt that in the world of the internal combustion engine the ancient rules and regulations for building a competitor would be rigidly enforced.

Was steam it? Lear recalled a bit of philosophy from a banker he had once worked with. "'Bill, if I think I can get through that stone wall, I don't care how bruised and bloody my head becomes,

I'll try; but if I'm convinced that I can't get through that stone wall, I wouldn't harm a hair on my head.' I think this is the position we must take today. Can we get through that stone wall?"

He was worried about the many safety devices that would be needed. "We cannot start our turbine before we are sure that all the water has been removed," Lear said. "This calls for a safety device. We cannot start our boiler until we are sure that it has liquid in it. This takes another safety system, and so on. You'll remember, in the beginning of this discourse I said reliability is inversely proportional to the number of components. It's even more proportional to the number of systems, because a system has many components. Any of these systems can fail and, in general, when one fails, the whole thing breaks down.

"We have the problem of developing a pump to pump the fluid, whatever it's going to be. Up to now I imagine we've spent, conservatively, $100,000 on the development of a pump. We haven't been able to buy one that would fit inside an automobile that would do the job."

The memory of Bill Besler's little steamer still bothered him. "I'm sure we can make a system that is twice as efficient as his but that still leaves much to be desired," Lear said.

When the meeting had lasted three hours, it was time to vote. Should they go on as they had been doing, giving the full effort to steam? Should they abandon steam and go all out to the gas turbine? Should they keep on with steam but on a reduced scale, giving the main push to the gas turbine?

Lear reminded them that Detroit was going to stick with the internal combustion engine, making no serious effort to develop something new. Therefore, as the air went on being filled with combustion poisons, there would be a growing demand for a clean propulsion system. The market for a clean automobile engine, Lear estimated, could run as high as $300 million a year.

"So now each of you take a piece of paper," he said, "and I want each of you to write about five lines on what you think is the move we should make. Remember now, this is your company, this is your money, and you are deciding what you are going to do with it."

"I for one can't express myself in five lines," Al Simonson said.

"Take a lot!" Lear replied. "Take six."

"My answer is far from yes or no," Simonson explained. "I see a system that has all the advantages of the old Stanley Steamer and I . . ."

"State it! State it!" Lear interrupted. "Remember, we're talking about combustion, noise, efficiency, cost, weight, space, and so forth."

The vote heavily favored the gas turbine, with work on steam to go on but sharply curtailed. The gas turbine power plant was simpler and closer to being perfected than a steam system, it was argued, offering an earlier solution to the problem of exhaust pipe poison.

The man who would lead the gas turbine effort was tall, polite Peter Lewis, twenty-eight, who had been working with gas turbines for Ford in Detroit. A native Californian, interested in "exotic, off-beat cars" as a teen-ager, Lewis had gone East after he earned his master's degree in mechanical engineering at Stanford University.

Over coffee in Apartment 20-K at the Arlington Towers, where he and his wife Roberta, a schoolteacher, had spent their first night in Reno, Lewis obligingly did what he could to get through to me on the rudiments of the gas turbine, patiently sketching in my notebook. Yes, technically, the gas turbine was an external combustion engine, the same as the steam engine. The combustor was on the outside, and the fire was sustained rather than being a series of confined explosions as in the internal combustion engine.

The gas turbine, therefore, should be as clean as the steam turbine, or any other steam system.

But there was still much to learn about gas turbines, Lewis said. Little had been written about them. "You have to grope around and find out for yourself—such things as blade size and angle, for instance." These were both critical because of the speed of the turbine.

But one of the biggest unknowns appeared to be on the way to resolution. This was what to use in place of scarce and costly nickel in the high heat areas of the turbine. The promise lay in ceramics, the same stuff as flower pots are made of. Being available in limitless supply, this was far cheaper, and it was easier to work with.

Yes, the gas turbine was the way to go—or was it?

15: ASK HOW THEY'D LIKE THEIR CROW PREPARED

In the steam part of the program, attention shifted to a radically new direction. The center of interest was an air compressor, consisting of two interlocking screws. Why not run steam through it? The steam, expanding as it advanced between the screw threads, turned the rotors, delivering power. The involute screw expander was, in effect, an endless cylinder.

The Gardner-Denver Company of Quincy, Illinois, pumpmakers for the past century or so, had suggested the screw during the summer.

"Look into it," Lear told Al Simonson.

A handsome young Swede with buckeye brown eyes, Simonson was a newcomer to Lear Land. Brainy and articulate, he had studied history and German at Uppsala and Heidelberg, and earned his engineering credentials at Syracuse University.

A preliminary evaluation of the screw machine looked good, and one was procured from Gardner-Denver for further experimentation. It arrived on the same day as word from California that Lear Motors had been included among three winners in the bidding to install steam power in a bus for San Francisco and the Alameda-Contra Costa Transit District, but with Lear Motors given the least chance of succeeding.

The state had been able to shake loose a few more dollars from the Urban Mass Transportation Administration in Washington, as Chairman Mike Wenstrom had said might be possible at the May 12 meeting in San Francisco. For the first time since the cash began to flow out, it looked as if there would be some coming in.

With something tangible to shoot for, a crew worked eighteen-hour days to get the screw expander mounted for testing on the dynamometer, getting scant help from three willing but baffled Gardner-Denver engineers. "We never put anything through it but air," they said.

Lear was out of town, but, as always, kept in touch by phone. His voice sounded strange as he checked in with instructions for Hugh Carson late in the forenoon on the day of the screw tests. "Where are you?" Ginny Hamilton asked.

"About eight miles up and a hundred miles north of you," Lear replied. He had been in Los Angeles overnight and was on his way to Seattle to make a luncheon talk, testing his new shipboard telephone as he flew.

A crowd collected at the dynamometer cell as the test began. In the control room Mike Wood slowly twisted the red handle that allowed steam to flow to the screw expander from the vapor generator test laboratory behind. A red light flashed over the door. Gauges fluttered. Superheated steam shooting invisibly from the bypass line outside the window of the building grew to a shrieking roar.

Ev Alford arrived as the uproar eased off. "Was it a good test?" he asked Ken Rudolph.

Rudy shrugged. "It didn't fail. You take one little step, then another."

There were more run-ups—more little steps—each a little higher than the last. The screw ran with a smooth, steady hum.

Old test expert Ed Lenheim was impressed that even with wet steam and low pressure the screw had shown power. "The thing that makes it more appealing than anything else," Ed said, "it's so goddamn simple. Nothing changes direction."

Lenheim had joined the steam force after Lear, in Wichita for a Lear Jet board meeting, ran into him in the Lear Jet plant. "How're things going?" Lear asked.

"Oh, I don't know, Bill," Lenheim responded slowly. "Things are not the same. . . ."

"Be on board at three!" Lear ordered. "I need you in Reno."

Four days after the first test, the screw developed one hundred horsepower. It gave promise of a stall torque (twisting force) five times as good as with the equivalent internal combustion engine.

The performance of the screw expander seemed to vindicate Al Simonson, who had championed it from the time it was first mentioned in mid-August. Lear sent him to Stockholm to see the originators of the machine, Svenska Rotormaskiner, as well as the company's former employe, Professor Alf Lysholm of the Royal Technical Institute. The company had tested the screw in power applications with good results, they reported. Simonson's old company, Atlas-Copco, who took over the screw's manufacture, said it would be five months before they could make a pair for him.

"It's a real interesting concept," Simonson said as he spilled tobacco from the can of Prince Albert on his desk over a cigarette paper. "In fact, it's the only one with real promise of long-range answers."

He listed the strong points about the screw motor. It had only two moving parts. The screw turned to advantage things that made trouble in the conventional steam system such as scale and dirt in the water. These it put to use sealing clearances between rotors and housing. The steam could be put through the screw at five times the speed of sound, meaning more efficiency, for the faster it ran the less it leaked.

To brake or reverse the screw-powered car, one simply reversed the steam flow. The boiler, chief space hog in a steam system, could be cut nearly in half compared to the size otherwise needed.

The screw engine would be cheap and easy to produce, Simonson calculated. The rotors could probably be made by extrusion, at $1 or so for the pair. Machines capable of extruding cold steel already existed. There was one in London. Altogether, Simonson estimated, a 190-horsepower screw motor, about the size of a shoebox and weighing 92 pounds, could be turned out for about $80 each in volume. To Lear, though, it all sounded too good to be true. "I want you to start thinking of an alternate in case the screw machine doesn't work," he directed Hugh Carson.

"Of course, you know what that will be," Carson answered.

"Yes—the piston engine. Can we make one work?"

"They've been making them since 1705," Carson said, having

in mind the steam engine built by Thomas Newcomen, later improved by James Watt.

"Let's get started," Lear said.

In San Francisco the next night, flying over in his Lear Jet after the day's work, Lear told a dinner audience of engineering college deans and professors of his efforts to achieve a low emission auto engine, getting them on his side at the outset by saying how glad he was "to talk to all you educated people."

The teachers sat forward like attentive pupils as the man who taught himself showed them some of the ideas his men had worked with in Reno, using the flip chart prepared by Bill Moore and Bob Davids. When he finished, following a question period, the audience rose and applauded.

In the heavy air of sea level and with the fuel load lightened by the outbound trip, Lear rammed the jet seemingly straight up into the night for the return to Reno, the lights of San Francisco falling away like a dropping elevator. Reporter Wolfgang Will of Berlin grimaced nervously. In Germany, he explained, one experienced this kind of thing only in military planes. Over the Sierra foothills at the approach to Reno, the air suddenly became violent, making great blanket tosses of the airplane.

Back on the good earth, Lear drove away, swung his car around and came back, rolling down the window as he came alongside my rented Volkswagen. "If you'll come up to the Brave Bull I'll buy you a drink."

At near midnight, after a day that had started at dawn, he still had energy to burn.

Next day Lear flew to Los Angeles to take part in a symposium at the California Institute of Technology at Pasadena, drawing, as one student observed, "a bigger crowd than Billy Graham."

Back in Reno after the weekend, Lear found a memo from Hugh Carson, advising that Hugh had bought a Valiant-6 engine from a salvage yard and giving his plans for converting it to steam.

"Go ahead—full speed," Lear directed, pleased.

Two weeks later the Valiant ran on steam for the first time. The results were scarcely encouraging, the engine having shown itself to be a poor match for the brute stresses of steam, which left it bent and warped.

Lear, in Washington to address the International Taxicab Association, approved Carson's proposed remedies over the telephone. Anyone but a good Lear man, therefore, might have been a little bemused to hear out of Detroit, mid-course of the changes Carson was making in the engine, that Lear had given up on steam. The word seemed to go out by all means except smoke signals and carrier pigeon after Lear had spoken to the American Society of Automotive Engineers at the University of Michigan. There was an eager I-told-you-so quality about the news, reminiscent of what happened when the first Lear Jet went up in flames.

In Reno, the switchboard blinked and the postman dumped extra packets of letters on Leona Corrigan's reception desk. "That broadcast must have had the highest Nielsen rating in history," Red McDougall remarked dryly.

"You can't do this!" the callers and letter writers protested. It was as if Lear had betrayed them.

The disappointed outcry came not alone from ordinary citizens who had been looking forward to a new age of steam, maybe with a steam car of their own; the sounds of dismay came as well from the makers of power equipment. Cummins Diesel typically had been counting on Lear in their plans to convert from Diesel electric to steam turbine electric. Had he really given up?

Many wanted to help. "If it's the boiler that's giving you trouble, I've got some ideas that may be useful," one man said. The scavengers checked in like carrion crows, wanting to buy up engines, boilers, and any other remains Lear wouldn't be needing any more.

Suppliers asked if they should keep sending materials. "As long as we pay our bills," Hugh Carson replied laconically.

Lear issued a "clarification" of his remarks at Ann Arbor. He had not given up on steam. Steam was fine as an interim solution to the automotive air pollution problem, but the ultimate answer, Lear contended, was the gas turbine.

"Give up?" Lear asked as I arrived on a new visit to the plant. "Ask them how they like their crow prepared." He grinned broadly. "I'm more enthusiastic than I ever was."

The latest Valiant engine was "running like a sewing machine." Only a few days before it had turned in a performance that startled everybody, delivering 500 foot-pounds of torque at 1300 rpm. This was unheard of by any engine. The 1970 Cadillac engine, nearly twice the size of the Valiant, delivered but 50 foot-pounds additional at more than twice the rpm.

Seated at his desk in blue shirt sleeves, Lear went on philosophically as Hugh Carson, Ev Alford, Pete Lewis, and Bill Moore listened. "You can do things empirically and come up with results," he said. You paid no attention to those who say it's impossible. "There are whole libraries written on why things can't be done, like the RAF's five hundred pages on why the jet engine will never replace the propeller," he went on. "You put intelligence into it, you put it together, and you try it out. More often than you think, it works."

In the fabricating shop, the Polara seemed well on the way to the tryout stage Lear spoke of. The two radiators, twice the standard thickness, were in place side by side, accommodated by removing the inside member of each double set of headlights. The pancake boiler was being fitted into the trunk. Although only one fourth the size of the old Doble boiler, Mike Wood pointed out, it made ten times as much steam.

"We have gone from two cubic feet per one hundred horsepower to one cubic foot," Mike said.

They also had a pump. Without that, to keep the cycling fluid whirling along, none of the rest mattered. The requirements were stringent. The pump must turn at 3000 revolutions per minute, and withstand 200 degrees of heat and 3000 pounds of pressure per square inch. It must be sealed against leaks and provided with fail-safe lubrication.

No such pump existed anywhere in the world except in massive sizes. So Max Winkler, a blond, crew-cut German from Milwaukee, designed one. The Lear 9-cylinder radial pump was about the size of a saucepan.

How the components of the steam system worked linked together they expected to know soon. They planned to drive the Polara by mid-January, a month hence. There were hard reasons to hope it would run. It was late 1969. The outlay to now, Joe Walsh said, was $5,238,000, all from Lear's pocket.

Meanwhile, into the engine driving the car on that day must be incorporated the lessons learned from successive generations of Valiant steam engines. It must have more precise valving, a stronger crankshaft, a new cylinder head, a new kind of lubrication system, and so forth.

Within days the newest Valiant conversion, fitted with racing car valves, was on the dynamometer, ready for testing. The shop filled with thunder as 800-degree steam was valved into the engine and the excess shot from the bypass outside window.

Like a doctor checking a chest, Hugh Carson moved about the engine holding a stethoscope to its sides, listening for "noises that don't belong." At low speeds, he heard popping sounds, as from preignition in a gas engine. Not good. When the test ended and the engine cooled down, it was found that the oil scavenge pump had failed, causing the engine to fill with oil and blow out the oil seals. Other things went wrong.

After a day-long discussion, it was decided to abandon the Valiant, along with a couple of Dodge engines and a Chrysler, in favor of a four-cylinder International. Being a truck engine, this was more rugged. It was also more compact, so that it could lie flat on the bottom of the engine compartment under the hood, leaving room for pumps, reservoirs, and plumbing on top of it.

Lear, just back from Washington, didn't believe poppet valves could ever be made reliable at high speeds, so for the International engine Hugh Carson thought up a rotary valve which would function when the engine was running at 4500 rpm, far too fast for poppet valves, which move up and down.

The idea for the rotary valve came to Carson as he lay awake during the small hours at his apartment in University Foothills unaffected by Bea's insomnia prescription of aspirin with milk and brandy, alternated with creme de menthe. "Sometimes there are problems that *must* be solved," he said. "You either solve them or it's the end of the line."

The rotary valve afforded more simplicity. The springs, cam shafts, lifters, and all the rest of the rigmarole that went with poppet valves would be gone. The full trade-off was 142 parts for eight.

As layout work on the new valve approached the finish, Lear flew to Washington once more to plead the cause of a clean engine, about his tenth assault of the year on Fortress Inertia on the Potomac. The opportunity was an invitation to testify before the Subcommittee on Air and Water Pollution of the Senate Committee on Public Works, which was cautiously mulling a proposal that the federal government lend a hand in getting the automobile cleaned up.

The proposed action, embodied in the federal Low-Emission

Vehicle Procurement Act, provided that the government, which buys some sixty thousand vehicles a year, stipulate that a certain percentage of them must be equipped with low-emission engines, thereby stimulating their development.

"The automobile companies appear unwilling or incapable of transcending the internal combustion engine," said Chairman Warren Magnuson of the Committee on Commerce in introducing the bill, Number 3072, on October 27, 1969. "They have announced that the main battle against automobile air pollution has been won, but this is not the case. . . . The time has come to launch a government program which will stimulate the development, production, and distribution of low-emission vehicles. . . . Congress should create a legislatively guaranteed market for innovative developers."

That meant such as Lear Motors of Reno. Introduced by Senator Jennings Randolph, Lear questioned whether the measure would do what it was supposed to do. Engines developed by the "innovative developers" Senator Magnuson referred to would have to be sold to the big car makers, for use in their cars. Why would they buy them, Lear asked? They had an engine of their own.

The other way around, with the engine builder buying the cars and installing the engines himself, didn't seem much better, either, because of the problem of getting the cars at wholesale prices. And the man with a new engine couldn't afford to build the car himself at the specified statutory price plus 25 per cent in the relatively small lots the government would want.

"A much more flexible pricing structure should be adopted," Lear said. "Otherwise the legislation would assist and encourage only the existing automotive industry."

It would not help the independent developer, who was really the best bet. "In the past," Lear reminded the senators, "brilliant innovations and break-throughs in an industry have come from outside that industry. Xerox and Polaroid are such examples."

Supporting only Detroit would merely lead to more "patch on patch" devices on the internal combustion engine already tried and not working—and which, a Lear study showed, would cost the public $6 billion a year in useless maintenance. That was the same as what the nation paid for medicine and drugs.

What was needed was an inherently low-polluting engine, "one not requiring frequent and costly maintenance," Lear said. The government should get behind the development of such an engine by putting up the money for a gas turbine, which Lear felt was the long-range answer to the need for a clean auto engine. It was as clean as steam, the interim solution, and considerably simpler.

It would cost $300 million—$25 million to develop the prototype, $75 million for plant facilities and tooling, and $200 million in working capital to get the engine into production.

Perhaps it went through the minds of the solons that this was just over the amount the government gave the aviation industry to develop the supersonic transport, which not everybody agreed was needed.

It was no use looking to Detroit for salvation. "The automotive industry," Lear said, "is totally committed to the status quo. They don't want a new engine if they can avoid it. They are going to save the internal combustion engine which has taken sixty-five years to develop, no matter what the cost."

It was going to take some outside force—like the government —to get them off the dime, because the industry is run not by the owners but by managers hired by the stockholders. "If they don't do the job the shareholders like, they will be replaced," Lear said.

He assured them, in reply to a question from Nevada's Senator Howard Cannon, that regardless of what Detroit's house organ, the *Automotive News*, said, he was still in the steam business. "I am continuing if for no other reason than to keep somebody in the future from saying I couldn't do it."

Cannon wanted to know if Lear thought the government should apportion its Research and Development money for a gas turbine "among a number of competing independents."

"I think if you want to throw the money away, it would be better to throw it down the sewer," Lear replied bluntly. "You wouldn't have to administer it that way. It would be like handing out four or five NASA contracts to four or five different contractors to build a spaceship to go to the moon. These small, paltry sums—I call them nickel and dime R and D efforts.

"The first step," Lear continued, "is for the government to pick a company that can do it for the money—build a gas turbine for the $25 million. Perhaps you can find someone to put up the other $275 million to tool and produce it. But you will never get anyplace until that first step is taken.

"We think we can do it for $25 million. The automobile companies laugh us out of their offices when we say that. They say it's ridiculous." He paused and smiled. "They said the Lear Jet couldn't be built for $10 million. They said $100 million. We did it for ten."

Meanwhile, until there was action to produce a clean engine, Lear asked the senators to consider "how many pounds of transportation it requires to move 185 pounds of humanity around." He suggested that a way be found to limit the size of cars. He noted acidly that Detroit, despite the pollution emergency, was coming "out with what they call muscle power engines. What for? Because they get more money. And because somebody wants to hear the tires skid."

There was no response to this. Senator Cannon asked if the extra 25 per cent allowed under the bill would "provide enough incentive for the production people to go ahead and produce cars," once a low emission engine had been developed.

"Only mass-produced cars could compete," Lear replied. Anyone below the capacity of American Motors would be out. But there was no reason why the auto companies should buy the engine, he repeated, "because they have got an engine plant and would rather sell their own."

The best solution was for the government to use its leverage and get "one gas turbine, low-emission, lightweight car on the market at the right price and with the right performance," Lear said. "Then the competition among the companies will lead them into following. As a matter of fact, they will try to beat us to the market."

If nothing else, Lear's battle of attrition against Washington seemed at last to be awakening its interest in what was going on at his Reno plant.

He arrived home in time to welcome a distinguished deputation from the Office of Science and Technology in Washington. The Ad Hoc Unconventional Vehicle Propulsion Panel of nine came in elaborate secrecy, threatening to go back home at the mere suspicion of newsmen on the premises. They even insisted that they be briefed separately from a group of Californians, which included Dr. A. J. Haagen-Smit, chairman of the California Air Resources Board, and John Maga, his executive officer.

This made for problems at the last minute. Bill Moore and

THE INCREDIBLE STORY OF BILL LEAR

Bob Davids, already numb and red-eyed from a week of preparation, had to stay up another night to make an extra set of displays.

What the VIPs thought as they inscrutably listened to the presentations and toured the shop apparently was intended to remain as unrevealed as the visit itself. No comment was heard until the group came to the Polara. They eyed the side-by-side radiators, the dashboard controls which made things move under the hood, the pancake boiler securely bolted to its moorings in the trunk. They looked at the Valiant engine, canted over on its side and making a convincing stand-in until the smaller International with its rotary valve was ready, making room for the boiler under the hood instead of the trunk. "Lear" was the new name on the front of the car.

"Very impressive!" Dr. David G. Wilson, associate professor of Mechanical Engineering at the Massachusetts Institute of Technology, exclaimed. "Fantastic!"

Dr. Wilson also committed himself on the involute screw idea, prompting Al Simonson to observe later that at least there was one friend in the crowd. "I am impatient with those who are quick to say the idea is no good," Wilson said to me.

Perhaps a clue to what the rest thought lay in the comment of Dr. Haagen-Smit, who had arrived as a skeptic. "I feel much better about it," he said as he prepared to go home. "I am glad to see General Motors get a good competitor."

The rotary valve, which had been the "white hope" of the steam effort, as Hugh Carson put it, proved to be another disappointment. Finally built and fitted into the International engine after giving the engineers more than two months of trouble over the design, the valve leaked too much. They had known it would leak some—one balanced this against the gains, such as the greater time it allowed the steam to enter and leave the cylinders—but this exceeded tolerable limits, as did the cost of reducing it further. They were back to buffalo chips.

Lear heard the bad news when he returned March 12 from addressing the American Society of Mechanical Engineers in Chicago. His hopes sank. "He feels the whole steam effort is a lost cause," Hugh Carson wrote. He was "more unhappy with steam systems each day."

One could feel the falling barometer all over the shop.

Then, on March 19, the brewing storm broke. The state of California stipulated they wanted performance from the Lear steam bus far better than the best by any gasoline bus currently on the road after a half century of development. It was much as if the Signal Corps, in its negotiations with the Wright brothers, had asked them to build the Lear Jet.

On top of this, they chiseled on the money, cutting it to $320,000 from the $450,000 Lear had bid.

As Lear sat simmering in his office, mentally matching two years' effort and $6 million against the California proposition, feeling more beaten and foolish by the minute, Joe Walsh came in and dropped a check for $300,000 on the desk for his signature.

"What's that for?" Lear asked.

"February's expenses," Walsh replied offhandedly.

Walsh's manner was the spark in Lear's tinder. "Well, this is the last $300,000 month!" Lear flamed.

He needed Buzz Nanney to drive him home that night. Moya offered no sympathy at the day's events. "I don't want to hear any more complaints," she said sharply. "You built the Lear Jet in a year. Why does it take so long to put an engine in an automobile? Let's do what we started out to do or say we made a mistake and forget it."

As always in a crisis, Moya was at Lear's side at the office next morning. He was punching the buttons to call the press when she and the others in the room prevailed on him to wait.

"We had to save him from retiring because we all knew that wouldn't work," Moya said.

There was a conference around the table. The status of the various projects—the brushless motor, the new automatic pilot, both nearly finished—was discussed. Things were not as black as they seemed. The bus deal, though, as the terms stood, was out. It was decided to cut back the work force to slow the outflow of capital, and thirty-eight employees were painfully laid off.

The news that Lear had turned down the bus contract traveled fast. Before the day was over, Carlos Villareal of the Urban Mass Transportation Administration, phoned from Washington. "Bill, you can't do this!" Villareal cried. "We want you to try it so we can say steam won't work!"

"I'm not putting another dime into it," Lear growled.

"We'll write you just the contract you want," Villareal pleaded. "I'm sending a man out first thing Monday. Don't make a move till he gets there."

The Washington emissary Charles Daniels had the manner of a friendly passer-by who had stopped in to see the farmer's vegetable garden. He listened attentively as Lear told of investing $1 million to develop a boiler putting out ten times as much steam as the old Doble boiler, at one fourth the size—of searching the world for a feed water pump and finally building one here, at a cost of $200,000, and of other successes.

"It's quite evident you've been working on the problem," Daniels said admiringly. "You're the only people I've seen who are totally dedicated to it."

After hamburgers at Joe Gardner's Bordertown Club on the California line up the road, with Daniels telling his share of the jokes, the visitor was shown slides giving the cost of proposed measures to keep auto pollution down—of "keeping a patch on a patch"—rather than getting rid of the cause. Nearly $2 billion a year—that would be the tab for nationwide facilities to provide two inspections a year on two hundred million automobiles. This would be what the motorist came up with in extra taxes to support the boondoggle after he had paid as much as $67 billion to buy the gadgets in the first place, and had been gaffed additional billions to keep them in repair.

And, of course, it all wouldn't make much difference. There would still be pollution from automobiles, since the internal combustion engine was inherently dirty and, from the evidence, not amenable to being cleaned up. Exhaust control devices had been on cars since 1966. They still didn't work.

Al Simonson intrigued the visitor with some things about the screw engine, illustrating with slides. Among other critical advantages, calculations showed it allowed a 45 per cent reduction in the size of the boiler over the size needed in a piston system. The screw was light and simple, weighing only a pound per horsepower and having only two moving parts. Installed in the Dodge Polara, it would take the car to 60 miles an hour in seven seconds from a standing start and give it a top speed of 128.

"We feel this is a very promising system and we'd like to work on it if we go ahead with steam," Simonson said. "But it can't be done with backyard equipment. It will take money."

"It's a fallacy to expect somebody in a garage to come up with it," Lear affirmed.

Lear strongly objected to having anybody look over their shoulders. "If that's the way it's going to be they can take their contract and shove it!" he said feelingly. "Four hundred and fifty thousand dollars overhead on a $600,000 contract! I call that getting in the way." There had been too many delays already. "We've lost six months just waiting for that goddamned contract to come back."

Joe Walsh came in with a yellow pad to take down the conditions for accepting the bus deal, as dictated by Lear. First, he mentioned the $450,000 they were to be paid.

"Three hundred and twenty," Walsh corrected. "Everybody gets the same"—meaning each of the three winners.

Lear stood up, his face turning red. "That does it! Forget the whole thing!" He strode from the room.

Daniels smiled abashedly. He lamely explained that he felt the purpose of the bus project had been "misunderstood." It was only for feasibility—a "quick and dirty" feasibility demonstration.

"In that case it would be no better than the Doble," Simonson replied with surprise. "The feasibility part was done years ago."

"The government's position," Daniels said, passing quickly on, "is that they put up something and the other party puts up something."

"Lear has already put in $5 million," Joe Walsh retorted quietly.

The man sent by UMTA Administrator Villareal ostensibly to give Lear what he wanted, and whose visit had tied up key people all day, had no authority to negotiate. The negotiating, Daniels said, would have to be done with the state of California.

In the shop outside, Daniels ran into Lear, who was controlled and polite. Daniels complimented him on how far ahead he was and said he would be in touch with him next day. "We want you in on this, Bill," he said ingratiatingly.

It had been a long day. In the hangar the Lear Jet was ready. Ed Lenheim hollered across to the apron from the office some five hundred yards away, his words carrying clearly in the cool air of early night. "Fill her for Palm Springs!" Palm Springs took a little more fuel than to Los Angeles.

The enclosing mountains threw back the thunder as Lear took off, and the running lights were quickly lost among the stars.

Buzz Nanney put on his hat and went home, waiting for another time to tell Lear about the present he was getting him, a drawing of which lay on his desk. It was an unusual .38 caliber Italian target pistol.

It fired backward.

16: HERE COMES STEAM!

It was April Fool's Day and Lear had gathered his men in the office. After a week's rest and reflection in Palm Springs, he was back, spoiling for action.

"If you guys had your ass up against a buzz saw and you had the enemy coming at you in front, what would you do?" he asked. He mentioned Moya's words about the time it was taking to put an engine into an automobile.

Nobody answered.

Al Simonson spoke up. "I'd make a steam system."

"How long will it take?" Lear asked.

"Five months." That was the time Atlas Copco in Stockholm had said it would need to build a pair of rotors.

"Too long," Lear said.

Simonson reminded him that on his second trip to Sweden, failing to find a pair of ready-made rotors on the shelf, he had brought back copies of the patent papers on the screw and had picked up other know-how from talking with his old employers, Atlas Copco, who took over the manufacture of the screw after its development by Svenska Rotormaskiner.

Within the hour, three of them—Lear, Simonson, and Carson —were at forty thousand feet, streaking for Los Angeles, where a gear manufacturer assured them he could make the rotors. This arrangement shortly bogged down, however, and Gardner-Denver, who suggested the screw in the first place, took on the job, offering to make nine sets of rotors at cost, or $7500. It would take not five months, but eight to ten weeks.

By mid-May things were looking so good with the screw that Lear was indulging a side interest. He told about it over a $4 hamburger at The Bistro in Beverly Hills. It had to do with a new process for extracting precious metals from the surface ore found all over Nevada.

"If this works," he said, not altogether jokingly, "I'll have enough money to buy and sell Howard Hughes—not that I'm interested in that, but it's fun."

The ore indicated an assay of $1500 a ton, in silver, gold, and some platinum—and there were one hundred million tons of it. "That's—let's see . . ." Lear scribbled on a napkin. "That's $150 billion."

Commodities broker David Callahan, a son of Terre Haute, Indiana, looked at him across the table. "Gee, Bill," he drawled in Hoosier accents, "I was going to buy the lunch today. Now I think I'll let you buy it."

In Reno that evening, the mood of the shop, like the boss's, was upbeat. The screw motor looked more and more like the big winner. The one problem that had threatened to be sticky appeared to have been beaten, Hugh Carson said. This was how to seal the rotors so that no steam leaked past them, causing loss of power. A coating material was testing out promisingly, giving zero clearances.

With the screw at front and center, the piston engine had been set aside. "Fifty per cent of its drawbacks—skipping, banging, knocking, untoward sounds of all kinds—are in the same category as those of the internal combustion engine," Carson said. "So we were adding IC problems to steam problems. There were too many parts. It was too heavy, too bulky, too complicated."

They still had the Valiant, though. "It's a good engine," Hugh went on. It packed three hundred horsepower, twice its output on gasoline, and had the same torque as the Lincoln Continental engine. That was a lot better than the Stanley and Doble, with thirty and eighty horsepower, respectively.

Lear came in, saying he was "depressed." Bill Moore followed a few steps behind like an equerry, bearing two half-gallon measures of restorative. There was general restoration.

At home next morning, Lear furiously pedaled his mounted Sears Roebuck bicycle, like the boy riding the gift bike in the store window long ago. He pedaled to exhaustion, working off a few more ounces. Down to 196 pounds from 210, he was going for 186. He combed his hair and was heard by Moya to mutter as he put the comb down, "Okay, bring on your goddamn wildcats!"

At the breakfast table he picked up the *Wall Street Journal* and, recalling his early wireless days, read off the name of the paper in the dots and dashes of the Morse code, Moya following. Gunnar Christensen handed him a package. "Your shoes came yesterday," Gunnar said. Lear unwrapped and inspected his new Corfam shoes, two pairs for $14.95.

As he tried them on, he told of having fun asking shoe store clerks for Corfam shoes and being put down with a haughty "We don't carry them. I tell them, 'That's your problem! You ought to!'"

Lear handed me a pair. "Try these on."

They fit perfectly.

"Okay, you keep those and I'll get some more."

So now I was in Bill Lear's shoes.

Pushing the breakfast plates aside, he and Moya filled out an order blank for shirts, ties, and other items, including a pair of white summer shoes. Plastic footwear requires no stops at shoeshine stands, saving time. With both the clock and reciprocity in mind, Lear also favors washable, non-wrinkling Farah slacks, reasoning that since Farah flies two Lear Jets the least Lear can do is wear Farah's pants.

Being a millionaire has bred no pretensions in the man who made it on his own. He once yielded to a suggestion from Buzz Nanney that a man of his wealth and station ought to have a chauffeur. "It's more dignified," Buzz said.

The chauffeur promptly drove through a traffic light as they were setting out for Santa Ana and was stopped by a policeman. Lear, sitting in the back doing his best to look dignified, roared at the cop, "Give the son of a bitch a ticket! I saw him do it!" For the rest of the trip, Lear drove and the chauffeur sat in the back. That was the end of chauffeurs.

On his way to work, wearing his new $7.50 shoes, Lear made up time by hitting one hundred miles an hour, driving the American Motors' Hornet from his stable of cars. He was going to Las Vegas that day to take part in a panel discussion at the thirty-second annual convention of the Aviation/Space Writers' Association at Caesar's Palace. But first he went up to test the new auto pilot with LeVell Tippetts, returning in an hour.

"Not good enough," he pronounced as he walked away from the ship. "It was perfect when we tried it on the breadboard," he added perplexedly. "It'll need more work."

It was now lunchtime. At the Bordentown Club, up the road on the border with California, Lear got into a bantering exchange about reducing. "I once drank fourteen cans of Metrecal in one day and I still weighed the same," he said. He matched owner Joe Gardner for the beer and sandwiches, double or nothing, and lost. He accused Gardner of using a two-faced coin.

Back at the plant, Lear had some further business at the office. "I'll see you for dinner," Moya said as she prepared to drive away in her white Mercedes roadster. There was no reply. "All right—maybe I won't see you then," she added, half to herself.

As we waited by the jet in front of the hangar, Buzz Nanney drove up inquiringly, looking at his watch. It was one o'clock. Lear was due to speak in Las Vegas at two. "It's only four hundred miles," Bill Moore said assuringly. "Forty-five minutes is plenty of time to get there."

Lear arrived. He went directly aboard, wound up the engines even as he was sitting down, and took off, making a steep climbing turn into his course over the hangar. At altitude, he turned the wheel over to Clyde Martin, moved to a seat in the cabin and in deep concentration fell to sketching on the back of a large manila envelope. He was working out a way to air-condition the ship in flight as well as on the ground, he explained after we landed in Las Vegas. "I think I got it," he said.

At the ASWA meeting, where he walked in exactly at two o'clock, Lear was presented last as "the frosting on the cake." Since the theme had been one of lament against the federal government, specifically charging cavalier treatment of general aviation, the door was wide open on one of Lear's favorite topics. He had "worn out shoe leather and made the seat on my pants shine" trying to get action on air pollution, and with an eye on the two Federal Aviation Administration men present, he was now ready to advance it as a law that federal bureaus expand to use up their funds for administration, leaving nothing to get things done.

When the meeting ended, newsmen gathered around Lear on the stage, the New York *Times*, Boston *Globe*, Philadelphia *Enquirer*, Reuters, NBC, CBS. Others waylaid him in the corridor. He obligingly waited an hour to do a taped interview with Clete

Roberts of CBS, or he would have made it home in time for dinner.

Moya and Tina greeted him with relief. They had heard him on the short-wave receiver as he talked to the Reno tower on the way in. Five-year-old John Christensen, with eyes as blue as a Norse fjord and hair the color of rye straw, climbed into Lear's lap, calling him "Uncle Bill."

The next day got off to fair start by any reasonable standards when Lear received a phone call soon after he reached the office. "I've got 145,000 shares of stock I didn't know I had," he said when he hung up the receiver. He thought a moment. "Hell, that's a million dollars even at today's prices!" He picked up the phone again. "Excuse me while I take care of this matter," he said.

Joe Harris, newly hired from Wichita, turned to Buzz Nanney. "What do you do when you find a million dollars lying around the house you didn't know about?" he asked.

"I don't know," Buzz answered. "I've never had the problem."

The amount turned out to be closer to a half million than a full million dollars. "For a while there I thought I'd found some fairly important money," Lear said, dismissing the subject.

In the shop outside the door, his people carried forward toward the more significant fortune. Now that they seemed at last to have found true north in the search for a modern steam engine, Lear had loosened the reins. "I want you to make decisions," he told his men. "Don't hold up on something just because I'm not here."

Senior designer Paul Studer, a big, rugged man from Pomona, California, was preparing to make more tests of the all-important coating material for the rotors. He had already tested the product under conditions far more stringent than it would ever meet in the screw. Studer applied the material, called Sermetal, to a piece of metal, then held the metal in a 700-degree steam jet traveling one thousand feet a second. This only appeared to make it stick even better. Moreover, it seemed to distribute itself about the surface as needed, according to the profile.

"It gives us the precision we don't get with machining," Studer summed up. "We feel it will do the job."

Red McDougall, grinning shyly, stood up to explain that he was looking for ways to make the boiler smaller still. For the bus, it was now down to 32 inches in diameter by 8 inches thick, described by Al Simonson as merely "the difference between the ridiculous and the excessive."

As the components of the screw were being honed to their final form, Bob Davids tentatively showed on his drawing board where the components might be placed within the car, guided by the amount of space the engineers said each needed. The screw, allowing more room for maneuver than other systems they had pursued, was making life easier for Davids. "The engineers sometimes wait several minutes before they start cussing me out instead of right away," he said wryly.

Handsome Bob Millar, who liked to drop in at the Mapes Hotel's Coach Room in the evening and exercise his lyric tenor voice with airs from light opera, was at his board working out how best to place the components from an engineering point of view. "This is the most promising thing we've had in two years," Bob said of the screw.

Nearby, Dick Kudlicki was filling in the details on Millar's larger canvas. A free-lance engineer, who had been with AiResearch in Phoenix, Arizona, when he learned of the Reno project "from a magazine the guys were passing around," he was pleased to be back on steam.

Al Simonson, the philosopher, measured the turning point from far back along the way. "It began," he said, "when we started getting honest with ourselves. That was a necessary condition— beginning with the firing of Wallis. We have gone forward ever since despite setbacks."

Simonson fashioned a cigarette of sorts, drizzling tobacco on the desk and floor. "It's now just a matter of plodding," he said. "The excitement begins when we get the rotors and start putting them together."

Hugh Carson agreed. "Up to now we've really been taking it easy, learning the feasibility of ideas," he said. "It's been research —no development. The push comes when you start engineering. That's also when the surprises come. The things you worry about don't materialize, and the things you never dreamed of go wrong."

Whatever the surprises might be, Ev Alford didn't think they would amount to much. "This is the one that makes the most technical sense," he said, striking a match to his pipe. "I think it's going to go all the way now."

At the end of May, California capitulated on the bus contract, agreeing to Lear's terms—$450,000 and execution on a "best effort" basis. The agreement was signed on May 28, just over a year from the state's initiation of the project. For bureaucracy and politics, it was business as usual while the environment perished.

For Lear it was good to have this out of the way as he flew to Los Angeles the next day to deliver the commencement address at the Art Center College of Design and to receive an honorary doctorate of science. "We climbed out at nine thousand feet a minute this morning," he said as he arrived at the school, grinning broadly, Bob Davids at his side.

Old honor grad Davids, Class of '67, described how Lear then put the ship on auto and went to work on his speech. Lear added more lines on the pad as he sat at the place of honor for a box lunch, finally completing the text perched solitarily on a stool at a long table in an empty classroom.

Facing his audience in the bright, hot sun, the self-made man told of always having been able to avoid doing what he didn't like to do—of quitting a paying job at seventeen for a non-paying job with the air mail service, causing his mother to doubt his sanity—of staying close to electricity ever since his interest was awakened by the *Titanic*'s wireless calls for help in 1912.

But that was another time. Getting by without a formal education was no longer realistic for anyone who wanted to earn a living, he counseled. "I speak as one who has tried it both with and without money. Believe me, it's better with money."

It took schooling, such as at Art Center.

The news that Lear once again was going forward with steam brought a new flurry of interest from the news media. "We'll drive the car up the White House steps," he told John Babcock of KABC-Radio in Los Angeles, discussing Washington's persisting inertia about what he was doing. "Maybe then we'll get their attention."

Lear believed again that steam power, giving off almost no pollution, was in fact the ultimate answer to the internal combustion engine after all, rather than the gas turbine. "When I didn't think so for a while," he told Babcock, "it was because we hadn't yet made the break-throughs in the components—the boiler, the feed water pump, the condenser—that now open the way."

Things were still falling into place in late June. "I'd almost guarantee we'll have the Polara running in October and the bus in December," Hugh Carson said when I stopped past his house before heading back to Los Angeles. "Better not stay away too long this time."

I drove out to River House. Lear and Moya were on the sun porch, seated on the wicker couch with the TV set pulled close before them. The program ended and Lear twirled the dial.

"Turn it off," Moya said.

Lear turned it down.

"Turn it off—all the way off," she commanded.

Obeying, Lear drifted off to sleep, lulled by the river and the somnolence of a summer Sunday afternoon. Old Lear man Mel Beener, at the house to make a stereo installation in the hi-fi set, appeared in the door from the living room and motioned to Moya. She left the porch and I followed shortly, leaving Lear to his nap and to salvage what he could of the restful weekend he had planned before discovering that he had to be in Washington in the morning.

In the story books this might have been a good place to end it. The goal he had sought seemed to be in his grasp. The biblical lines were his to say: "I have fought a good fight, I have finished my course, I have kept the faith." Tina was disciplining herself to master a Mozart concerto during the summer, Moya said proudly, shutting herself away with a piano in a small trailer parked next door to teacher Gunnar Johansen at Gualala, California. David had been accepted by the California Institute of the Arts at Valencia. Suddenly, all was well with the world.

There was a commotion on the porch and Lear came bursting into the room, waving his arms. The sleep had charged his batteries to the full. "Come on! Come on!" he said excitedly. "We're going to see *Patton!*" The picture was playing on South Virginia Street.

"Settle down," Moya said soothingly, taking hold of his arms but without effect. "You settle down."

"Follow us," Lear directed as we reached the cars, parked nose-in against the stone abutment edging the yard. I trailed them up the drive and onto the freeway. When my speedometer read 85, I rescheduled *Patton* for another day. There wouldn't have been time to see it all anyway before plane time.

As the days passed, the bright promise of the screw began to dim. The machine which had looked so simple, with only one moving part, became more and more complicated and less and less efficient. Instead of having only one set of rotors, obviating the need for timing gears, it had three, in series. The tally of pieces ended up:

six rotors, six timing gears, thirteen reduction gears, eighteen sets of ball bearings, three high pressure casings, three connecting shafts, a high pressure lubrication system, and a water cooling system for the housing. And the efficiency was only 13 per cent. The internal combustion engine claims 19, half again as much.

This cheerless development, however, was offset by something else which had been happening in parallel with the screw project. This began when the mail brought copies of the patent drawings on a "low volumetric flow steam turbine" from its inventor, Jerry D. Griffith, late of the nuclear project at Fort Belvoir which ran out of money.

The turbine wasn't much but then came a letter from Representative Gerald Ford of Michigan, containing, besides a second set of drawings, a paper on the turbine written by Kenneth E. Nichols of Barber-Nichols, consulting engineers of Denver, Colorado, who had been project engineer on the Griffith turbine.

Lear phoned Denver and talked to Robert E. Barber, Nichols' partner. He told of the problems they had had with steam turbines, using water as the circulating fluid.

"Why don't you go to organic?" Barber asked.

"We have, but it blows up." The first Learium was both flammable and toxic.

"Nonsense! We've been working with it for years."

"Can you build an organic turbine?" Lear asked. "If you can, I'll give you a contract."

"Of course! That's how we make our living." Can a blacksmith shoe horses?

"Why don't you come and see us?"

At ten o'clock Saturday night, two days later, Hugh Carson picked up Barber at the Reno airport and drove him to River House, where he impressed Lear and Carson with his knowledge of turbines. The talk went on until three Sunday morning. After a few hours' sleep, it was resumed at the plant with other Lear men on hand, called from their homes. "Mr. Lear very enthusiastic," Carson wrote in his log.

Barber wanted a two-week contract to pinpoint the particular fluid best for this application, but Lear and Carson already had a family of fluids picked out, any one of which would work fine. Barber, along with a go-ahead to design the turbine, took a sample of Learium back to Denver for tests. He reported back by phone the next day. "I'll be goddamned!" he said. The Learium sample was exactly on the mark.

Lear had hoped to get appropriate new equipment in which to install the turbine from General Motors. He had written to GM president Cole after the California bus contract came in, taking Cole up on an earlier suggestion that GM might supply him a bus. (Flxible had taken theirs back.)

"I would like nothing better than to co-operate with you on this," Lear wrote to Cole. He cannily added the thought that he didn't "think it would do General Motors any harm in the realm of public relations to have the world at large know that you are assisting in our effort."

Lear continued, "As a matter of fact, don't you think it would be one of the smartest and lowest-cost public relations moves that your corporation could make, as it would demonstrate the substance of your interest in aiding in the development of a fundamentally low-emission propulsion system?"

The state of California, he wrote Cole, offered him a beat-up old bus with four hundred thousand miles on it, "but I think this system is far too modern and, I feel, too good to put into a junk bus. This situation led me to recall your suggestion of the past to use a General Motors bus. If you believe there would be any advantage to you . . . in cooperating with us . . . we would be only too happy to work with you."

There had been no reply to this overture.

Then, at San Francisco's annual Bohemian Grove outing Cole kidded Lear in a speech pushing General Motors, breeching the rule against "weaving" at the Grove. In his contrition, Cole gave Lear a brand-new bus, a 1971 Chevrolet Monte Carlo, and "anything else you want."

Hosting a dinner party at the Beverly Wilshire Hotel in Beverly Hills after the Grove festivities, Lear gave me an actual-size print of the turbine, contained on a sheet of 8-by-11 typing paper with room to spare. "It should be good for three hundred thousand miles," he said in high spirits. "It cost us $7 million to find it, but I'll guarantee you we have it now."

Events were quickening—it was time I made a new trip to Reno.

Buzz Nanney was in a philosophical mood as, following lunch at the Holiday with Norman Biltz and John Heizer, we drove to his house to pick up a birthday cake for Ed Lenheim baked by Ursula. Buzz spoke of the "perimeter of design"—how you never know how wide it is when you set out to find something new, as you don't know where the walls are in a dark room. He remarked on the discipline it took to admit error and change course, as Lear had done so many times in the search for a new engine.

At the plant, Joe Walsh was being coolly patient about this latest change of course. "The bloom is off the rose," he admitted of the screw, but its development would be carried forward up through tests, collaterally with work on the turbine, then a choice would be made between the two. "That's what I choose to believe," he said, with humor in his pale blue eyes. "It's known as the Walsh theory. After fifteen starts I'd like to see something finished."

In the design department, surrounded by sketches, Bob Davids was busily putting the final strokes to the lines of an ultra-modern bus for the Los Angeles Rapid Transit District. With only three weeks to meet the deadline for the bid, he had had to work fast. "General Motors would have had a hundred people working on it," he said, referring to his alma mater.

He was amused that while the RTD clients had said they wanted a bus "with innovative features which add to the vehicle's comfort, attractiveness, and social acceptance," they soon betrayed in their specifications that their hearts weren't really in it. As they warmed to the particulars, they even spelled out the trade names of the parts and components they wanted used, helpfully listing the addresses of the makers.

The engine should be a "V-8 gasoline type." A Chrysler 413 would be fine. The windows were to be the familiar "sliding type," and the doors "slide-glide." For the radio antenna, acceptable standards were represented by Antenna Specialties of Cleveland; floor covering by RCA, grab rails by Elion National, varnish by Pontiac. American Number 6432 would do it for the passenger seats, National 70-1 for the driver's seat, and Exide for the battery. Not much here of the stuff of Columbus.

Lear struck down these barriers to a new world by declaring to his RTD clients that he would bid only on the basis of the first page, where they were still on "innovative." Then he told Bob Davids in broad outline what he wanted, and let him go ahead on his own. The result was an airy, graceful coach for eighteen with large fixed windows and a one-foot step, as different from the cumbersome behemoths of today as the Lear Jet from the World War I Jenny.

For sure, it would *not* have a Chrysler engine—or any other kind of internal combustion power plant.

Bob Barber arrived from Denver at 10 P.M. Hugh Carson met him at the airport and brought him to his home, where Bea and I waited. A small, lean young man with shrewd blue eyes, Barber fully shared Lear's enthusiasm for the turbine engine. "This is a winner," he said. What made it so was the fluid. "The Rankine cycle is old," Barber reminded us. "What's new are fluids of molecular weights heavier than water. These open the door to new applications."

During breakfast at the Mapes next morning, Barber had more to say about the turbine-power system. It would take up the same room overall as the internal combustion engine, but weigh only half as much. While it operated for about the same, it would cost less to build—and go almost indefinitely without maintenance, the wheel being the only part that moved. It should be good for five hundred thousand miles.

In Lear's office soon after, with Hugh Carson and Ev Alford on hand, there was action, as Barber had put it, "to see that our pieces fit their pieces—make sure our turbine mates with Lear's gearbox, and so forth." This was the interfacing often heard about in the Lear shop.

Lear found time to glance at a paper to be delivered by one of the panelists in a discussion of steam power for automobiles before the American Society of Automotive Engineers, meeting in Ontario, California, in which he was slated to participate. "Ignorance places no limitation on verbosity" was his smiling comment.

As the meeting ended near noon, Lear riveted Ev Alford with an Ancient Mariner's glittering eye. "I don't want this running in November," he said. "I want it running thirty days from now!" He brought his fist down on the table.

"Yes, sir," Ev replied, chomping his chewing gum.

The SAE meeting at Ontario, presided over by Arthur Underwood, lately retired after forty-one years as head of General

Motors' research laboratory, had much the atmosphere of an old-timer's picnic, devoted less to steam's future (if any) than to its past. There was little sign anyone had discovered the space age. Lear was the fellow from out of town who didn't quite belong—a brash interloper who still didn't know the facts of life.

"Bill Lear is a piker," Underwood said as he started the meeting. "I spent a half billion to put the internal combustion engine out of business," he went on, leaving the audience to make the distinction between spending corporation money and one's own, as Lear had done.

William Besler, who as builder of one of the two steam cars General Motors showed to President Nixon's cabinet at Newport Beach the year before, accounted for part of the figure Underwood referred to, waspishly began by saying, "I'll sue for slander the next guy who says I sold out to Detroit." With a glance at Lear, he added, "It seems to be something to tell how much money you've spent."

He had been forty years in steam, Besler said, and he fondly reminisced about the old steamers. "I just made one for General Motors," he observed, identifying the car he had built as a "Doble." "They told me to," he said, adding that there was no reason not to. "There is nothing better than that."

Besler ended by calling up Warren Doble, brother of the late Abner, from the audience. "He taught me all I know," Besler said, eulogizing Doble as the elder statesman of steam. As Doble reached the platform, a tousled-haired ancient of oddly rustic aspect, Underwood said deferentially, "I won't set the clock for him."

Plainly, for Doble the clock had stopped some time ago. "I can very clearly remember the 1906 Stanley that we had," he began in a reedy voice, conjuring lavender and old lace. All the good belonged to the past. Why, in 1900 the Germans had steam engines that were more efficient than anything built since. "There might be some hope in looking back on their work," he suggested cautiously. On the whole, however, he was pessimistic. "I gave up steam back in 1935 as a bad job."

Doble was puzzled, therefore, by the present goings-on. "I've seen so many strange predictions about steam," he said doubtfully. "Mr. Lear talks about a reduction gear for a turbine going 45,000 rpm. He doesn't tell us how he's going to do it." He shook his head. "I'd like to hear more about that."

He wasn't sure about the need for steam anyhow. The audience laughed appreciatively at his proposal that motorists use Scuba gear against smog. "If it's good enough one hundred feet down in the sea, it's good enough for the Santa Ana Freeway."

General Motors agreed that steam was no use, flatly saying so in a paper delivered at Thursday's SAE session by Paul Vickers of GM R & D Division. It had learned the truth from the two steamers it had built, one through Besler, the other in its own shop (actually conversions of a Chevrolet and Pontiac) and shown at Newport—though Vickers insisted, "Our goal was to build the best steam engine possible."

What they got, Vickers read, was an engine far worse than what they now had. The oxides of nitrogen pouring from it exceeded the government's standards for 1975 and were several times the level wanted for 1980 by the Department of Health, Education and Welfare. The same was true of hydrocarbon emissions from the engine. It used up to three times as much fuel as its IC counterpart. It performed poorly. It was complicated, unreliable, and hard to repair.

The paper concluded, "Since the vapor cycle engine offers no exhaust emission advantage over a spark ignition engine with advanced emission control systems, it must be judged on its other characteristics. The higher costs of construction, increased maintenance, poor performance, and lack of fuel economy make it an unattractive alternative to the properly controlled spark ignition engine."

In short, the steam engine not only had no advantages over the internal combustion engine; it fell several miles short of it all around. So why bother with it?

The verdict by the world's largest builder of automobiles that there was no hope for steam gave Lear no pause. He had Bob Davids make up a model of the turbine. Carrying the mock-up in a wig box lined with red satin, he flew to Los Angeles, and after conferring with engineers at the AiResearch Manufacturing Company about making the wheels, he sped to the Civic Center and told the public about his turbine by way of a televised press conference at the offices of Warren Dorn, chairman of the Los Angeles County Board of Supervisors.

With Dorn at his side in a county helicopter, he then flew to the NBC studios in Burbank to repeat the news of the new engine in a TV interview with Art Linkletter. The audience applauded as he held up the turbine for all to see. Shaped like a large spinning top, it suggested Aladdin's lamp. Perhaps it would be as fabulous.

Lear's studio reception was rather better than that from Herb Klein, President Nixon's press secretary, entering the building as Lear and Dorn left. Klein squinted silently at the model. "It looks good," he ventured finally. "It looks good." He turned and walked on.

Back in downtown Los Angeles, after giving an interview to Ted Thackrey of the Los Angeles *Times,* from Dorn's office Lear phoned Moya at River House, five hundred miles north. It was six o'clock. "We'll be back up there at seven-fifteen," he said.

"If we were to tell people what we've done today," he said as we crossed Temple Street toward the chopper pad in the parking lot beyond, "they wouldn't believe it."

The blades were already swinging in windy hubbub as we approached. Lear walked briskly aboard. He closed the door, waved jauntily, and the machine went cartwheeling off into the fever-red blob that marked the setting sun through 14,000 tons of poison, the daily dumpage on L. A. County, delivering him to his waiting jet at Flying Tigers.

By early September, with the design of the crucial wheel and other parts of the turbine done and the fabrication proceeding, Lear got an idea for simplifying the system. The plan had been to use two turbines, one to drive the wheels of the car, the other to supply the auxiliary power requirements—for the brakes, steering, and so forth. This was necessary because when the car stopped, so did the main turbine. Only the pilot light was still going.

But two turbines oppressed Lear. He wanted to eliminate the second and find a way to make the main turbine do it all.

Hugh Carson was out of reach, he and Bea having slipped off in the family Bronco to indulge in their favorite weekend sport of exploring ghost towns. His frustration at trying to find Carson ended when Hugh made the tactical error of checking in at the

end of the day from Merced, over in California; he and Bea
had run into a snow storm in the high Nevada country. "That's
only 260 miles from here," Lear observed, thinking in terms of
jet distances. "Drop in on your way by in the morning."

Driving most of the night, the Carsons slid down the road out
of the mountains past River House at eight-thirty Sunday morning—too early, they thought, to stop. They drove on home and,
after a badly needed forty winks or so, Hugh phoned Lear. "Where
have you been?" Lear demanded. "I was up swimming at
seven-thirty."

They met at the plant and by day's end they had the problem
of the second turbine under control. The answer was to use a
torque converter, which is a kind of clutch. With this, the main
turbine could be disengaged from the wheels, allowing it to idle
and thereby do the work of the second turbine. Using a torque
converter, Carson said, having two turbines was "like wearing
both a belt and suspenders," in some quarters known as the def-
inition of pessimism. A crew was rounded up for Labor Day,
including Ken Rudolph and Ev Alford, and the tracks laid down
by Lear and Carson on Sunday were pounded into place.

To save time, it was decided to go ahead with the two
turbines for the Monte Carlo, as planned, reserving the advancement of a single turbine for the Hornet. The bus would have
two, in any event. "In heavy applications there will probably
always be two," Carson said.

Hurry was the watchword. At midafternoon Wednesday, Lear
called "everybody that's got anything to do with this" into his
office for a long-distance interfacing session with Bob Barber and
Nichols in Denver. "I got all my gang here to talk to you," Lear
said into the talk box on his desk, getting things under way. The
positioning of the various components, as well as sizes and re-
lationships, were carefully gone over again, each man in turn
sitting forward toward the box as the area of his concern came up.

The talk turned to the problem of using the engine as a
brake. "I'll come up with something in a couple of weeks," Barber
said.

"Naw, come up with it in a couple of days," Lear replied
disappointedly. He added, "You know, when Christmas comes
and I don't have my toy to play with, I'm going to be hard
to get along with."

"Harder," McDougall muttered, probably a little louder than he intended. There was an explosion of laughter, and the meeting ended.

Late in the afternoon Lear's nose began to bleed. Hugh Carson, called in from his own office, carried out a red-filled vessel. When he returned, he suggested that Lear lie on the couch. Lear gave him an argument. "Mr. Lear," Carson repeated with an uncustomary tone of command, "will you lie down, please!"

Lear lay down. The bleeding slowed and finally stopped. The interval of rest apparently was salutary in another way. Getting up, he sat at the table and sketched a place to put the air conditioner in the steam system. This had troubled him.

From the windows the mountains lay in purple twilight when Lear put on his coat to call it a day. "Let's take one more look around," he said, turning back at the door. He led the way to the mock-up of the bus Bob Davids had sketched for the Los Angeles Rapid Transit people, having pointed out that a full-scale model was "much better than pictures" to convey what the bus was like. With the diligent help of Paul Morris and Leif Chapman, majors in transportation design at Los Angeles' Art Center School, Davids had already made it an object of pride to Lear, who frequently came and sat in it during the day with visitors, somberly enjoining them not to overlook the fare box, pencil-marked "15 cents," as they came aboard. Lear sat in the make-believe bus again now. Then he went home.

The nose bleed disquieted Moya, with memories of a time before. She made an appointment with Dr. Barton in Beverly Hills. "He feels he's running out of time," she said as we hurtled south, as usual traveling in the stratosphere. It wasn't easy to hold him down and see that he got proper rest. "You have to put a knee on his chest and close off the telephones," she said.

Lear made up for poor sleep with cat naps during the day—as he was napping now, in the captain's seat. His head hung low on his chest. Moya moved forward and touched him on the shoulder. The head came up and he was the jet pilot back on the job.

Waiting at Flying Tigers was an old friend, actor George Mann, a big, affectionate bear of a man who had known both Lear and Moya since his days in the cast of *Hellzapoppin'*. Someone —he left it a mystery—had phoned him that the Lears were coming and would need transportation. (David had driven the Los Angeles Cadillac to Reno.)

The news at the doctor's was good: blood pressure just right, heart strong, general health sound. Nothing wrong with the nose except for a susceptibility to the effects of dry air. Doctor Barton had one bit of advice: Hold the alcohol down to six ounces a day. Since this was more than he was getting now, it was jocularly noted as we rode away that he would have to step up his intake to comply with the doctor's orders.

"We're on the home stretch," Hugh Carson assured soon after I arrived for a final look. "We're out of the blue sky. You know what blue sky jobs are? Those are engineering jobs that call for work in areas that aren't known. We've been out of there a long, long time."

Ken Rudolph hoped to have the complete turbine and gear case in hand by November 1, ready to put on the dynamometer and test. But, as a veteran of Bob McCulloch's steam effort in Los Angeles, Ken was keeping his sights low. "The first time we put that thing in a car, we're not going to drive it," he said. "The first time we put it in, we are going to find that somebody didn't wire the car right and the ignition key doesn't work— like what happened at McCulloch."

He uncovered a couple of pictures on his desk. In the first the driver was being handed the key to the car. In the next, outside the door, the car was being swarmed over by nonplused mechanics, trying to find why it wouldn't start. "Somebody hooked up the wires wrong," Rudy said. "It's going to be some little, tiny, idiotic, foolish thing like that that makes everybody feel foolish—like forgetting to put fuel in the tank or forgetting to connect the fuel line."

To Ken it would not be excessive if the car didn't run the first ten times. "After all," he said. "we're doing something there are no textbooks for. Detroit has had seventy years of development, and we're going to try to do it in two! Put it another way: We're going to build the Model-T, then the Model-A, and then the V-8—all in a couple of years. I say if it'll go around the block and I can drive it back into the building, it'll be a success."

Meanwhile, Lear looked ahead to the next step: to get the engine produced. This was beyond the resources of any one man. He wrote to his friend Ed Cole at General Motors.

Dear Ed: October 8, 1970

THANK YOU FOR THE BUS!

THE MONTE CARLO!!!!!

AND PARTICULARLY THE HELP FROM THE HARRISON DIVISION.

Ed, I would like to take this opportunity to suggest that General Motors and Lear Motors join forces to work closer together on a development program for a low emission steam system for the automobile. I am convinced that making a low emission steam powered prototype that will meet 1990 HEW standards is now feasible, but the problem of production requires our joint participation.

I have come to you first because of your obvious faith in what we're doing which is evident in your generous support and because of our fine past relationship.

Our program here is so encouraging that I believe we will produce a prototype system by year end which would be better on every count than an internal combustion engine *with* clean-air devices added.

Now is the time for us both to begin discussions on a joint development program to take us to the production stages of such a propulsion system.

I make this proposition to you with the greatest seriousness. A low emission steam program in which General Motors is participating would obviously be one where the benefits could more quickly be made available to the general public. Please let me hear from you as soon as possible, so that if you are interested, detailed discussions can take place without delay at your convenience.

                                        Respectfully your friend,

                                        Bill Lear

It was time, also, to explore abroad—for markets and for sub-contractors. Lear flew to Santa Ana, California, and brought back three men from Japan's Kawasaki Heavy Industries, Limited: Tim O'Brien and Roy Warnock of Kawasaki's Santa Ana office, and Fumihiko Kato, manager of Kawasaki's motor cycle division, at Akashi, who was on his first visit to the United States. Lear showed them through the plant, the tour including a sit-in at Bob David's bus mock-up, then took them to River House for the steaks he had ordered by radio from the Silver State Meat Company as he flew in.

The conversation flowed until ten-thirty, ending when Lear rose from the table. Finding the guest house filled, he arranged accommodations for his guests at Harrah's. Gunnar Christensen drove them to Reno.

It had been a full day: More than one thousand miles of flying, an appointment with Pacific Airmotive in Burbank, where he let Moya off to visit Tina at the California Institute of the Arts; and three appointments in Orange County, with Sam Auld, Martin Aviation, and the Stevens Boat Company, on his way back stopping at Burbank to retrieve Moya, several hours' work at the plant and, finally, hosting dinner.

O'Brien, market research manager for Kawasaki, told next morning of having spent a rough night, too excited by the potentials of Lear's turbine to sleep. "My mind kept going off in all directions, thinking about the things we could do," he said.

While O'Brien and Lear picked up where they left off at the dinner table the night before, Larry Orr gave a technical briefing to Kato and Warnock in the conference room, blueprints covering the table. Kato-san, speaking cautious English and only occasionally venturing a question, made frequent entries in a small notebook.

Sunday was another day. Lear and Carson, palavering in Hugh's office, sketching, arguing, and having repeated recourse to Hugh's new desk computer, hit on a way to cut the condenser in half while having it do the same work. Since the condenser, because of the room it takes up, traditionally has been the main limitation on horsepower in steam, this meant they had suddenly lifted the barrier to steam for all uses.

"This is going to be a marvelous break-through," Lear said as they broke for lunch. "If somebody offered me $10 million for the patent on it right now, I wouldn't take it."

For a moment toward the end of the day, it looked as if

divine approbation might have been signaled. In Hugh's doorway appeared an unkempt figure in shoulder-length hair, beard, and bare feet, staring silently into the room. He had wandered in through the open door, unseen by the guard. He was "interested in gliders and power plants," he explained as he was ushered out.

"I thought, 'Jesus is back!'" Lear said afterward.

General Motors President Ed Cole's reply to Lear's letter proposing they join forces was to come and see him. Cole arrived with his wife and Vice-President Paul F. Chenea of GM's research laboratories aboard a company jet Sunday night, October 25.

Hugh Carson filled me in by phone. After a social evening, Moya took Mrs. Cole to see Virginia City Monday and the men got down to business. "Mr. Cole was like a boy with a new toy," Carson said. "He was notably enthusiastic."

The upshot of the Cole visit was that he appointed Don Manning, assistant chief engineer of GM's Truck and Coach Division, to serve as liaison with Lear, to watch closely and lend a hand during construction of the prototype steam system. There were no problems. "The parts for the turbine are coming in—the wheel, gears, shafts," Carson said. "It'll all be in by next week. Our cut-off date for having the turbine together is November 3.

"I'll give you a call. . . ."

17: THERE SHE GOES

"Let's do it!" Ev Alford called out.

The crew, wearing yellow plastic aprons over white smocks, headsets clamped to their ears, put on neoprene chemical masks which, extending well below their chins, gave them a grasshopper look.

In the control booth, speaking into a face mike, Lee Blodgett read through a check list, then threw a switch. Lights came on. The laboratory filled with uproar. There was a whine, quickly rising to a screech.

"There she goes!" someone shouted as the turbine cut in.

The new power system which could put the internal combustion engine out of business was running for the first time. As the speed mounted, the voice of the turbine settled into a smooth, steady hum, full of authority and promise.

Pleasing as it sounded, the crew had a good idea this was the way it would go. They had already run the auxiliary turbine a number of times, beginning eleven days earlier. They celebrated that occasion by drinking up the whole magnum of scotch brought in to displace the small, one-slug bottles kept on hand as antidote for the accidental ingestion of Learium. Then, in the small hours, they had boldly telephoned Lear at his home, prefacing the good news by saying, "Goddammit, you call *us* in the middle of the night!"

They knew Lear would want to know—as today during further runs of the auxiliary turbine and preparations to fire up the main turbine that night, he had kept in close touch from New York. "He keeps calling every fifteen minutes," said Dorothy Olson, his secretary.

"Jesus Christ, I wish he'd come home!" exclaimed Ev Alford as he rushed from the lab to take Lear's latest call, shedding his mask as he went.

In his final contact of the day, told of the snowstorm raging in Reno, Lear replied facetiously, "Good! Then you won't be able to get home tonight and you can get a lot of work done."

This led to banter as the work went on. "You'd yell too if you were spending ten thousand dollars a day of your own money," Alford reminded the others. "That's what it costs to keep the doors open, whether anything is accomplished or not."

Bill Moore, heavy-lidded from lack of sleep, offered to share his "dinner" of a candy bar with Alford. "Thanks, I had mine," Ev answered.

Lee Blodgett methodically set up a camera to monitor the test gauges, using a spray gun with blue paint to mark the three points on the floor where the tripod would stand.

"They put more man hours on that little operation than a recorder would have cost," Paul Studer observed critically.

Ken Rudolph suggested they suspend Byron Hanchett and the camera from the ceiling with a hoist, letting him down each time they wanted a picture taken.

At nine-thirty, with the clock racing on and many things yet to be done before the test could begin, somebody appealed to Alford, "Ev, can you postpone tomorrow a couple of hours?"

There was debate whether to call Lear when the test was over. "We'd get chewed out," it was observed.

"Hell, we'll get chewed out anyway!" the others retorted, laughing.

"It seems like R and D work is always done late at night," Rudy mused, implying that the boss would understand.

Then came Alford's "Let's do it!" and the turbine ran. Suddenly, the tumult died and all was quiet again.

"What'd you do that for?" Ev demanded of Red McDougall.

"I thought you said shut down," Red replied, looking more startled than usual.

At eleven-thirty came another halt, this one because pressure in the flow lines from the Learium tank had fallen off. The crew conferred briefly, accentuating the Martian look of the scene as they bobbed about in their masks, lifting the lower portion for conversation. There were more stops.

At twelve minutes past midnight the test was ended. "Pretty good," said Lee Blodgett, smiling, his voice hoarse, as he left the control room.

Total running time was estimated at a half hour and the turbine had reached its intended operating speed of 46,000 revolutions a minute. "Not a howling success," Rudy remarked as Ev scribbled a telegram to Lear in New York after a short post-mortem in Ev's office, "but more a barking success." Reflecting a moment, Rudy added cheerfully, "But it was a long way from the bad days when *every*thing went wrong."

In the tingling, star-lit winter night outside, snow was scraped from windshields and the ice beneath slowly melted by starting engines and getting defrosters going. Bob Davids had the additional problem of one of his newly mounted snow tires rubbing against the muffler. Patiently he set about jacking up the car and taking off the wheel so he could make adjustments.

Now that they had moved from the drawing board to the test chamber, trying out actual hardware, they were soon knee-deep in the workings of Murphy's law, that rule of perversity which assures that whatever can go wrong will go wrong. At the next run of the turbine, two days after the first, the fluid leaked past the turbine and spilled into the exhaust, portending far worse things such as bearing failure. Mysteriously, a deep groove was found to have been worn in the face of the metal seal all around, apparently by an abrasive.

Told of the problem when he phoned from Washington, where he was seeing Nixon and members of the Environmental Protection Agency, the latest bureaucratic growth dedicated to environmental salvation, Lear seemed more puzzled than upset as his voice came over the talk box; perhaps because he was too weary to be upset, he sounded tired. Making some suggestions, he appealed wistfully to his crew as the conference ended, "Give me some kind of encouraging telegram tonight, will you?"

"We'll do that if you'll pray for us," Ev Alford replied.

"I'll do that," Lear said quietly.

Next, the Learium ate through the boiler. The temporary expedient of nickel-plating the inside of the boiler tubing came to nothing when the plating failed to go on evenly. At another stage, a different kind of fluid in use turned the system into a miniature plastics factory, manufacturing Teflon and sand, and badly fouling up the system. When water was added to the fluid to make up a deficiency, the combination devoured the aluminum of the regenerator.

These troubles with Learium were on Joe Walsh's mind as preparations were under way for another test run of the screw expander, thought by some to have possible applications in heavy, off-the-road machinery. Walsh waggishly listed the advantages of "Walshium" or water (somebody suggested "Walsh-Ade"), which would be used as the working fluid in the screw. "You can drink it, make tea out of it, or swim in it," Walsh said.

There was difficulty with the fuel vaporizer, which was prone to burn out. The happy answer, found by Hugh Carson, was to change from a machined device costing $600, to a spiral coil of tubing that cost 30 cents and was ten times more effective. The solutions were seldom so congenial.

One of the more stubborn problems was the pump, which had the critical function of keeping the fluid whirling on its way around the cycle. Max Winkler's pump, fine for water, did less well with Learium, which corroded the seals. This intrigued Dr. Giovanni Savonuzzi, courtly director of research and development for Fiat in Italy, who toured the plant with Lear on a Sunday after breakfasting at River House, following a flight from San Francisco.

Pausing at the bench where Max Winkler and Lyn Davis were working with the pump, Savonuzzi picked up one of the damaged seal diaphragms and silently examined it. "You know," he said at length, "I would like to work on that."

Savonuzzi's parting words as he left the plant were heartening. "Congratulations!" he said to Lear. "I have far fewer doubts now than before I came. This is the most serious approach I have seen." He shook Lear's hand. "You will do it!" he said firmly. "You will do it!"

The frustrations of the pump hung on. Each new sealing material sooner or later showed itself no better than the last. Different types of pumps, needing no seals, proved to have shortcomings of their own. Oil mixed in the fluid for lubrication only brought new complications such as fouling of the system and lowering the effectiveness of the condenser.

The solution came, not by changing the seals or the pump, but by changing the fluid. This resulted when Douglas Heinz of the Dow Chemical Company, who had been keeping an eye on this vital aspect of Lear's steam project, set up a meeting between Lear and his own people at the home plant in Midland, Michigan. Lear spoke for an hour, defining the problem. In the question period that followed to pin down the target, a Dow man ventured that a stock item of the company, an ordinary chemical solution costing about $1.40 a gallon, basically contained the properties needed, requiring only minor chemical changes and the addition of water.

Heinz ordered a fifty-four-gallon drum of the fluid shipped to Reno from Dow's plant at Pittsburg, California, for trial. Sealing troubles with the pump promptly ended. So did corrosion of the boiler. Also, the new fluid was non-toxic and non-flammable, and it was stable, unlike the fluid which had turned into Teflon and sand. Finally, it was well suited to the Rankine cycle.

"It looks like the final answer to our fluid problems," Lear said.

There was one trade-off for the new fluid. Its molecular weight was only 34, as compared to 80 for the fluid it displaced. This meant that the turbine would have to be run at 60,000 rpm instead of 46,000, and that there would have to be some redesigning of the nozzles admitting the vapor to the blades—much as the mariner trims his sails to suit the wind.

Devising controls for the new engine remained a lingering challenge. The system must be foolproof, with built-in, automatic protections, Lear insisted. The car must be as simple to operate as today's car, the driver needing only to turn a key to start, know where the throttle and brake are, and how to steer. "Everything works fine by itself," Pete Lewis remarked one day. "The problem is to get them to work together."

Nor was it a small thing to get the entire system packed under the hood. In the old steam cars the boiler took up all the room in front, the engine going in the back. There would be none of this dispersal in the Lear car. This responsibility fell to Bob Millar, who supervised construction of the Monte Cart, a small angle iron truck on casters named for the waiting Monte Carlo which was to be first to receive the new power system. The Monte Cart afforded an opportunity to work out the positioning of the components in advance and to test them in the relationship they would occupy in the car.

For a time the engine seemed to take unkindly to this intimate association of its parts on the Monte Cart. "The first couple of days nothing went right," Hugh Carson said, flipping on his Panasonic recorder and filling the office with what could have been the playback of a riot. Out of the melange of sound came shouts, curses, and words of disgust. There were many start-ups, followed by quick shutdowns. Several times the lab was evacuated as leaking fluid threatened a cyanide gas attack. But as the days passed the hullabaloo subsided and little by little all became quieter and smoother. The turbine was settling down to the future.

"It does nothing but run," Hugh Carson said enthusiastically when the turbine had logged thirty hours. "Its acceleration and horsepower capability are shocking. It goes almost instantly to its maximum power—from zero to 10,000 revolutions a minute in one to two seconds, and to 40,000 in another half second." He explained that efficiency improved as the speed went up, opposite to the nature of the internal combustion engine.

Something else about the turbine differed from the IC engine as well: It was *clean*. With the fire contained in the combustor at the center of the boiler, out in the open, rather than taking place as a series of rapid explosions in the confines of a cylinder, with time for only part of the fuel to be burned, emissions came to nearly nothing.

"Unburned hydrocarbons, a bare trace," the measurement read. "Carbon monoxide, essentially zero. Oxides of nitrogen, less than .07 grams per mile," a slight fraction of the mark allowed under federal standards for the next several years. Visitors from the Kawasaki and Mitsubishi automobile works in Japan, home of "Yokohama asthma," the smog disease, were deeply impressed by this showing from Lear's engine.

In mid-January, in a snowstorm that hid the hangar from the office, Lear took off for New York to appear on Hugh Downs's "Today Show," taking along the turbine and a bottle of compressed air to run it with. Over the show's TV network, millions saw the little wheel spin and heard Lear tell what it could do. More would hear about the turbine through a press conference at the Overseas Press Club of America afterward, attended by newsmen from throughout the world. With men walking on the moon, few things any longer seemed to fire the mass imagination quite so much as the thought of a new kind of automobile engine—one that ran on "steam," one which was clean.

On the banks of the Potomac, however it was as if word of

Bill Lear's existence hadn't yet penetrated. Not long before, the Department of Transportation had issued a request for proposal (RFP) from fourteen firms to "design and develop a 'new look,' 15- to 25-passenger bus that will perform well in low speed stop-and-go urban driving, will accommodate present-day and developing propulsion systems and will be non-polluting. . . ."

Lear Motors Corporation of Reno, Nevada, which already had just such a bus mocked up, to say nothing of the engine to go with it, was not among the favored fourteen on the DOT's list.

The explanation could hardly be that the DOT didn't know what Lear had. Carlos Villarreal, chief of the DOT's Urban Mass Transportation Administration, had personally visited Lear's Reno facilities when the bus was in the planning stage and learned all about it as well as the engine. Lear had filled him in again, later, as they rode in a taxicab in San Diego, although Villarreal's fixed stare as Lear talked prompted Moya to observe to Lear afterward, "Do you realize he didn't hear a word you said!"

When Lear reminded Villarreal of this conversation in a later visit to Washington, Villarreal responded with a lecture on protocol. "That's no way to deal with a government administrator," Villarreal scolded, referring to the talk in the taxicab. "You write him a letter."

Lear now wrote the letter. "As you say, a letter puts things on the record and the events of my recent visit to Washington do need to be recorded," he opened.

Recalling his unavailing efforts to reach Villarreal and others of UMTA by phone, until he left a message saying he would take his case to the President if necessary, Lear wrote, "Let me now add that I will go further: I will go to the taxpayers of this country who are footing the bill for the boondoggling being sponsored by your department in what it alleges to be an honest effort to develop a low-pollution engine to displace the internal combustion engine. . . .

"You emphatically denied knowing anything about an RFP for mini-bus designs, as if it were perfectly reasonable for the UMTA administrator not to know about this. Then, when I confronted you with the published list which the RFP was being sent, asking why Lear Motors was not included, you found it expedient to drop the pose of ignorance and accept exposure for mendacity as the lesser embarrassment, tacitly admitting . . . that you knew about the list all along.

"The whole situation needs to be thoroughly looked into. As a citizen who has spent a fortune of his own money to do a job which the Government should be doing, since the issue is of critical concern to all, I am respectfully asking Secretary Volpe to do so forthwith."

At the California capital in Sacramento, nobody even knew about the DOT's list, published by the United States Department of Commerce in its *Commerce Business Daily*. Jeanne Woodrow, secretary to Mike Wenstrom, research analyst in the Assembly Office of Research, who was project director for the California bus program, was shocked. Speaking of the current project, in which Lear Motors had been rated the least likely to succeed, she exclaimed, "Wouldn't you think they'd wait until they see how that comes out?" She shook her head sadly. "This double-up stuff is why we don't have enough money."

Why was Bill Lear being left out? Bruce Samuels, in the office of John Francis Foran, until the 1970 election chairman of the Assembly Transportation Committee, had an answer. "Lear has not produced an engine," Samuels said. "The only people who have are the Williams Brothers." He looked up. "Do you know about the Williams Brothers?"

"Their engine, I'm told, is basically the old steam system," I replied, having in mind Hugh Carson's description of the Williams car as "a fit museum piece," made by their father in the 1930s.

Samuels bridled. "Just what do you mean, 'basically the old steam system'?" he demanded.

Under the circumstances it seemed more than passingly interesting that Samuels' card read "Consultant to Assembly Transportation Committee."

Lear's letter to Villarreal brought a phone call from him, in which he made a garrulous, ingratiating attempt to explain Lear Motors' omission from the list of fourteen firms solicited by UMTA to submit proposals for a new bus.

"Bill, I'm delighted you're coming to Washington," Villarreal began, his voice singing out over the talk box, in what may have been the high point of what followed for the next twenty minutes. "Well, Bill . . ." Villarreal kept saying. "Well, Bill, there are a lot of better things to do than work in the government." He was doing it out of patriotism, he indicated, ascribing the same motives to Lear. "We're doing it for our country," he said.

Near the end, Lear restated his intention to "put the giraffe outside the capital," paraphrasing the story of the farmer who, visiting the zoo and seeing a giraffe for the first time, said, "There ain't no such animal." Lear's car was the giraffe.

There was silence at Villarreal's end. "You mean a real giraffe or a stuffed giraffe," he asked, puzzled.

Lear explained.

"Oh, you're not talking about the animal!" Villarreal exclaimed as the lights came on.

The conversation ground to a close with Villarreal saying, "Bill, you're a great American. I love you because you're just like an old lovable teddy bear."

Whatever it may be worth to be called an old lovable teddy bear, worse lay ahead in Washington, at the hands of Robert A. Hemmes, assistant administrator for program demonstration at UMTA and a classmate of Villarreal's. Having listened to Lear tell of the millions he had spent in the search for a clean engine, Hemmes retorted harshly that Lear had no right to spend money for things that didn't work. Hemmes rendered this surprise advisory service of UMTA in tones which suggested that Lear had been using not his own money but the public's (the kind Hemmes and his 130-odd fellow bureaucrats use).

Shaken, Lear replied that while they had all sorts of fine engineering skills in his organization, clairvoyance was the one thing they were short of. He refrained from asking if next time they have a new idea in Reno, they might check it out with Hemmes before they put any money into it. Lear explained that although it was nice to be able to go directly to the thing that worked, for those ordinary mortals with no special gifts of prescience, it was generally necessary to feel one's way there, finding out and discarding what didn't work as one went. In short, you learned what worked by first learning what didn't. He quoted Henry Ford's remark that his greatest asset was his "junk pile," since it represented knowledge he had arrived at the hard way and could be sure of.

And from the junk pile they had amassed in Reno, Lear went on, they knew that there was no excuse to spend $4 million of the taxpayers' money to develop a small, clean bus for city driving, as UMTA proposed to do under its pitch to the fourteen firms to make proposals. To do so was sheer boondoggling. It could be done for $1 million, or possibly even for half that, thanks to the "mistakes" they had made in Reno.

"We can save the government a lot of money," Lear said. Neither this nor much else of what Lear told Hemmes could have been news to him. Son John Lear and new marketing director Ed Uhler, calling on Hemmes later, found the walls and ceiling of Hemmes' office festooned with Lear documents, ranging from newspaper clippings and letters to charts and diagrams, including a drawing Lear had made for Villarreal.

At one point in an hour-long diatribe against Lear, Hemmes banged the desk with his fist, saying, "And everything in this office is public property!"

"Really—including that tape you've been making?" asked John Lear, who had noticed the wire leading from under the papers Hemmes was shuffling to a recorder nearby.

Taken aback, Hemmes replied, "Well—I guess so." He promised his callers a copy of the tape. It had not arrived in Reno weeks later.

While the prophet seemed to be without honor on the Potomac, this was not so in Detroit. To the auto men, whatever their thoughts on the record, Lear was one to admire—and to give them disquiet—this man who walked alone, daring to do by himself what they in their collective might said couldn't be done.

At lunch in the General Motors restaurant, during a visit to see President Ed Cole, who reiterated his offer that Lear could have anything he needed, including an airplane to fly his car to Mesa, Arizona, for testing, Lear noticed as he entered that the dining room was packed. "What's the occasion?" he asked.

"They came to see you," replied Don Manning.

Lear was soon receiving handshakes and good-luck wishes from an encircling crowd at his table. "We're all for you," they assured him with feeling. When he rose to leave, all but a few abandoned their lunches and left with him.

As the turbine behaved better and better each day, like a bronco gradually submitting to its rider, Lear's faith in it hardened. "I think it may be the ultimate answer after all, instead of the gas turbine," he said.

He had just come from a medical check-up, the doctor finding him to be "suffering from a malady called good health," and he made straight for the combination conference room, kitchen and dining room, to stir the caldron which that day displaced hamburgers for lunch, taking over from Dorothy Olson. As he walked, Steamer, the black poodle, at his heels, he launched into a convincing imitation of W. C. Fields.

With the Sisyphean stone finally brought near the crest of the hill, there were more moments of levity. Holding court in his office one Sunday afternoon, Lear phoned broker Dave Callahan in Beverly Hills and for fifteen minutes, speaking with a thick accent, got away with the pose of an outraged commodities buyer named "Learsky" who had bought stock which went down instead of up.

"All right, Bill Lear," Callahan at last said sheepishly, "I get you."

There was the horseplay one sundown after Joe Walsh answered obliquely to a query from the chairman of the board. Lear, wearing a pistol in his belt, drew the gun and said, "I'll give you one minute to answer the question!"

Hugh Carson held up a hand. "Mr. Lear, for something as serious as this I think you ought to give him a minute and a half."

"Okay, I'll give him a minute and a half," Lear agreed.

Disappearing, Carson ran to Lear's office and returned with a gun for Walsh. "Now," Carson said, "this argument can proceed on an equal basis."

For Lear, as always, the rough times were the weekends. "The worst days of my life are the enforced holidays of Saturday and Sunday," he said as he hosted a chili party at River House on the final Sunday in March.

On this day, in addition to the burden of being idle, he was tired and disgusted, having just returned from Washington and a new encounter with the Urban Mass Transportation Administration. "They don't want answers," he said wearily, "only problems."

He brightened as he told how Saturday at the plant had been "one of our best days." He had invented something that did away with the small puff of smoke given off at the combustor at each start-up of the engine. It was not enough, he had stressed to his men, that the engine ran clean once started—it must start clean. The I-told-you-so crowd would be waiting to pounce like starved barracuda at the least imperfection.

As the testing on the Monte Cart continued, duplicate components were installed in the waiting Monte Carlo, so that, as Dave

Camomile said, "When the tests are done all they have to do in the car is turn it on."

The installation work followed a sort of two steps forward, one step backward progression as components in place were removed for further refinement according to last-minute findings on the test stand. The car must do more than merely run the first time it was tried, Lear said; it must perform as near to perfection as could be, the way the Lear Jet did. Nothing was to be omitted, including air conditioning.

The forward steps prevailing, the car had reached the stage where it looked as if it could be driven off any day, when Washington finally went too far in its treatment of the man from Reno. The Environmental Protection Agency named the Aerojet Nuclear Systems Company of Sacramento, California, as the winning bidder for the "design and development of an automobile propulsion system utilizing a Rankine Cycle Engine (Organic Working Fluid, Rotating Expander)."

This was Lear's engine.

Moreover, Aerojet's bid to build an engine already built was considerably higher than the joint bid of Lear Motors and Barber-Nichols, designers of the turbine. Aerojet bid $562,831, Lear and Barber-Nichols, $518,365.

Lear Motors, never contacted by the EPA to learn what progress it had made, got the word by undated form letter after the agency had denied for two weeks that a decision had been reached. Joe Walsh wrote to the EPA's contracting officer, Martin K. Trusty, asking for a debriefing. The agency replied by phone, asking to come to Reno to do the debriefing in person rather than by mail. It later canceled the debriefing altogether.

Again, the EPA gave the nod to Steam Engine Systems of Newton, Massachusetts, to build a steam car in the next year, the specs containing the provisos redolent of Stanley days that ways be found to keep the water from freezing and to get up steam fast. SES' bid was $570,000, Lear Motors', $485,406.

The SES case included the interesting sidebar circumstance that a director of the firm was Dr. David Ragone, chairman of the President's Ad Hoc Unconventional Vehicle Propulsion Panel, from the Office of Science and Technology, which had visited Lear's plant early in 1970, thoroughly informing itself on Lear's progress.

Richard Morse, president of SES, likewise had enjoyed special

THE INCREDIBLE STORY OF BILL LEAR

opportunities to gather proprietary information from private sources, having been chairman in 1967 of a committee formed under the Secretary of Commerce to examine "the technical and economic feasibility of present and future automotive power sources and to recommend an appropriate role for the Federal Government." The committee panel included Dr. David Ragone, as noted now a director of SES.

Fed up at last, Lear wrote an angry letter to President Nixon, key members of his Administration, all 533 members of the United States Congress not excluding resident Commissioner Jorge L. Cordova of Puerto Rico, and various private parties such as consumer advocate Ralph Nader and S. Lyn Sutcliffe, counsel to the Committee on Commerce—upward of six hundred all told.

"As you know," Lear began, "for over three years I have been developing a steam engine as a replacement for the air-fouling internal combustion engine. Despite many technical difficulties and disappointments, we are now at a point where success is imminent. . . . This has been achieved with almost no help from the government, and at a cost of about $8 million from my personal funds.

"I would consider this money well spent if now, with the co-operation of the government, we could move ahead quickly and produce meaningful quantities of hardware. Instead, our considerable bank of research knowledge has been almost totally ignored by the governmental agencies charged with administering the clean air act. The funds appropriated by the Congress to allay air pollution are being shamefully squandered and ineffectively administered."

Getting down to specifics, Lear wrote, "Over $4 million has been allocated by the Urban Mass Transportation Administration to procure a low pollution passenger bus. Previous to this, Mr. Carlos Villarreal, UMTA administrator, visited our plant in Reno. He was briefed on progress we had made toward design of a low-pollution, small-sized passenger bus. After this visit, UMTA issued a request for proposal calling for a 'systems management' and research study for a 'new look' passenger bus. The RFP describes a bus closely resembling the one we designed and carried through to the mock-up stage. The RFP was sent to fourteen companies. We were excluded.

"This was in spite of the fact that we were in a position to offer quickly, almost exactly what was being called for in the RFP. Furthermore, I offered to build the bus for less than $1 million. Yet UMTA seems determined to go through the 'systems management' approach to select some company to write another RFP to select another company to obtain the bus. UMTA, I am told, has 129 employees. Surely they could and should write their own proposal instead of hiring other people to do their work for them. The $4 million can be easily spent by this 'systems management' approach without ever procuring any hardware. Meanwhile, valuable time is lost while air pollution steadily worsens."

Lear took up the matter of the two contracts given to other firms to cover ground already covered by Lear Motors, the low bidder. "We already had hardware successfully operating that conformed closely to the RFP requirements," he wrote. . . . "In spite of this, we did not win either bid."

He described the winning SES corporation as "a paper company" with "about a dozen employees," and cited the advantages enjoyed by SES officers Morse and Ragone in going about the country armed with government authority to find out what everybody doing research and development in low-pollution systems, Lear Motors among them, had turned up.

"At the very least, it seems highly unethical that Mr. Ragone and Mr. Morse should be in a position to bid against us for a government contract in this technical area," Lear wrote.

Furthermore, he went on, the award to SES was for $570,000, while Lear's bid was only $485,000.

"Finally, the Steam Engine Systems Corporation proposal utilizes a reciprocating type engine," Lear went on. "We have thoroughly investigated and developed a number of reciprocating type steam expanders and found them to be totally impractical for today's automotive vehicle. Had the proposal decision team chosen to investigate our research activities, which we have freely made available, they would have realized that the reciprocating type engine is the wrong way to go. So $570,000 will be wasted to find out what we already know."

Concerning the contract which the government awarded to the Aerojet Nuclear Systems Company of Sacramento, to develop the identical vapor turbine engine developed by Lear and nearly ready for the road, Lear made two points in his letter: "Aerojet has shown no particular history of competence regarding Rankine Cycle systems" and "The award was made to Aerojet for $562,831. Our bid was for $518,365. I can understand the government's desire to help the aerospace industry, but not at the expense of progress in air pollution."

His company had neither been consulted nor questioned during the time both proposals were being considered, Lear wrote. "In effect, the government chose to completely ignore our three years and $8 million worth of valuable research, although the information could have been obtained for the asking."

He summarized, "The tragic waste of both time and money toward a solution for the serious air pollution problem is outrageous. People are dying while studies are being made of studies, while the wheel is being reinvented, and reinvented again. . . . I earnestly solicit your help." He signed "Respectfully yours, William P. Lear."

To some addressees Lear included a cover letter, as this to the President:

"The attached letter details the facts concerning my disillusionment and disgust with the way the air pollution problem is being handled. I don't like to be critical of your administration, but considering the increasing importance of air pollution, I know you certainly want to be aware of the facts. . . ."

Before he could load this considerable correspondence into the mails, a chance opportunity came to place its contents before the public. KABC Radio's John Babcock phoned from Los Angeles for an interview, and Lear read the letter on the air, valiantly keeping his voice under control as he read. The Associated Press and United Press International picked up the story and sent it to the nation's two thousand-odd radio and TV stations as well as most of the country's newspapers, and that night Lear's barrage against Washington was a lead item in the network news. His charges continued in the news for some time, like the aftershocks in an earthquake. One broadcaster was heard reading Lear's letter with rising emotion out of Washington on the third day.

One of the first officeholders to be heard from was Senator George McGovern, avowed presidential candidate, who arranged to visit Lear in Reno. EPA chief William D. Ruckelshaus checked in, inviting Lear Motors to take part in a conference with auto men to see what progress they had made in controlling tailpipe pollution. There were calls from writers, newspaper and magazine editors, and from TV and radio stations, wanting copies of Lear's blast; and from the public who only wanted to say hurrah.

Then began the mail, flowing like a wave swamping beaches

from a disturbance at sea. Many writers enclosed copies of letters they had already gotten off to their representatives in Washington. "If you think it will help, I will see if the *Eagle-Beacon* will publish this letter to Senator Dole," wrote Howard R. Moore of Wichita, enclosing a letter he had written to Kansas Senator Robert J. Dole. "It may put more pressure on him to get something done besides politicking."

"We urge you to give your serious consideration to Bill Lear's letter concerning his frustrations in his efforts to solve the pollution problem with a new motor," typically wrote J. E. McGraw of Los Angeles to California Senator Alan Cranston. "There aren't many Bill Lears left now—and his experience with the federal government makes it discouraging, rather than rewarding and inspiring, for private industry to make any further contributions."

Meanwhile, as the mountain snows receded and the Washoe Valley slowly turned to green in the third springtime since it all began, installation of the vapor turbine engine in the Monte Carlo came at last to the end, and the space-age steam car, which everybody said couldn't be built, was ready for the road.

Well, almost—almost.

"Everything is in the car," Lear told Art Linkletter on the phone April 13. "As soon as the controls are perfected, we'll be off and running."